CONTEMPORARY COLLECTING:

THE DONNA AND HOWARD STONE COLLECTION

CONTEMPORARY COLLECTING: THE DONNA AND HOWARD STONE COLLECTION

JAMES RONDEAU
WITH AN ESSAY BY JUDITH RUSSI KIRSHNER

THE ART INSTITUTE OF CHICAGO
YALE UNIVERSITY PRESS, NEW HAVEN AND LONDON

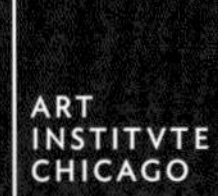

Yale

CONTEMPORARY COLLECTING: THE DONNA AND HOWARD STONE COLLECTION was published in conjunction with the exhibition *Selections from the Donna and Howard Stone Collection*, organized by and presented at the Art Institute of Chicago from June 25 to September 19, 2010.

First edition
Printed in the United States of America
Library of Congress Control Number: 2010926569
ISBN: 978-0-300-16548-7

Published by
The Art Institute of Chicago
111 South Michigan Avenue
Chicago, Illinois 60603-6404
www.artic.edu

Distributed by
Yale University Press
302 Temple Street
P.O. Box 209040
New Haven, Connecticut 06520-9040
www.yalebooks.com

Produced by the Publications Department of the Art Institute of Chicago, Robert V. Sharp, Executive Director

Edited by Elizabeth S. Zinn
Production by Carolyn Ziebarth and Kate Kotan
Photography research by Joseph Mohan

Designed and typeset by Jeff Wonderland
Separations by Professional Graphics, Inc., Rockford, Illinois
Printing and binding by GLS Companies, St. Paul, Minnesota

This book was produced using paper and materials certified by the Forest Stewardship Council.

Editor's note: In the illustrated checklist, objects labeled "gift" or "promised gift" represent works given or promised by Donna and Howard Stone to the Art Institute of Chicago.

CONTENTS

FOREWORD

All great museums are collections of great collections. The Art Institute of Chicago is no exception. Since our earliest days, the generosity of local collectors has helped shape the course of the museum's history. Through the support of individuals like Frederic Clay Bartlett and his wife, Helen Birch Bartlett, masterpieces like Georges Seurat's *Sunday on La Grande Jatte—1884* have become the timeless, cherished works that our visitors have come to know and enjoy intimately over the years. Other names come to mind when defining our museum's modern and contemporary collections. Arthur Jerome Eddy, the great champion of Modern art, gave twenty-three objects by artists such as Kandinsky and Manet to the museum in 1931. Martin A. Ryerson's vast holdings—spanning the fifteenth to the twentieth centuries in all media—came to the museum in 1933–38. In 1982 Lindy and Edwin Bergman made a very important contribution of Surrealist works, including thirty-seven of Joseph Cornell's signature boxes and collages. And in 1997, we acquired over one hundred objects from Lannan Foundation, which strengthened our holdings of artists such as Gerhard Richter and Bruce Nauman.

I am pleased to add the names of Donna and Howard Stone to this distinguished list of benefactors. Over the past three decades, Donna and Howard have built a rich, intergenerational collection of art in all media. While there is a focus on 1960s and 1970s Minimalism and Conceptualism, including works by artists such as Dan Flavin, Sol LeWitt, Robert Ryman, and Fred Sandback, there are also substantial examples by younger artists such as Robert Gober, Felix Gonzalez-Torres, Roni Horn, and Gabriel Orozco, who were deeply influenced by the previous generation. Their collection has grown into a truly international representation of art-making practices during the last fifty years.

Donna and Howard are consummate Chicagoans. Their support of local universities and artists is unmatched, and their commitment to the Art Institute has been long-standing. Both have been highly active members of the Society of Contemporary Art for many years. Howard has served as a trustee and Chairman of the Committee on Contemporary Art since 2003, and Donna has been a key member of the Committee on Prints and Drawings since 2006. Their gifts and extended loans have long graced our galleries of contemporary art, exposing visitors to some of the most important work of our time. Underscoring their dedication to film, video, and new media, the couple gave fifteen works in this genre to the museum in 2007. These pieces, along with other examples from the Art Institute's collection, are routinely shown in the Donna and Howard Stone Film, Video, and New Media Gallery, which they endowed to celebrate the opening of the Modern Wing in 2009.

It is our great pride and pleasure to be able to present the first-ever public exhibition of works from the Stone Collection, organized by James Rondeau. In addition to the fifty-nine objects featured in the show, this publication includes an illustrated checklist of 231 works that will serve as a record of the Stones' holdings for years to come. The exhibition and catalogue also celebrate a major gift from the Stone Collection. Fifty outstanding works have been designated on this occasion as promised gifts to the museum. These paintings, sculptures, and drawings were carefully chosen to add to our existing strengths and fill long-standing gaps in our collection. The fifty works will join forty-two objects the Stones have given or promised at previous times. For this, we owe them our deepest and most profound respect and appreciation.

Taking its place among the Art Institute's other legacy gifts, Donna and Howard's contribution reminds us that all art was once contemporary. As our visitors come to know and love the galleries of the Modern Wing, they will undoubtedly find works that speak to them on the same level as our other beloved masterpieces. The Stones' gifts will most surely be cherished among the museum's new classics.

JAMES CUNO

PRESIDENT AND ELOISE W. MARTIN DIRECTOR

INTRODUCTION AND ACKNOWLEDGMENTS

When I began my work as a curator at the Art Institute of Chicago in 1998, the museum's collection and programs of contemporary art were defined within a larger context of twentieth-century painting and sculpture. Since that time, much has changed. In 2002, prompted by the new millennium and in response to the support of several members of the museum's board of trustees, then-director James N. Wood began to define an independent and wholly revitalized role for contemporary art with the creation of a new and autonomous curatorial department charged with the care and oversight of objects across a wide spectrum of media dating from 1945 to the present. Under the current leadership of James Cuno, this re-thinking has made its greatest—and most obvious—impact with the splendid realization of the Modern Wing. There has been a parallel and at times less visible set of consequences as we have expanded the collection of contemporary art in markedly ambitious ways. It would be an understatement to say that Donna and Howard Stone have been an important part of this effort; they have, in fact, been an essential one. Howard has expertly led the Committee on Contemporary Art since 2003, overseeing an expansive program of acquisitions developed through both purchase and gift. During this decade of unprecedented growth, the Stones have been steady and persistent advocates of the Art Institute. For this we are deeply grateful.

To our advantage, the Stones' long history of generosity has been reciprocated by numerous artists, galleries, and organizations, all of whom have kindly granted our requests for images, information, materials, and permissions during the course of organizing this catalogue and exhibition. A sustained look at Donna and Howard's collection reveals deep commitments to and friendships with a number of artists. We would first like to express our sincere appreciation to all the artists who have participated in this project, either as a result of their inclusion in the present exhibition or in the Stones' collection in general. Many provided advice to us—either directly or through their studio assistants—about their works. These artists are represented in the catalogue's illustrated checklist, which serves as a chronicle of the collection, and we are proud to include them among our collaborators.

We owe special thanks to a roster of international gallerists, all of whom represent artists in the Stone Collection. These include in particular Roland Augustine, Marianne Boesky, Shane Campbell, Valerie Carberry, Carla Chammas, John Corbett, Jim Dempsey, Richard Desroches, Barbara Gladstone, Marian Goodman, Carol Greene, Max Hetzler, Rhona Hoffman, Lawrence Luhring, Matthew Marks, Glenn McMillan, Anthony Meier, André Millan, Shaun Caley Regen, Andrea Rosen, Mary Sabbatino, Samia Saouma, Lisa Spellman, Lucien Terras, Angela Westwater, Donald Young, and David Zwirner. On numerous occasions, we have called upon these individuals and their staffs for guidance and expertise, and they have contributed immensely—and with patience—to the production of this catalogue as well as to many aspects of the exhibition. Special thanks are also due to Amy Baker Sandback and Jennifer Smith.

As always, it has been our great pleasure to work with Judith Russi Kirshner, Dean of the College of Architecture and the Arts at the University of Illinois at Chicago. Judith has been close to the Stones for many years and has offered her cogent thoughts on their collection in the essay that follows. In this light, we would also like to respectfully acknowledge other colleagues, all in Chicago at one time or another, who have maintained an active dialogue with Donna and Howard over the years, including most especially Neal Benezra, Francesco Bonami, Amada Cruz, Douglas Druick, Okwui Enwezor, Susanne Ghez, Madeleine Grynsztejn, Mark Pascale, Jeremy Strick, Peter Taub, and Hamza Walker.

The Stones' interest in art has never been limited to a particular medium. Their collection is quite varied, including paintings, sculpture, drawings, ambitious installations, and an impressive group of both single-channel and multichannel video works, fifteen of which they gifted to the Art Institute in 2007.

As such, and in the process of readying each object for public exhibition, we have relied on conservators from all areas of the museum. For their attention and assistance, we are grateful to Valentina Branchini, Lauren Chang, Barbara Hall, Kelly Keegan, Kristin Lister, Sara Moy, Suzanne Schnepp, Doug Severson, Harriet Stratis, and Frank Zuccari.

Also at the Art Institute, Bernice Chu and William Caddick oversaw the design and construction of the exhibition, aided by the excellent services of Tom Barnes and his crew. Yaumu Huang was responsible for the exhibition's smart design. In the registrar's office, special thanks go to Angela Morrow for her superb organizational skills. Appreciation also goes to Craig Cox and John Molini. In the Imaging Department, we thank Robert Hashimoto, Robert Lifson, and Caroline Nutley. Additionally, our thanks are due to Michelle Lehrman Jenness of Protection Services, Kimberly Masius of Constituent Relations, and Lauren Schultz of Communications. As always, I would like to thank President and Eloise W. Martin Director James Cuno, as well as David Thurm, Dorothy Schroeder, Jeanne Ladd, Sam Quigley, and our entire legal department, especially Julie Getzels.

We are always proud to collaborate with the Publications Department on an exhibition catalogue. This project in particular presented a fair number of challenges as we sought to represent both a chronicle of the collection in the form of an illustrated checklist, as well as a detailed look at the fifty-nine works selected for the exhibition. To that end, Carolyn Ziebarth was instrumental in overseeing the book's production. Our excellent editor, Elizabeth Zinn, contributed to every aspect of the catalogue's development. Joseph Mohan worked attentively and with patience to coordinate permissions and reproductions for the more than two hundred images. Great thanks and admiration also go to Robert Sharp and Sarah Guernsey, as well as Kate Kotan and Molly Heyen. In the Department of Graphic Design, Jeff Wonderland provided the handsome catalogue design. Jamie Stukenberg of Professional Graphics was responsible for the majority of the photography, and the rest of the Prographics team provided the gorgeous color separations.

Donna and Howard Stone are very much a part of our family in the Department of Contemporary Art. Over the years, they have worked closely with our Collection Manager Nora Riccio and Technician Nicholas Barron, and this exhibition was no exception. Jason Stec's oversight of the installation was invaluable, as was his dependable assistance with photography. We also acknowledge the contributions of Charles Campbell, Lisa Dorin, and Jenny Gheith. Finally, and most importantly, Exhibitions Manager Maureen Pskowski was indispensable in coordinating the project. As always, Maureen administered all aspects of the exhibition with characteristic intelligence and great aplomb, and we are grateful for her efforts.

My final and most profound appreciation goes to Donna and Howard Stone. Professional protocols between curator and collector long ago gave way to a deep personal friendship, shaped by love and admiration. I am proud and grateful to have been a small part in facilitating what will surely be their enduring legacy at the Art Institute of Chicago.

JAMES RONDEAU

CURATOR AND FRANCES AND THOMAS DITTMER CHAIR OF CONTEMPORARY ART

A NARRATIVE OF COLLECTING

JUDITH RUSSI KIRSHNER

When Dan Flavin titled his early combination of fluorescent and incandescent lights *one of May 27, 1963*, he marked its making: date and title are the same. Among the earliest of about three hundred remarkable examples by major contemporary artists acquired by Donna and Howard Stone since the late 1970s, this work now seems emblematic of a moment when an astonishing shift in art practice occurred. Flavin had first explored unorthodox pairings in his series of "icons," in which he attached light bulbs to painted boxes. In the Stones' piece, ten small red bulbs in porcelain mounts punctuate a four-foot-long red fluorescent tube to insist on a quirky, almost musical register of technological illumination (see fig. 1). Such seemingly casual juxtapositions achieve emotional capacity from plain materials to become instrumental in the provocative dialectic in which first-generation Conceptualists and Minimalists restored subjectivity and significance to the relics of mass production.

Also in the 1960s, Robert Ryman (who, like Flavin, was employed as a guard at New York's Museum of Modern Art, selectively absorbing the Modernist lessons of his predecessors) reduced his palette to white pigments on unstretched canvas and other unconventional supports. Each gesture, edge, choice of fastener, and even the artist's signature thus becomes an eloquent

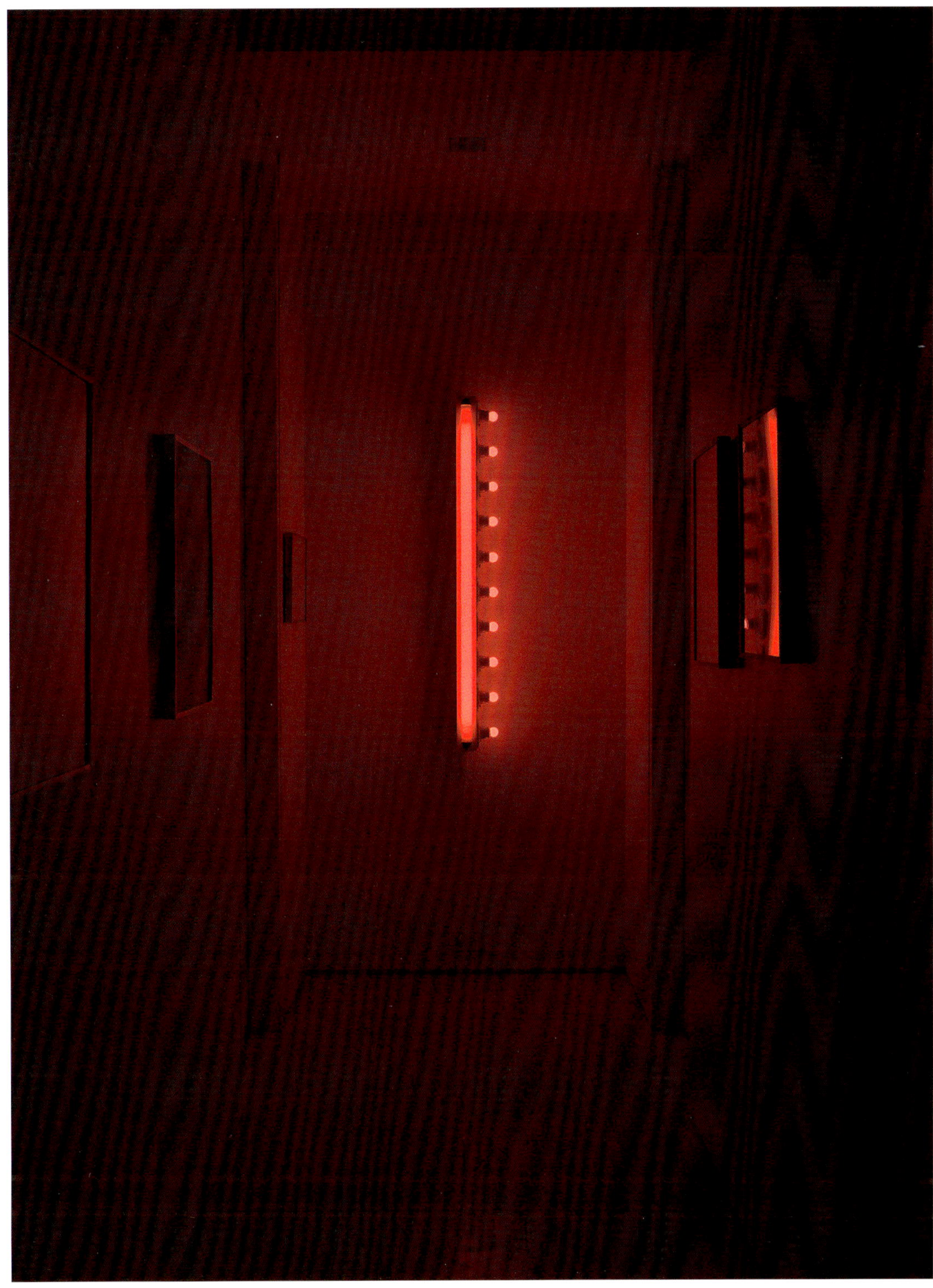

Fig. 1. The Stones' hallway, including Dan Flavin's *one of May 27, 1963*.

element in his stringent compositions. The swirling strokes of oil paint in the Stones' *Untitled* (1961) advertise their own autonomy on the paper support mounted on Masonite; like all Ryman's subtle compositions, *Untitled* measures straightforward components of the very means of painting against complex ideas, so that apparent plastic forms give rise to intellectual speculation about pictorial meaning. In a related enterprise, stretching gray-painted elastic cords from floor to ceiling for *Untitled, 1967* (1967), Fred Sandback drew enormous volumes from the thinnest filaments to imply a space that at first glance is barely visible yet in actuality is largely influential on our perceptual experience of the room.

That same year, Modernist critic Clement Greenberg published "Recentness of Sculpture," lamenting the substitution of ideas for aesthetics, the lack of expression and metaphor, and the preoccupation with the blurred margins between art and non-art so central to the enormous experimentation of the decade.[1] Unable to believe that the world could be transformed by art or that all works must be politicized, artists in the 1960s and 1970s nevertheless crafted stimulating models of resistance, critique, and intervention. By now these debates and imaginative meditations have been accepted as integral to the canon formation of contemporary art. The Stones' collection allows a unique opportunity to examine these past exemplars and the provocative dialogues that sprung from them.

Unfettered by institutional conventions of chronology or stylistic homogeneity, the Stones have built a rich, intergenerational collection of art. Certainly, there is a strong focus on Minimalist and Conceptual works, and this extends to more recent examples by artists who were the first to address issues of seriality, systems, and factual experiences. A unique sculpture by Stanley Brouwn, one of the more influential but less well known Dutch Conceptualists, produces a primer of measures. The work bears comparison with Sol LeWitt's earlier serial projects in its rational demonstration of a progression and, like so many of the objects amassed by the Stones, is abstract and conceptually driven. Although there are some outstanding figurative pieces in their collection, its expansive diversity is mostly grounded in the more intellectual lessons of Modernism. Cerebral and self-referential, Lawrence Weiner's linguistic proposition *MADE FRAGILE AT THIS TIME ON THIS PLACE TO A POINT OF NO RETURN* (2000) becomes specifically performative in its broken typeface—yet its potential for meaning might also apply to the spatial and temporal grasp of a younger generation of artists, including Gabriel Orozco and Robert Gober.

During a 1993 trip to Paris, the Stones were fascinated by Orozco's exhibition of terracotta construction rejects shaped into unrecognizable forms suggesting bread or body parts. They acquired *Made in Belgium* (1993), a roof tile that the artist salvaged before it was fired, then distorted and shaped with his hands. The ultimate global citizen, Orozco, whose sculpture, photography, and collage constitute an important cluster in the Stones' collection, often manifests a direct appreciation for corporal references—the importance of touch, for instance, in the small ink drawing *Palm* (2001). Cuts in space and time, Orozco's enigmatic works appear to defy gravity when suspended from the ceiling, like the giant spume *Under Tow* (2003), which assumes its ambiguous winged shape from poured polyurethane foam. Evoking the skeletal framework of an unidentifiable animal, airborne and perhaps prehistoric, it accentuates Orozco's selective historical inheritance, including fantastic objects like the hanging constructions of Aleksandr Rodchenko or Vladimir Tatlin. The progressive political aspirations and formal vocabulary of Russian constructivism may lurk in Orozco's variable practice and output (for example, in the geometric circular shapes of his airy, abstract paintings),[2] but there is another temporality circumscribed and deftly expressed in the collage *Eroded Suizekis 9* (1999), in which the rendering appears worn and the title itself implies time passed. Finally, the remarkable *Dent de Lion* (1998), a plethora of fabric discs attached to metal stalks, is both a delicate spectacle and an explosive blossom.

Robert Gober's magisterial wall-mounted *Double Sink* (1984) plays with representation through a process of making strange. Its soft curves and coupled sets of penetrations lacking hardware assume anthropomorphic associations; the four holes stare back at us and the painted enamel surface appears less like porcelain than skin. What appears at first glance as a readymade, moreover, has actually been hand-fashioned by Gober to evoke denaturalized purification rituals performed at the missing plumbing fixtures. Wrenched from its context and lovingly distressed, the utility sink is an oddly sorrowful reminder of loss and impurity. Its appearance as a readymade commands an imposing presence and reverses the irony of Marcel Duchamp's classic upside-down urinal to represent abandonment. *Double Sink* recalls art historian David Joselit's apposite claims for Gober's "poetics of the drain" and the fragility of functionality.[3]

In addition to Orozco and Gober, other artists of a younger generation also incorporated the everyday into their work; however, in contradiction to precedents of Modernist originality or legacies of aesthetic remove, many of them inserted a complex ethical and/or political argument into their production. This is seen most obviously in two works by Cady Noland: the still shocking bullet-ridden agony of Lee Harvey Oswald in *OOZEWALD*, and the curious line of assorted instruments in *The Big Slide* (both 1989). In the former, the flattened image of the assassin conveys the horror of the moment in its carnival pose, which is torn from the headlines but oddly reminiscent of the painful posture associated with the passion of Christ. *The Big Slide* also addresses issues of American dysfunction. In her depiction of a U.S. flag hanging next to a blind man's cane and handcuffs, Noland juxtaposed a potent American symbol amid uneasy implements of the handicapped and constrained.

Felix Gonzalez-Torres's *"Untitled" (Portrait of Ross in LA)* (1991) emerges from the tragic perspective of disease, personal loss, and regeneration. The glittering pile of 175 pounds of cellophane-wrapped Fruit Flasher candy represents the ideal weight of the artist's lover, Ross, who lost his battle with AIDS in 1990. In this poignant work, Gonzalez-Torres figuratively and iconographically offers to share goodness and beauty with his audiences. Viewers are invited to take a piece of candy from the pile, which is continually replenished. The ephemeral sparkle and diminishing materiality of the candies (which directly parallels Ross's diminishing body weight) also reinforce the social anxiety and public consequences of the AIDs outbreak. With such revelatory combinations—death and sweetness—Gonzalez-Torres aligned a particular occasion with the endlessness of mourning and the political realities of an epidemic. Bite-size bits of melting transparent treats become liquid in our mouths; their implied or real absorption into our bodies performs the far more overt dyad of *Ghost and Pool of Blood* (1988) by German sculptor Katharina Fritsch. Her dazzling Plexiglas pool is shiny and hard and although the shroudlike white garment posits a physical and even metaphysical sense of mourning, it relies on metaphor and historical association: the tall ungendered ghost recalls marble statues of the virgin, and the pool evokes the tears she sheds for her son. However, this haunting drapery could conceal *any* recognizable human form; drained of life, its fictional reflection is bloody rather than clear. The question of objecthood, even technical support, replacing subject, so central to Minimalist analyses, still applies as we ponder Fritsch's statue. Is there even a mannequin underneath or are we simply admiring an apparition, a vertical arrangement of folds?

Representations and roles of the viewer are also explored in Michelangelo Pistoletto's *Girl Drawing* (1979). Standing directly in front of the large mirror, a signature material for the *arte povera* artist, spectators can observe and ponder their own reflections as the subject matter of the young female artist. Moving away from the piece, our presence evaporates, while the depiction of the girl remains. Once again in this collection, the body is sublimated and psychic resonances trump physical and metaphysical considerations. More overtly, Janine Antoni takes her own body as the material of photographic investigations that signal the necessity of self-nurturing and the demand for female-defined sexual identity and autonomy. While theoretical and linguistic structures of feminist theory have made sexual difference a socially relevant theme, Antoni, like many other women artists of her generation, uses photography to represent women's otherness as powerful—to challenge the condition of unrepresentability but also to respond to the imperative that women's imagery not merely reproduce traditional masculinist depictions of the female body. Antoni's poignant photographs from the late 1990s achieve symbolic authority as she destabilized the boundaries of sexual difference, twisting her body to succor, sustain, and signify female subjectivity.

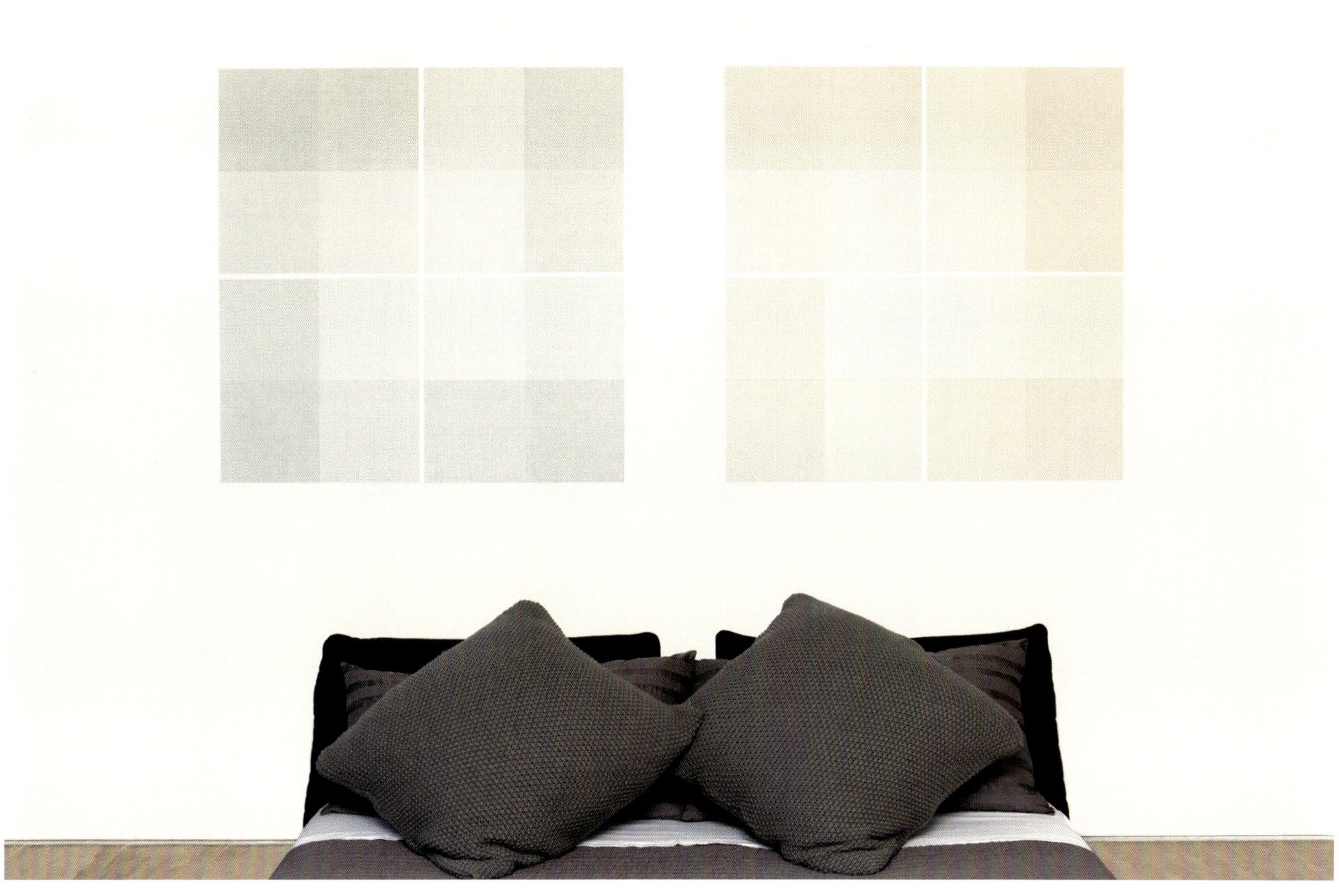

Fig. 2. Installation view of Sol LeWitt's *Wall Drawings #966–67: Drawing Series I 24 (B)*.

Her saturated color print *Mortar and Pestle* (1999) presents an unsettling close-up of an eye licked by a tongue, a comment perhaps on artistic vision, touch, and "taste," as well as the intimate, libidinal/erotic investments of viewing.

Illusion and appearance are obviously key issues for many artists in this selection. Gerhard Richter has observed, "Illusion—or rather appearance, semblance—is the theme of my life . . . . All that is, seems, and is visible to us because we perceive it by the reflected light of semblance. Nothing else is visible. Painting concerns itself, as no other art does, exclusively with semblance (I include photography, of course)."[4] In the Stones' collection, Richter's rich explorations of the possibilities of non-representational painting can be appreciated in *Gray* (1973), an early, nuanced disputation on non-color, as well as in the flickering, virtuoso *Abstract Picture* (2000). The monumental graphite and charcoal drawings *Set of Four* (2005) may reference the linear skeletons of the World Trade Center. Richter had planned to make a 9/11 painting, which did not

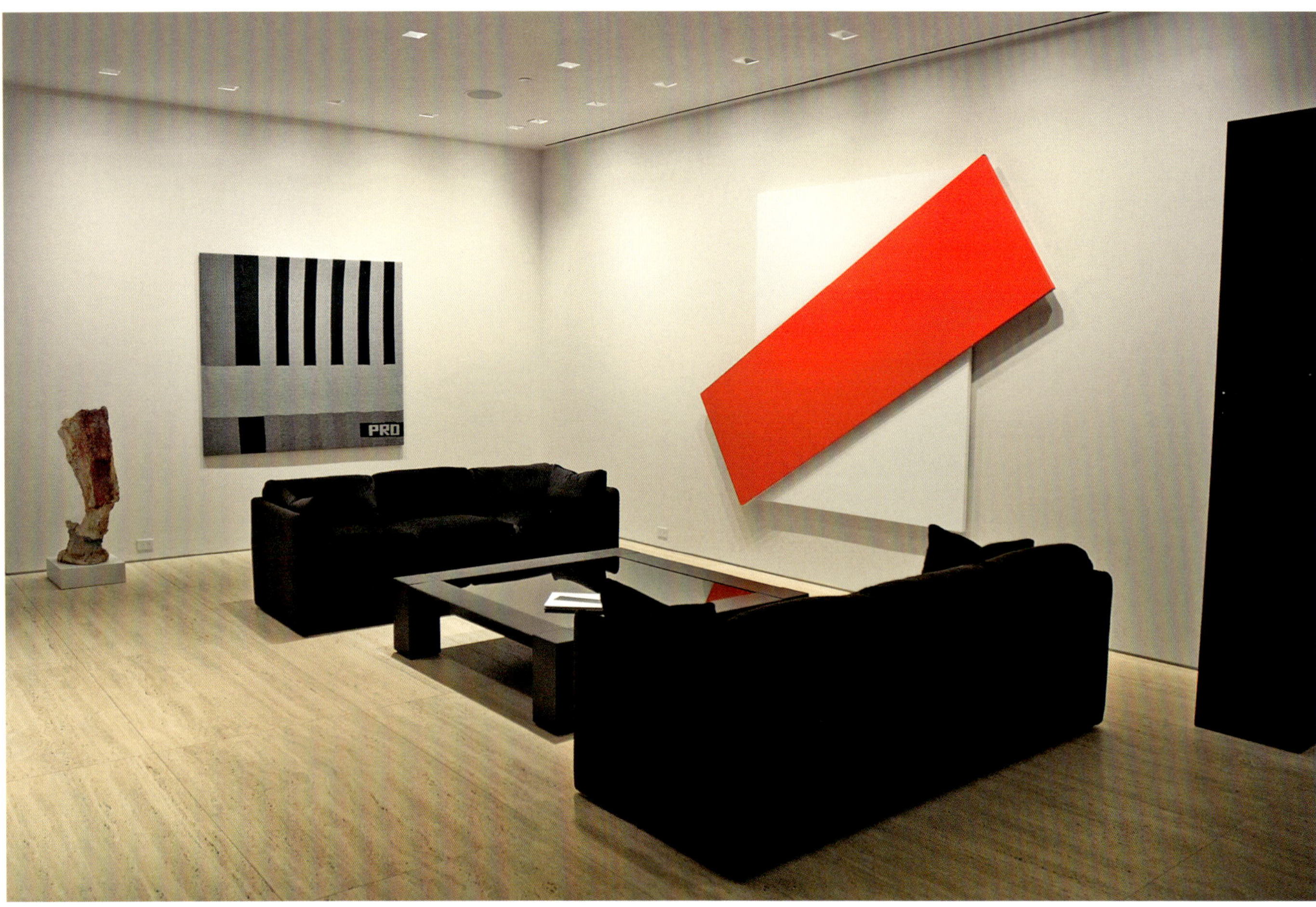

Fig. 3. The Stones' living room, including Ellsworth Kelly's *Red Diagonal*.

immediately materialize. "He then made the four drawings where the image of the World Trade Center seemed to appear subconsciously."[5]

Another take on the dyad of illusion and appearance occurs in the paintings of Sylvia Plimack Mangold. In *The Maple Tree with Pine* (2005), the artist turned her analytic gaze to the juxtaposition of difference in the declarative yet layered representation of two trees. Maureen Gallace and Judy Ledgerwood have also taken nature as their subject matter. In paintings like the small, detailed *Summer Rainbow, Cape Cod* (2006), Gallace magically arrived at a kind of idealized, pearly luminosity. Ledgerwood's large encaustic *Red Pine* (1990) begins with an arboreal reference but concludes on the border between what is known and unknown, bringing poetical allusions to visual speculations. Such investigations also animate the measured compositions of Julia Fish, where layers of paint applied in small repetitive brushstrokes become palimpsests in *Frost II* (1996), an eerily close approximation of its content. Here materiality and image are fused in what can also be viewed as a beautiful abstraction. In other works, such as *5811 South Ellis* (1995) and *Living Room: NorthEast, with lights, action* (2003–05), the gray masonry glimpsed through a window or the eccentric shapes on peach-colored ground derived from floor plans of Fish's own home reverse all categories of interior and exterior, vertical and horizontal. In a recent presentation at the Art Institute, the artist revealed to her audience, "I live in the subject matter of my paintings,"[6] which challenge spatial logic to occupy her canvases and our consciousness.

The Stones themselves are the subject of one of the works in their collection, Jim Hodges's *Untitled (Portrait of Howard and Donna Stone)* (1999). One of the artist's wall portraits, the piece depicts the collectors as two overlapping sets of concentric circles. The portrait invites comparison to another pair of wall drawings in the Stones' collection, two classic pencil works by Sol LeWitt (executed in 2001 but likely conceived in the 1970s). Installed in the bedroom (see fig. 2), they comprise two large squares (one black, one colored), each of which is segmented into sixteen equal components. Thin, precise, gridded lines add varying levels of shading to the different sections. Considered together, the Hodges and the LeWitt installations suggest a generous definition of the Stones' collection as a set of dialogues and relationships between individual pieces and the larger whole. While Hodges was moved by LeWitt,[7] the systematic precision of LeWitt's subtle geometries can be contrasted with the hand drawn, looping gestures of Hodges. Like the rings of two trees intertwined and measuring time together, the portrait also represents a collaboration between artist and collector; Hodges had the Stones select the colors of their circles (they chose French gray and black).

The Stones have built a home for art, creating a stage for vibrant intergenerational arguments, embracing works that ricochet between ideals of Modernist purity and a Postmodern appreciation of paradox and self-conscious representation. On this occasion, what enriches the narrative and allows it to expand is not only the Stones' subjective viewpoint but also the multiplying meanings these works will accrue as they are exhibited at the Art Institute. At home, the Stones installed one of their most recent acquisitions, Ellsworth Kelly's two-panel *Red Diagonal* (2007; see fig. 3), in the living room across from a floor-to-ceiling glass wall so that it becomes an abstract imperative, calling the high-rise architecture to order and competing in its purity and poise with the views of the gridded city at night. Transported to the walls of the museum, this personally cherished artwork will become an object of a public order of analysis and appreciation. It, and indeed all the artworks on display from the Stones' collection, will be seen in an art-historical context, transformed and amplified to satisfy our desire for fresh insights and unexpected visual experiences that underscore the making and interpretation of contemporary art.

NOTES

1 Clement Greenberg, "Recentness of Sculpture" (1967), repr. in Clement Greenberg, *The Collected Essays and Criticism*, vol. 4, *Modernism with a Vengeance: 1957–1969* (University of Chicago Press, 1993), pp. 250–56.
2 For examples, see *Gabriel Orozco: Trabajo*, exh. cat. (Galerie Chantal Crousel, 2003).
3 David Joselit, "Poetics of the Drain," *Art in America* 85 (Dec. 1997), pp. 64–71.
4 Gerhard Richter, *Notes, 1989*, in *The Daily Practice of Painting: Writings and Interviews 1962–1993*, ed. Hans-Ulrich Obrist, trans. David Britt (MIT Press in association with Anthony D'Offay Gallery, 1995), p. 181.
5 Phone conversation between James Rondeau and Marian Goodman, Art Institute curatorial files.
6 Julia Fish, lecture at the Art Institute of Chicago, January 14, 2010.
7 After attending the 1996 exhibition of LeWitt's prints at the Museum of Modern Art, Hodges spoke of his regard for LeWitt: "I felt a kinship with him and the profound humanness of his work. It was not as cool and analytical as I had previously thought." Quoted in Andrea Miller-Keller, "Varieties of Influence: Sol LeWitt and the Arts Community," in *Sol LeWitt: A Retrospective*, ed. Gary Garrels, exh. cat. (San Francisco Museum of Modern Art, 2000), p. 77.

JAMES RONDEAU IN CONVERSATION WITH DONNA AND HOWARD STONE

JANUARY 2010

JAMES RONDEAU Donna, you grew up in rural Wisconsin and Howard, you were born and raised in Chicago. These are two very different ways to experience childhood. Growing up, did either of you have much experience with visiting museums or knowing artists? When were you first exposed to art?

DONNA STONE I had no opportunity to visit museums, as there were none and even though we had access to Milwaukee and Madison they did not have good museums at that time. Our art curriculum at school consisted of a weekly program from the University of Wisconsin's radio station called "Let's Draw." It was a favorite. *Life* and *National Geographic* magazines were probably my first exposure to photography. In 1951 I came to Chicago to go to school and visited all the museums.

HOWARD STONE While Donna and I come from divergent backgrounds, each of us had our own experience with the arts. I spent time at museums with school groups and as a teen with friends. As young adults, first married, museums became a part of our life together. We went to the Art Institute and especially during cold winters we took our daughter, Julie, often. A friend took us to the Museum of Contemporary Art and we became members. In 1979 Donna retired and became a docent there. We had more time and began visiting local galleries. This was probably our first experience talking with artists. Also, artists often spoke to the docents. One of the first I remember was Jenny Holzer.

JR Early on, your involvement with the Museum of Contemporary Art was very important, I know, particularly Donna's work as a docent was an instrumental aspect of your development as collectors. Donna, you have often mentioned to me over the years the training you received, the people you met as a result of the docent program, and the great benefit of having to learn how to confront and explain new and challenging works of contemporary art. Can you talk a bit about your experiences in this regard—your training and your time as a museum educator?

DS You are right. The arrival of the MCA Calendar with an article that they were accepting docents in the fall of 1979 changed my newly acquired freedom to a new challenge. They chose me as a docent probably because of my work with children as a school nurse and nursery school teacher. It certainly wasn't for my knowledge of art. At that time Russell Bowman was the director of education. He was a great teacher. He could talk about the art with a sense of history and the present and always helped us comprehend it. Many of the exhibitions were the artist's first and we were dealing with work that had no written history to draw from. Understanding the art just seemed to come naturally to Russell, and he was able to communicate that knowledge to the docents. We also had the advantage of lectures and informal briefings from Judith Kirshner, who was the curator at that time. She had invaluable information and insight on the work, which she was able to convey to us, along with a sense of excitement. The addition to the museum had just been completed with the recent history of the Gordon Matta-Clark intervention, the Charles Simmonds wall, and the Max Neuhaus project in the stairwell. It was a very stimulating environment. Exhibitions changed almost every month, so it was very intense and challenging. One of the first I remember was Vito Acconci.

JR Howard, when Donna became a docent, had you already started collecting? When did you begin, and how? Do you remember your first purchases?

HS Yes, we had already started collecting. If I had to put a date on it, I would estimate somewhere in the mid-to-late-1970s. There was no focus, but it felt wonderful. It was exciting and one could feel the passion building, but there were very few funds. At that time we were collecting prints and drawings—Klee, Tobey, Miró, Gottlieb, and a Tristan Tzara limited-edition book illustrated by Miró, things like that. There were perhaps a few I'm not thinking of, but then out of the blue we were offered and acquired a small Jim Dine watercolor heart and a small Marino Marini horse painting. I still remember the joyful, exhilarating experience. Much later these were all sold to purchase other works. The first major piece we tried to acquire was not in the cards, as the gallerist did not know us and we were way down on the list. It was a Susan Rothenberg horse.

JR What was the gallery scene like in Chicago when you were starting out? Were you looking at galleries here and in New York, or both?

DS In the early 1980s, we joined the Art Institute's Society for Contemporary Art, and the programs—mostly lectures by artists—were very influential on us. Other important areas of our learning experience were alternative spaces like Randolph Street Gallery, then led by Hudson and later by Peter Taub, and the Renaissance Society, which is still under the wonderful guidance of Susanne Ghez. Later in the decade, most of our acquisitions were confined to Chicago galleries, however, with the advent of the Chicago Art Fair in the early 1980s, our trips to New York included galleries as well as museums. In Chicago we were actively visiting Young Hoffman, Robin Lockett, Feature (where we first saw the work of Charles Ray), Suzan Rezak (who first showed us Tom Friedman), Dart, Richard Gray, and Neva Benjamin, to name a few.

HS It is important to note this is when we began to formulate a direction and focus for our future collection. We were beginning to think about and become attracted to the Minimal and Conceptual work of artists like Sol LeWitt, Christopher Wool, Felix Gonzalez-Torres, Tom Friedman, and others. There were many wonderful exhibitions here. In New York, we were drawn to the East Village scene, where we first saw Jeff Koons's work. We truly wanted to own *Jim Beam J. B. Turner Train* (1986), but as it turned out we could hardly get the time of day from the gallery. We also were visiting Leo Castelli, Sonnabend, Luhring Augustine, Mary Boone,

Ivan Karp, and Diane Brown, among others. Things were heating up for our collecting future. We loved it, but hardly realized what the future would hold. Later, people like Angela Westwater, Marian Goodman, Barbara Gladstone, Matthew Marks, Andrea Rosen, Mary Sabbatino, and David Zwirner became important for us.

JR Were there collectors in Chicago when you were starting out that you particularly admired or learned from?

HS Certainly Jim and Marilynn Alsdorf, Lindy and Ed Bergman, Ruth Horwich, and Joe Shapiro were all role models. They not only were great collectors but they shared their collections with the community at large. The generosity of all these people to Chicago institutions was inspirational. In the early 1980s, we followed the activities of Susan and Lew Manilow and the direction they took in the international art scene. A bit later we met Gerry Elliot, who was in fact collecting Minimal, Conceptual work. Our first visit to his home was absolutely intriguing. We saw windows that were covered in order to install a Judd stack. It was the first time we saw a Judd stack in a private collection.

JR Are there stories or particular memories you associate with acquiring certain works of art in the collection?

DS Sometimes you can't get a piece out of your mind. This happened with a work by our friend Alfredo Jaar. We first saw *Cries and Whispers* (1988) in a New York gallery and fell in love with it, but we decided it was too large for us to have at home. About four years later, we were walking through the art fair in Chicago and saw his work in the booth of a European gallery. We mentioned that *Cries and Whispers* was our favorite, and they just happened to have it. This time we didn't let it get away. Ultimately, after installing it in our old apartment at 219 East Lake Shore Drive, we gave it to the MCA for their photography collection.

HS The Flavin we found by pure accident. We were in John Weber's gallery looking at an exhibition—I'm not even sure I can remember now what was on view in the main space—and we happened to walk into his office. *One of May, 27, 1963* was hanging above his desk, and we knew immediately we wanted to buy it. We had never seen a Flavin "icon" before and most of the relevant material was out of print; however, we knew how important this unique sculpture was and purchased it and the drawing, which was one of the few that Flavin did to document his work.

JR What has your family's relationship to your collecting been over the years?

DS Our daughter, Julie, and son-in-law, Bruce, do not collect; however, they live with some very nice paintings. Some were gifts and others they purchased before they began raising their family. Consequently, our three grandchildren have grown up with art at home, our collection, and visiting museums as they have traveled with us. Now that they are older they have more of an appreciation of what we do. They particularly enjoy the Modern Wing. It will be interesting to see what direction they take in the future or if they will think about collecting.

JR When I first came to see you in your old apartment on East Lake Shore Drive in 1997—after meeting you at dinner the night before, while I was in town interviewing for my job at the Art Institute—I saw an incredible range of work on the walls. What struck me then—other than, of course, the quality of the art on view and the ways in which they were installed—was the focus of the collection. You had clearly been drawn to Minimal and Conceptual art and had collected works across generational lines. So one saw great examples by Donald Judd, Dan Flavin, Sol LeWitt, Robert Ryman, and Gerhard Richter alongside works by younger artists like Robert Gober, Gabriel Orozco, Jim Hodges, Doris Salcedo, and Byron Kim, who had inherited certain aspects of those legacies. I remember so well seeing a LeWitt pencil wall drawing paired with one by Hodges, a white LeWitt structure next to a white Orozco "dandelion," the Gober sink directly opposite a Judd "bullnose," that sort of thing. The installation was quite inspired, and one sensed that it was wonderfully thought out. How intentional was this focus?

HS From the very first time we ventured into the area of serious collecting, we were concerned with finding the threads that connected the work. We were also interested in how the pieces would react to each other as we developed the collection. It has always been our contention that to install works properly we would need to understand why they belonged together. This gave us a feeling of immense comfort when we viewed the art. It is also enormously gratifying to hear that you recognized this when you first walked into our apartment. So yes, we did and do seriously think a great deal about installation. We should also say that we have not acquired our art for an intentional installation, rather, we selected things we wanted to live with. We then subsequently looked for the threads to put them together.

DS Howard has always had a very good sense of what goes together. I always say he does the installation and I have veto privileges that I seldom put to use. Our collection is all work we feel comfortable living with. Consequently there are artists whose work we recognize as important who are not represented in the collection because we didn't live well with them.

JR We keep mentioning the "old" apartment at 219 East Lake Shore Drive, a beautiful lakefront space in a 1921–22 brick Georgian building designed by Fugard and Knapp. The spaces were elegant and very traditional. Recently, you moved to a new apartment, a 1972 high-rise originally designed by Minoru Yamasaki and Associates—architects of New York City's World Trade Center—with an interior you commissioned by Chicago-based architect John Vinci. The new apartment is far more modern and minimalist in style. You also install works from the collection in your home in Arizona, where a hilly desert landscape predominates all views from the house. How have these different kinds of domestic spaces affected how you live with and respond to the collection?

HS Certainly, with the new apartment it was important for us to foster an environment that highlighted the art. As we mentioned, we think seriously about installation, and moving allowed us to create a living space that reflects the focus of our collection. Another thing we have always thought about collecting was outdoor sculpture; however, apartments are not conducive to this at all. When we purchased our first home in Arizona in 1989, we became very aware of the never-ending desert sky. Without much ambient light, we were able to enjoy the stars and sky in a way not possible in Chicago. When we purchased our present Arizona home, we began to think about a work relating to the sky and light and that, of course, led us to James Turrell. We met with him and he was taken by our site and wanted to cut into the side of the mountain, but the city would not allow it. So he designed our wonderful sky space, *Stone Circle* (2001). We love sitting in it at sundown and have had people visit us from all over the world.

JR Another aspect of your collection that I often think about is how successfully you have integrated the very best art being made in and around Chicago with national and international examples—one can often see the work of Gerhard Richter not far from that of Gaylen Gerber, Mary Heilmann near to Judy Ledgerwood, Luc Tuymans in proximity to Julia Fish, that kind of thing. I think the first time I noticed this was an installation in the old apartment of paper-based objects by Ann Hamilton and Buzz Spector, if I remember correctly. When I first came to Chicago, seeing your collection provided me with an important set of lessons about art in Chicago, not only in terms of seeing very good work but also in terms of seeing our great artists without any overlay of "regional" bias. It is most definitely evident in this catalogue and exhibition at the museum, and I know it is still something you are careful about in the changing installations of the collection at home. Can you talk a bit about your relationship to collecting art made in Chicago—early on and through to today?

DS If we provided an important set of lessons to you about Chicago-based work then that makes us very happy. It has always been our contention that work made by artists living and working in Chicago deserves to be integrated into our collection because it is just as important as work being created in New York, Los Angeles, London, and Berlin, etc. Therefore, we have paired some of the pieces in the collection as you have indicated. We are always looking for Chicago artists to juxtapose some of the international ones we originally found at galleries in Chicago, such as Gonzalez-Torres and Wool. We believe that there is a wonderful group of mid-career artists living and working in Chicago, and we continue to support the concept of integrating not just artists working here but young artists who are now coming into their own.

JR Your support of the Chicago art scene also extends to several of the key art schools here. You both have been active in helping the fine art programs at the University of Illinois, Chicago, and the School of the Art Institute of Chicago, where Howard is also a trustee. Strong art schools feed the creative community here in important ways.

HS Our involvement with the schools and young artists has always been important to us. We love talking to students and learning from them, and we are jealous of how much and what they read. We are mostly involved with the School of the Art Institute and the University of Illinois, Chicago, but we feel very fortunate that we have so many fine schools here. They definitely add to the richness of the art community—attracting young artists to the city and building communities to hopefully keep many of them here after graduation. We are very proud, for example, of the number of Chicago art school graduates represented in this year's Whitney Biennial.

JR You have always been very interested in film and video work. You supported a number of the Art Institute's important video acquisitions (by artists like Anri Sala and Diana Thater, among others), you made a substantial donation of media-based works from your collection to the museum in 2007, and you endowed the film and video gallery in our new Modern Wing. How did you get started collecting in this genre?

DS In the mid-to-late-1990s, we started to think about how important the discipline of film and video had become to contemporary art. Documenta X had several films that really peaked our interests. One was by the Belgian artist Johan Grimonperez, who did an elaborate, quasi-documentary film called *Dial H-I-S-T-O-R-Y* (1995–97) about airplane hijackings, and the other was William Kentridge. We vividly recall seeing *Felix in Exile* (1994) and *History of the Main Complaint* (1996) then as well, and this really was the beginning of us thinking seriously about video. After that we were in New York at D'Amelio Terras speaking with the gallerists, Chris and Lucien, when a young woman by the name of Shirin Neshat arrived at the gallery with a storyboard for her second film. Needless to say we engaged in a long conversation with Shirin and Chris and ultimately acquired *Rapture* (1999) directly from the storyboard, just before the finished work premiered at the Art Institute in the museum's *focus* series in 1999.

JR Yes, that was the first exhibition I organized at the Art Institute...

DS Of course, we remember that well...

HS After that we acquired approximately twenty films, none of which we ever managed to install at home. Today, sixteen of these, representing the best of what we had acquired, are in the collection of the Art Institute. It is very gratifying to see this happen.

JR For many years, both of you have been very involved with institutions, in Chicago and beyond. Donna is a long-standing trustee of the Museum of Contemporary Art, and both of you are in leadership positions at the Art Institute—Howard as a trustee and Chairman of the Committee on Contemporary Art and Donna as a key member of the Committee on Prints and Drawings. How do your roles within the institution help shape what you are collecting today, and how do they form your vision for the future?

HS Well, our close association with institutions like the Art Institute has exposed us to vast amounts of information we would not have had otherwise. It allows us to question and ascertain historical backgrounds and it provides direct contact with curators, writers, and historians, who in turn suggest readings that we use to further our own knowledge. This often prompts us to sharpen our vision of the future. But above all, these relationships with people in the contemporary art world have helped to keep us young. We rely on these encounters to inspire our future thinking as we both approach our eighth decade. We have, however, always felt that our relationship to the art world has given us much more than we have given. Above all, we feel the arts are the overarching element that tends to hold the world together.

Janine Antoni, *Mortar and Pestle*, 1999

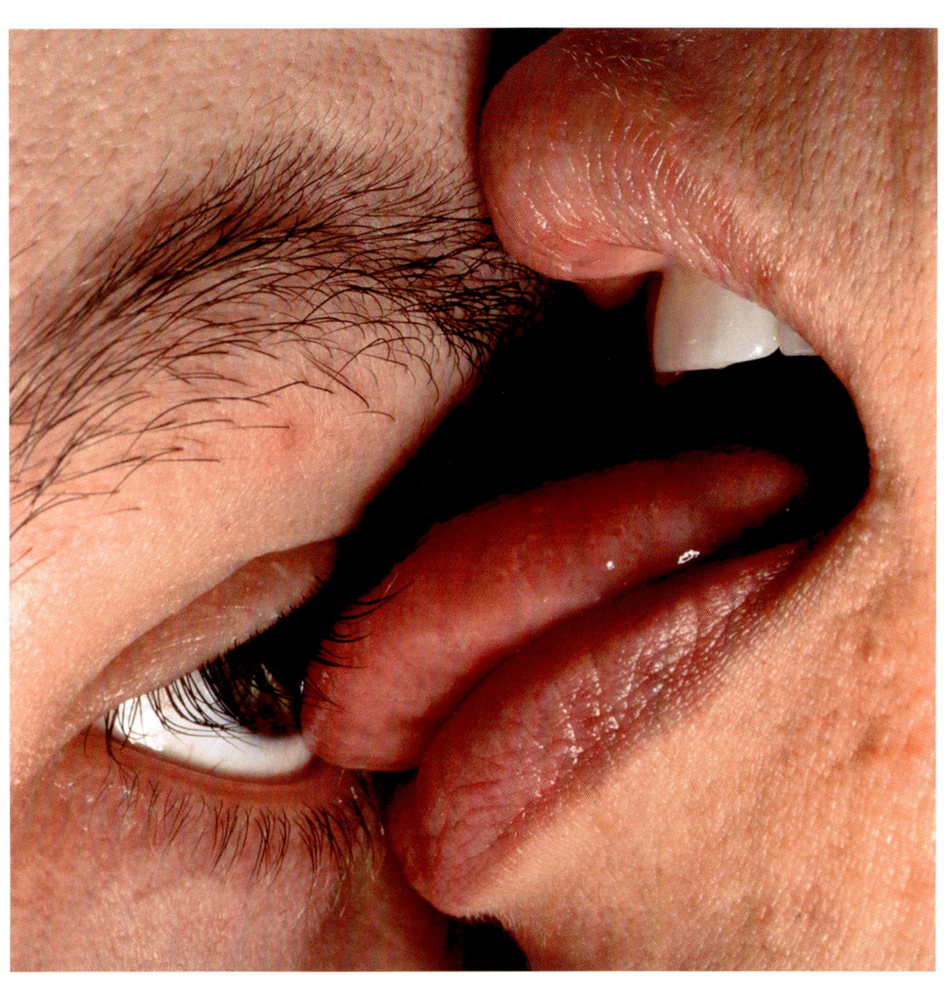

Janine Antoni, *Ingrown*, 1998 *Coddle*, 1999

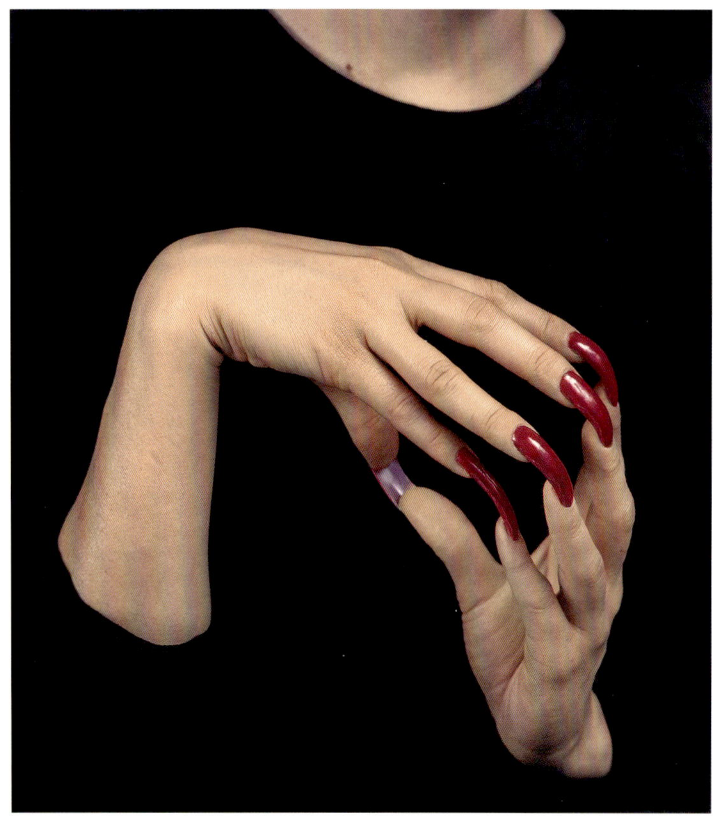

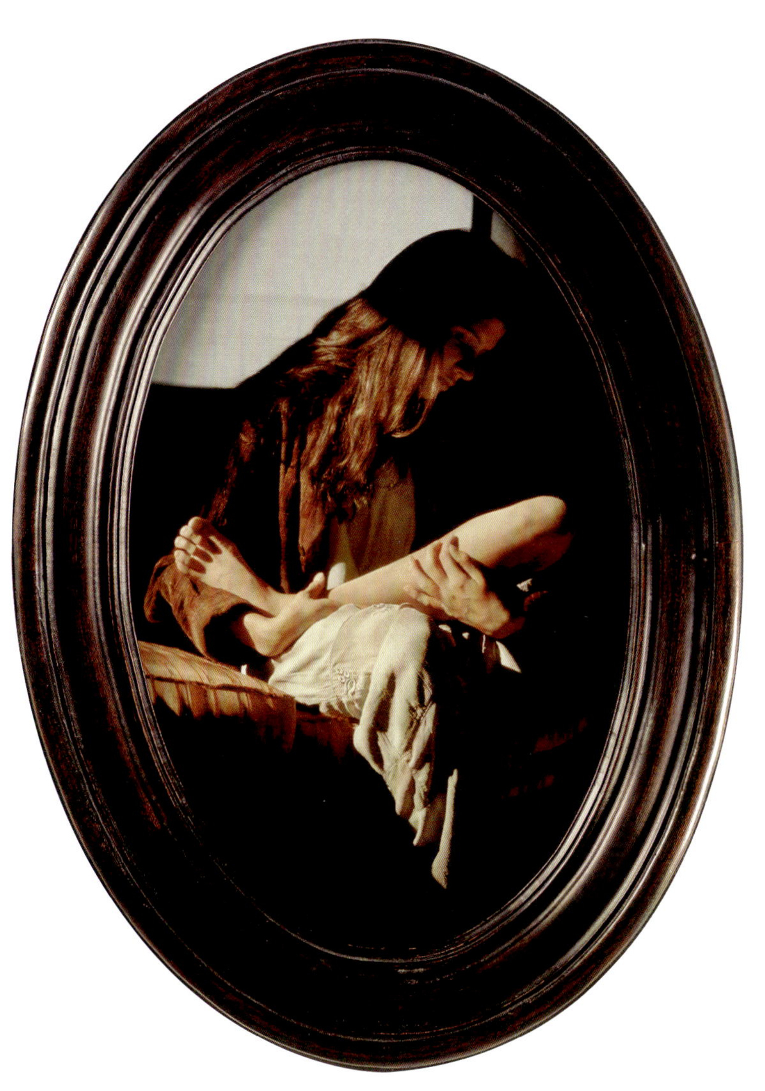

Janine Antoni, *2038*, 2000

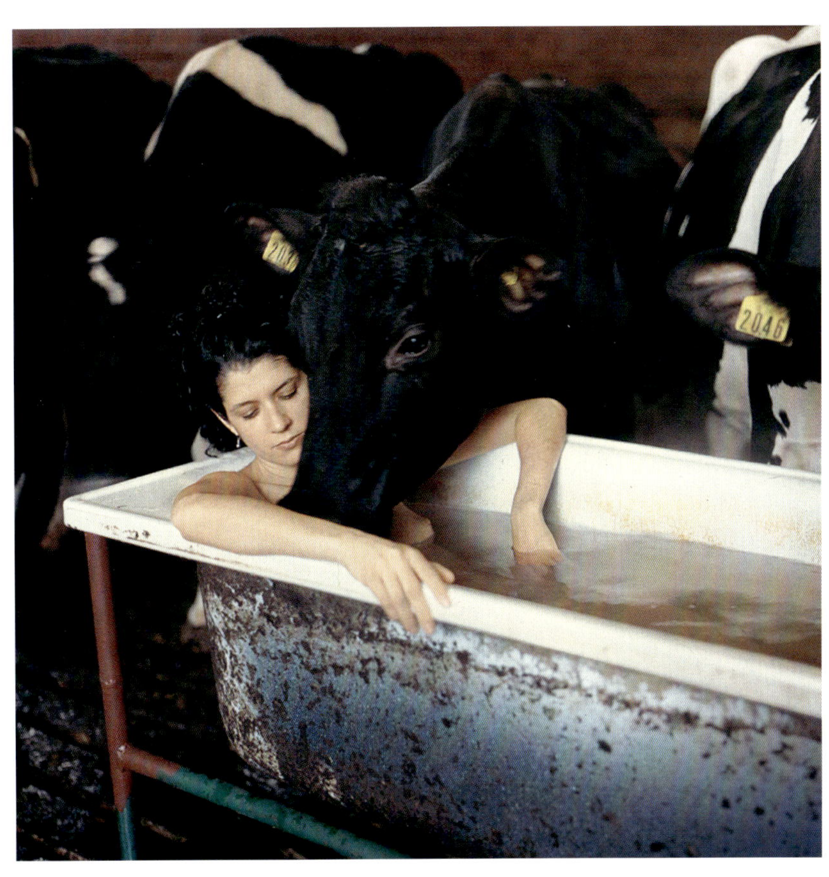
2046

Janine Antoni, *Caryatid (cobalt blue glazed porcelain with gold ceramic ornamentation)*, 2003 *Tangent*, 2003

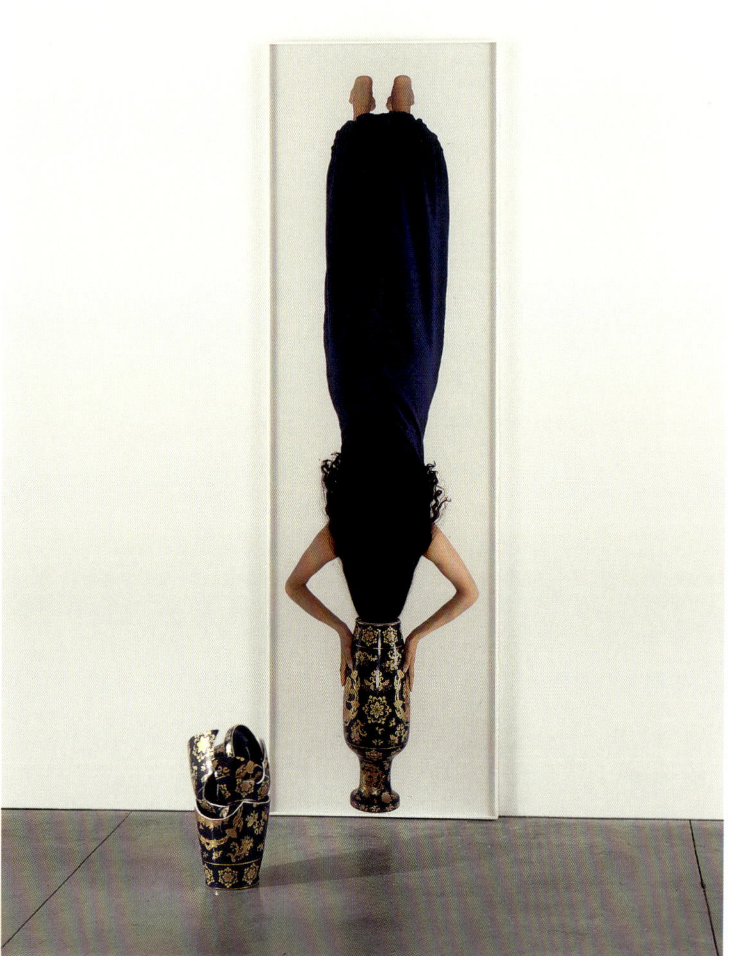

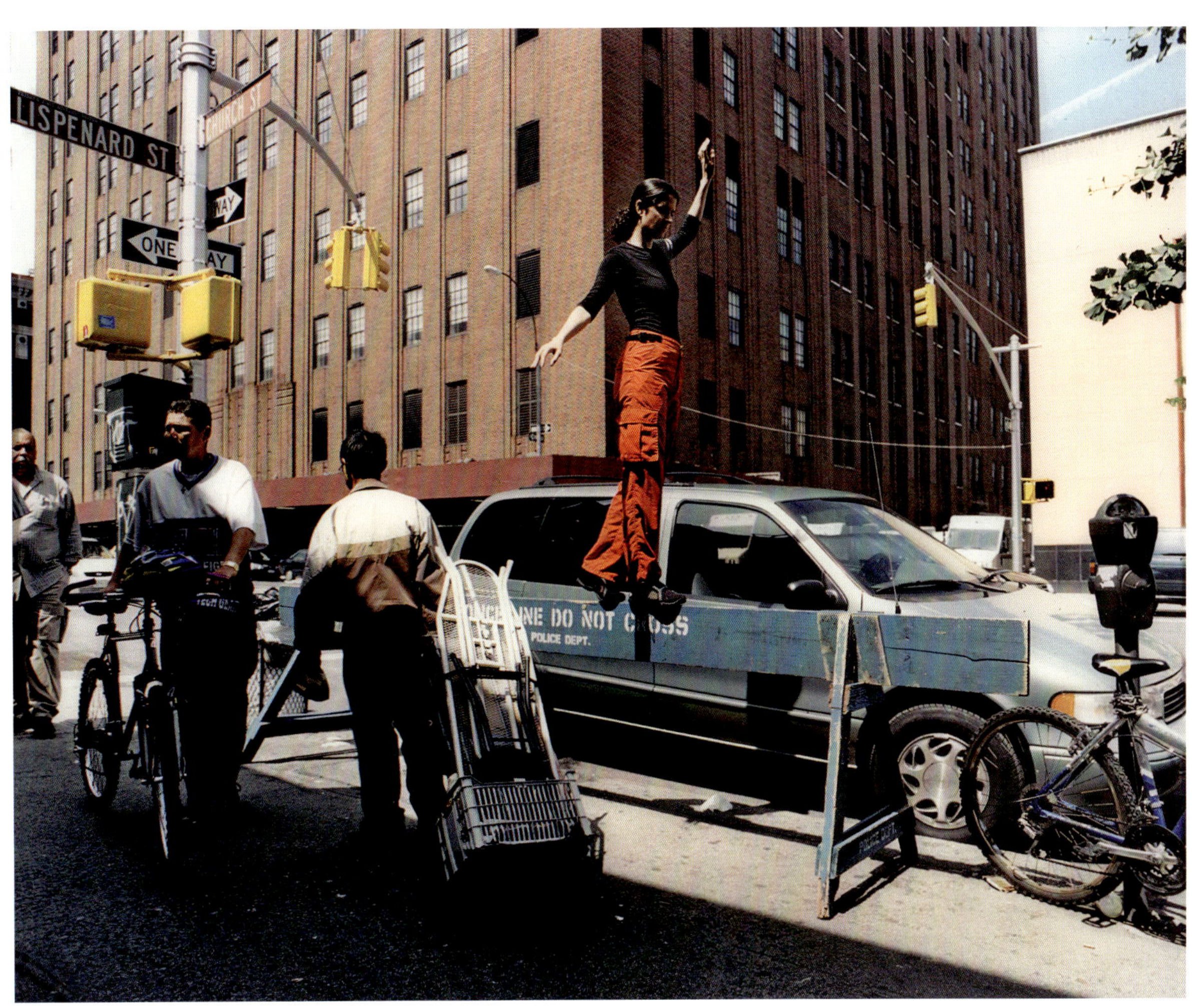
LISPENARD ST
ONE
DO NOT
POLICE DEPT.

Stanley Brouwn

In accordance with the wishes of the artist, no details of his life and work shall be published.

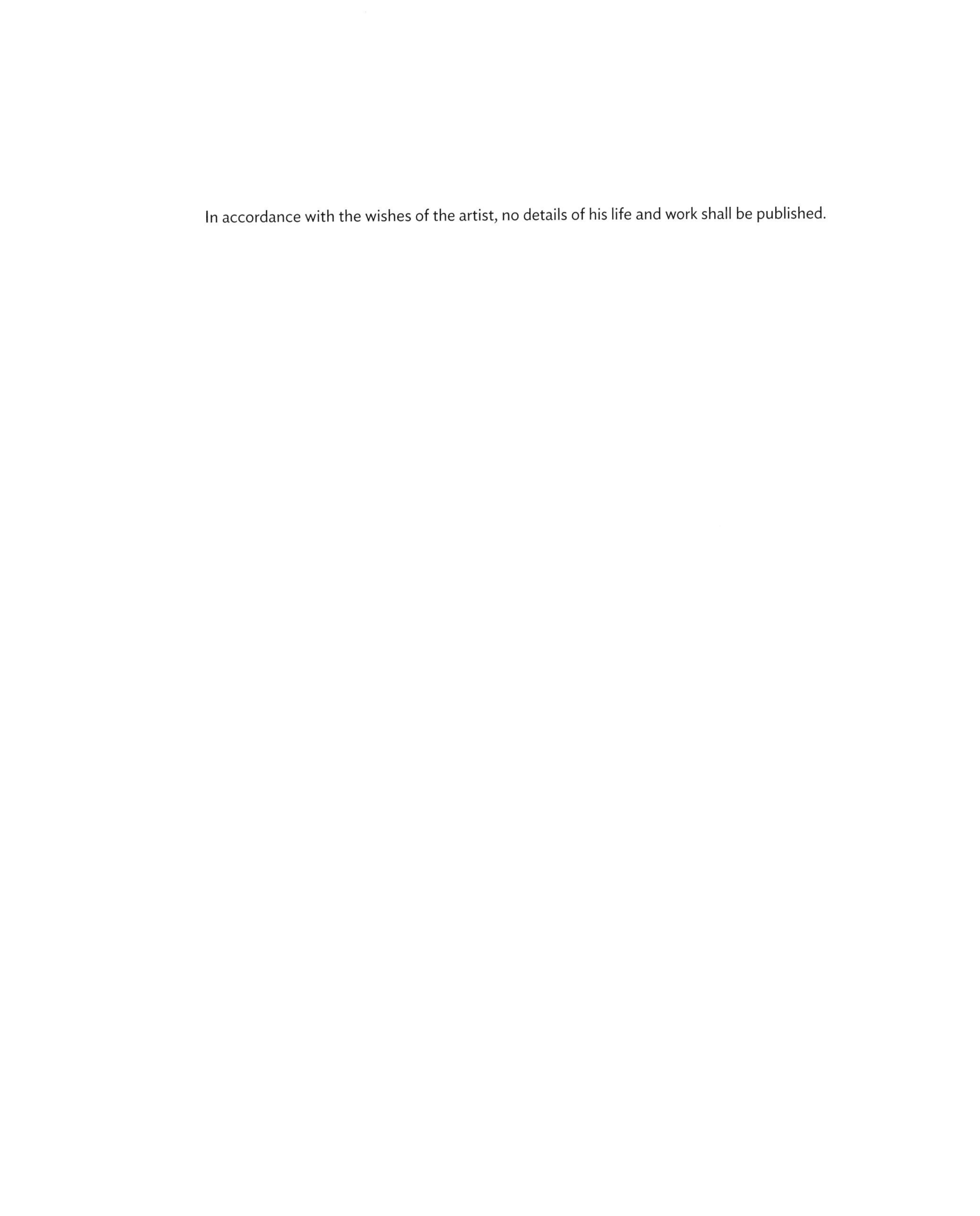

Marlene Dumas, *The Deceased*, 2002

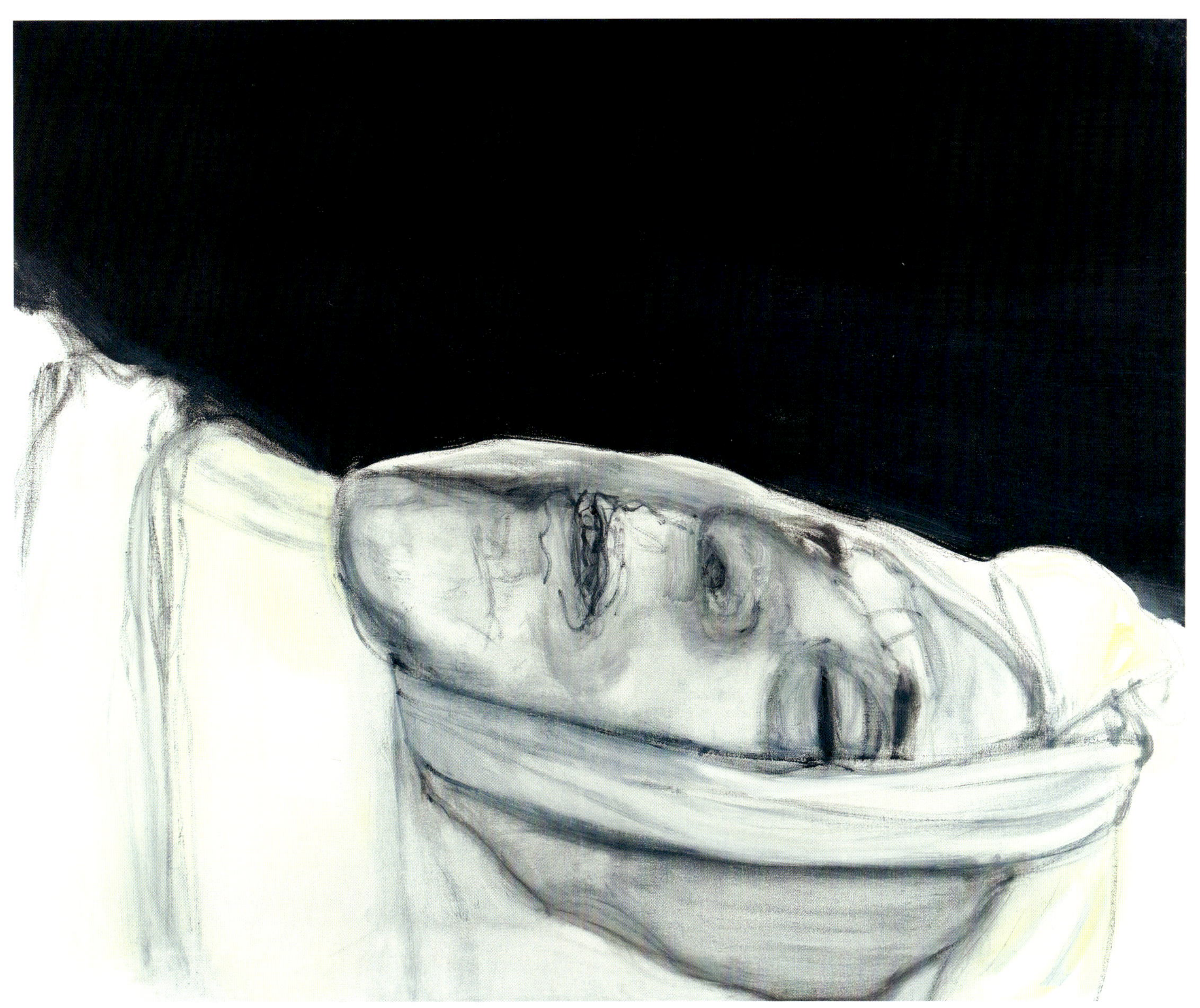

Vincent Fecteau, *Untitled*, 2008

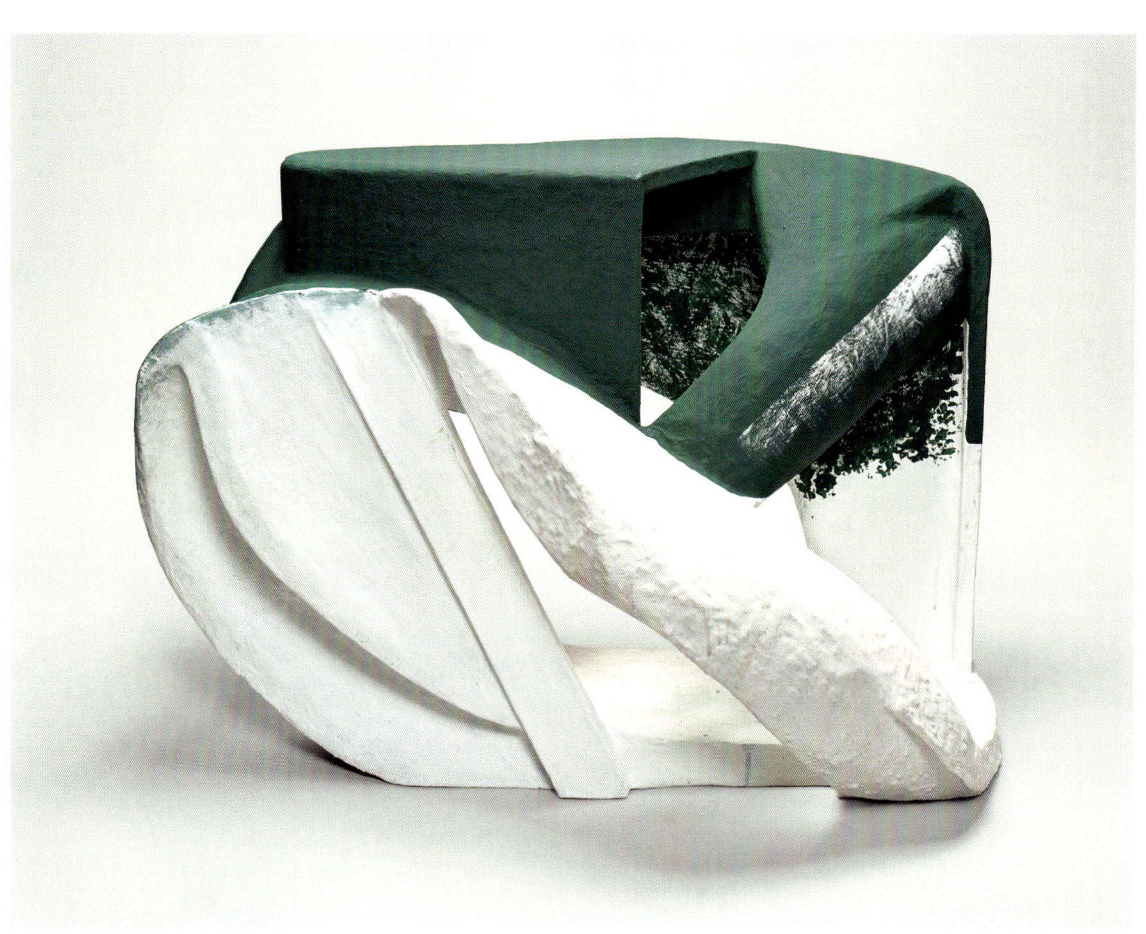

Julia Fish, *5811 South Ellis*, 1995

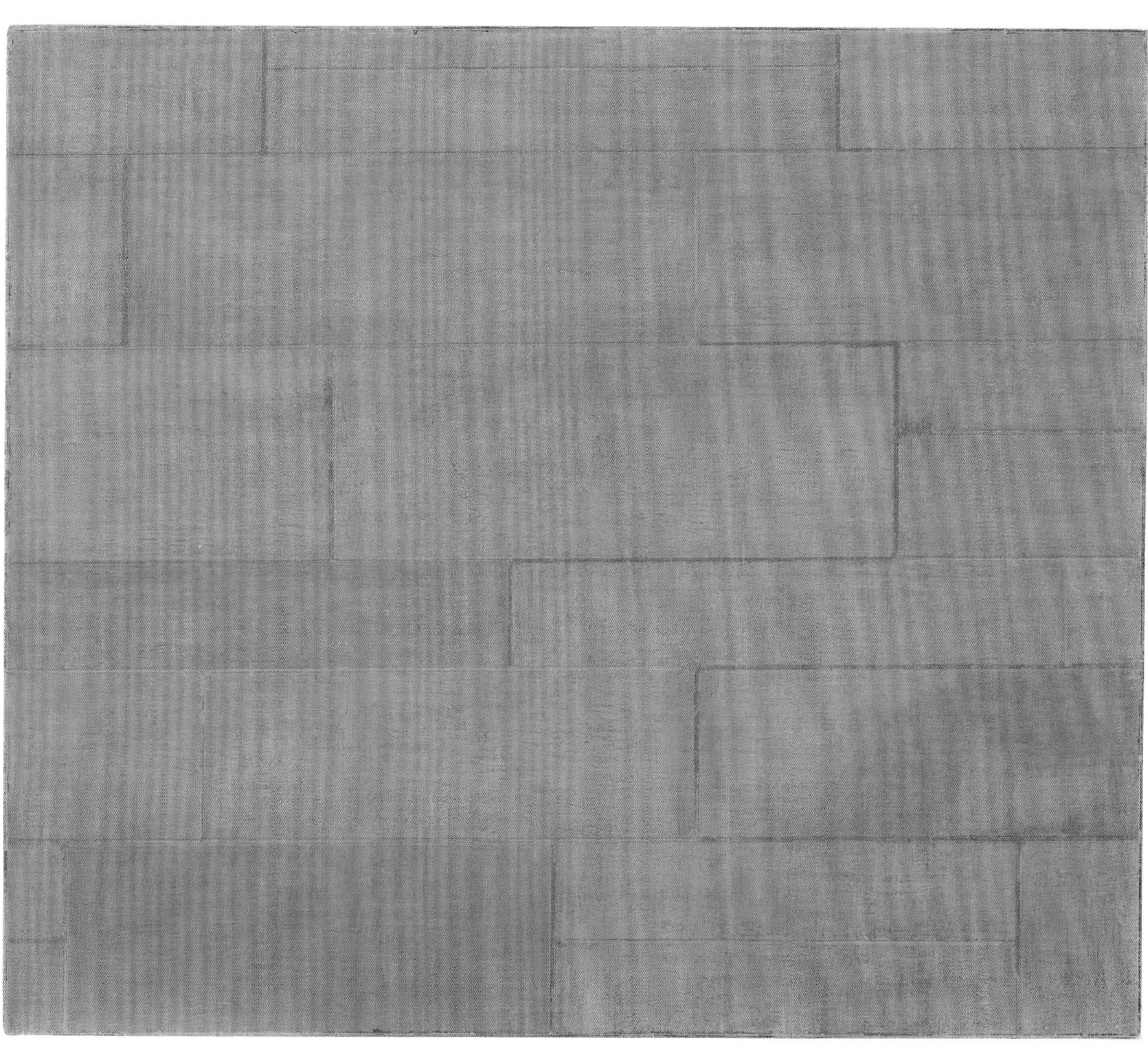

Julia Fish, *Frost II*, 1996

Julia Fish, *Living Room: NorthEast, with lights, action*, 2003–05

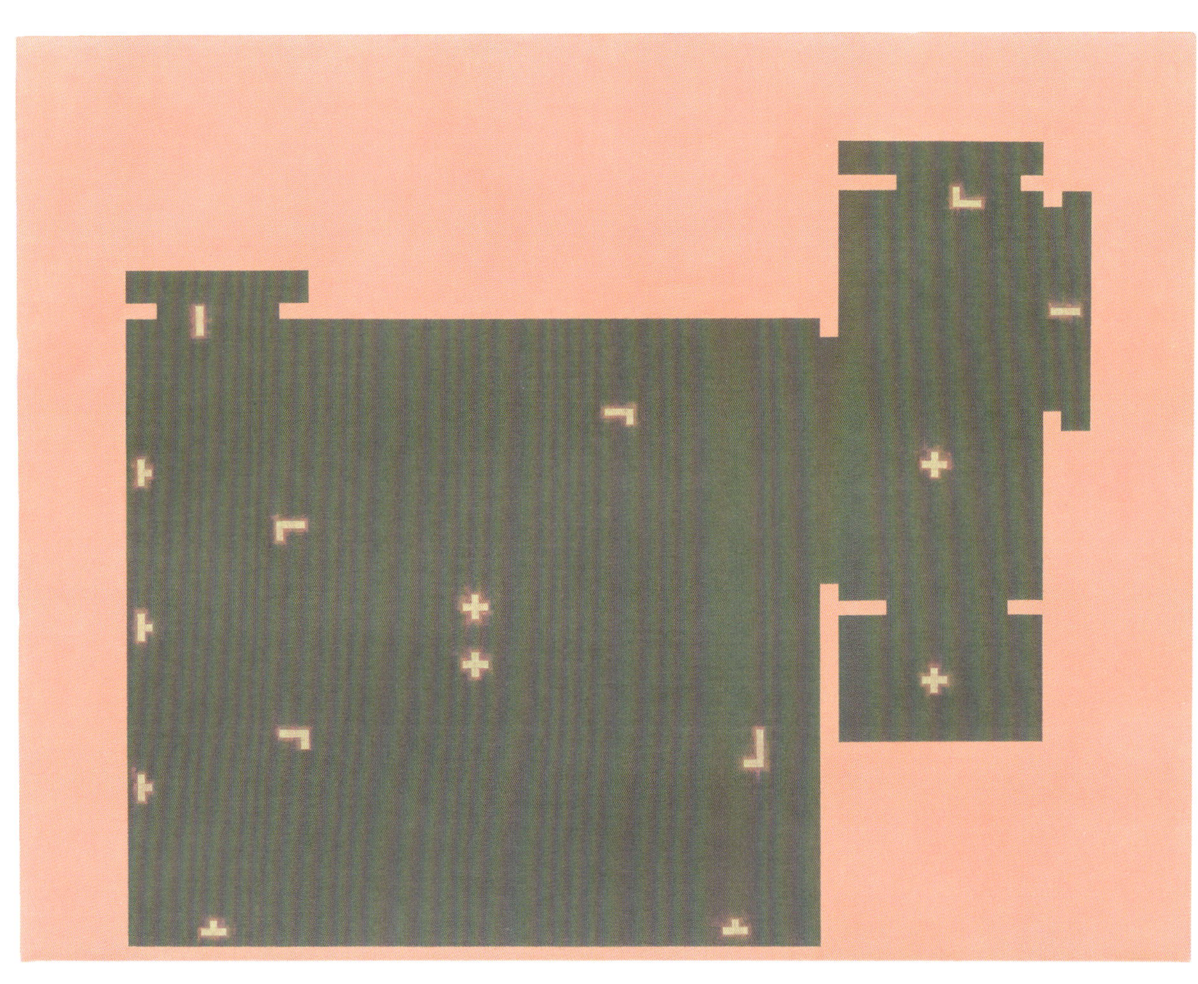

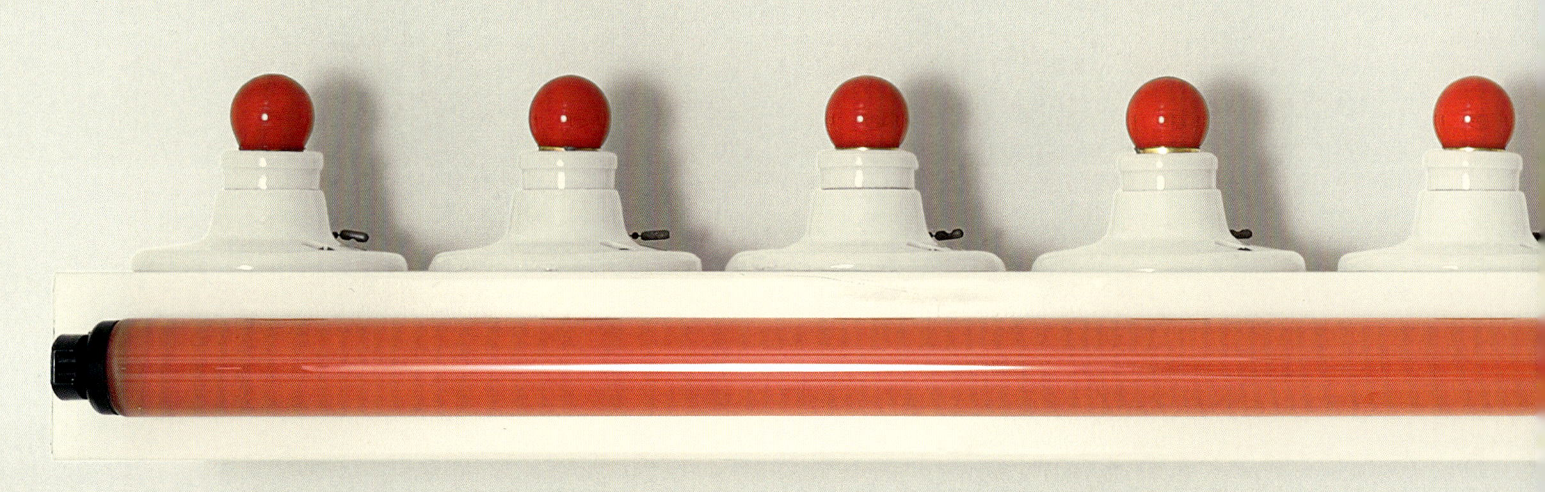

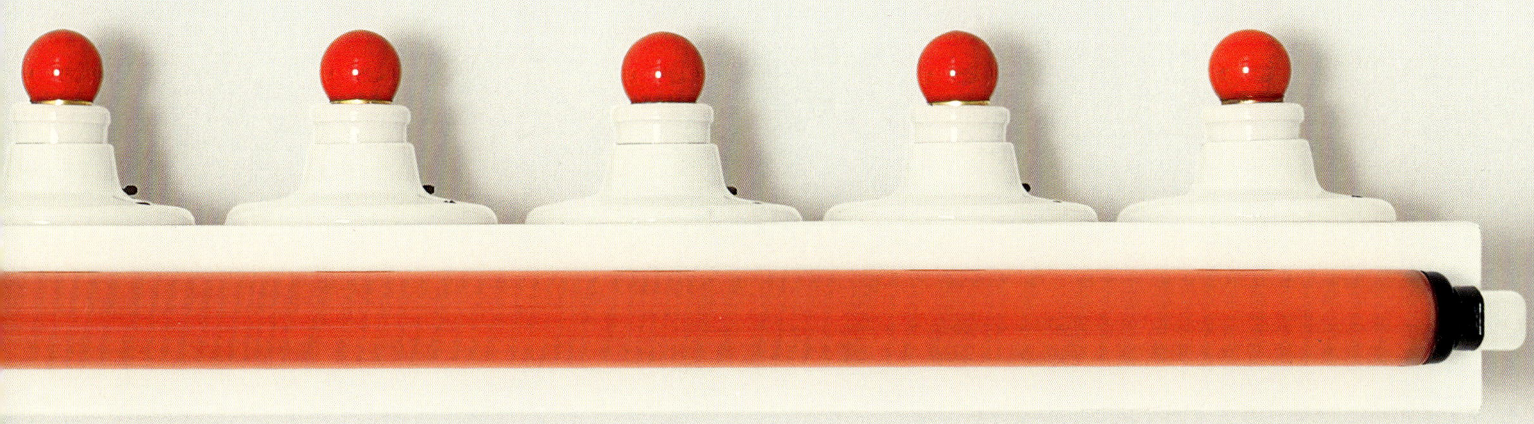

Dan Flavin, *one of May 27, 1963*, 1963

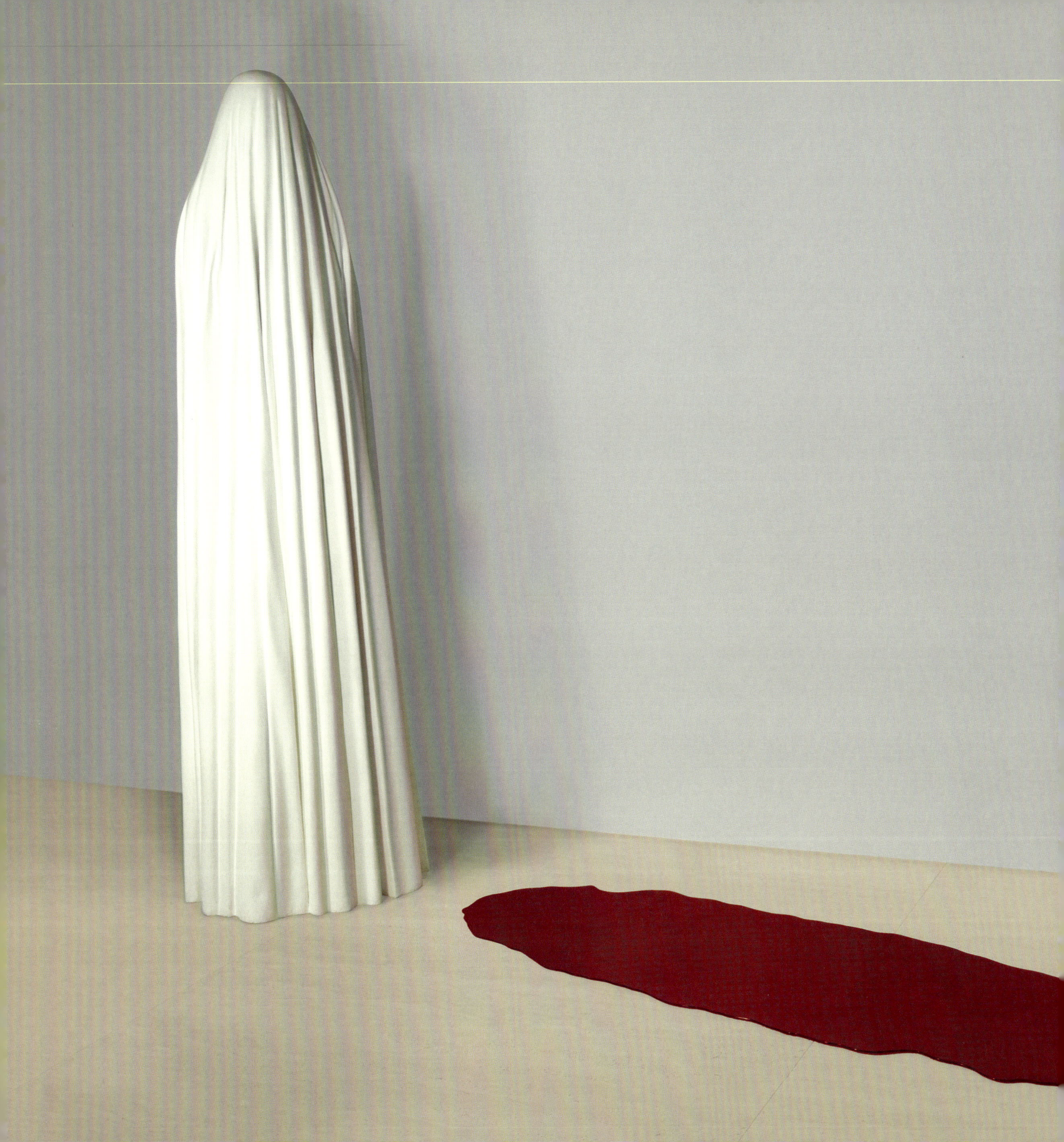

Katharina Fritsch, *Ghost and Pool of Blood*, 1988

Maureen Gallace, *Summer Rainbow, Cape Cod*, 2006

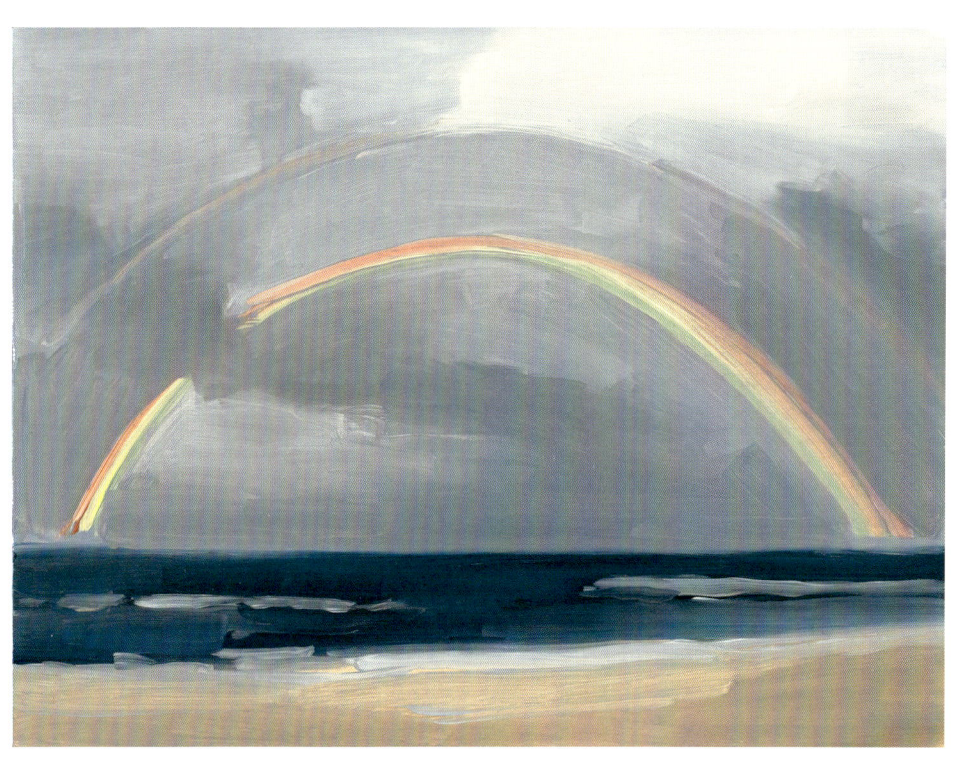

Robert Gober, *Double Sink*, 1984

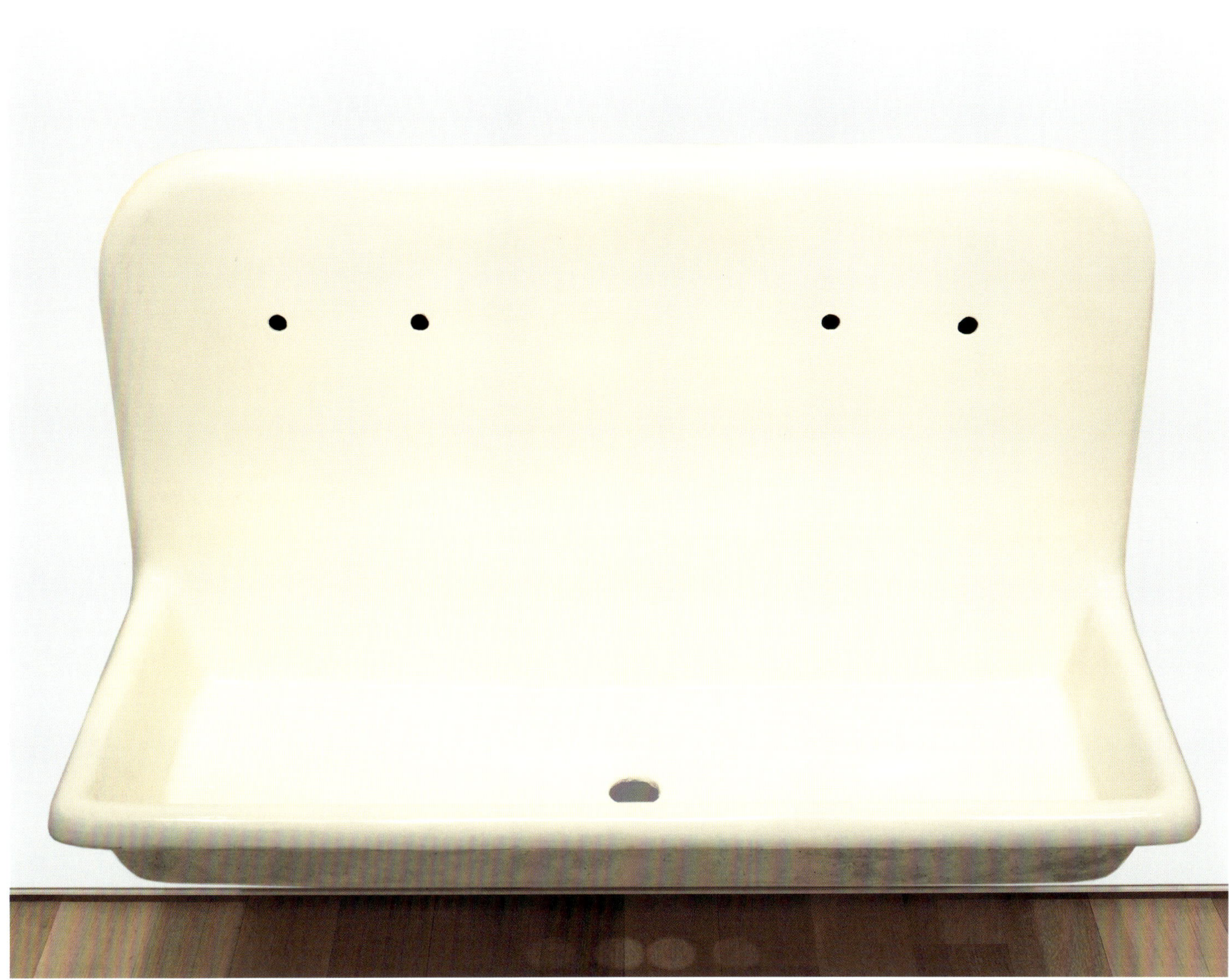

Robert Gober, *Untitled*, 2000–01

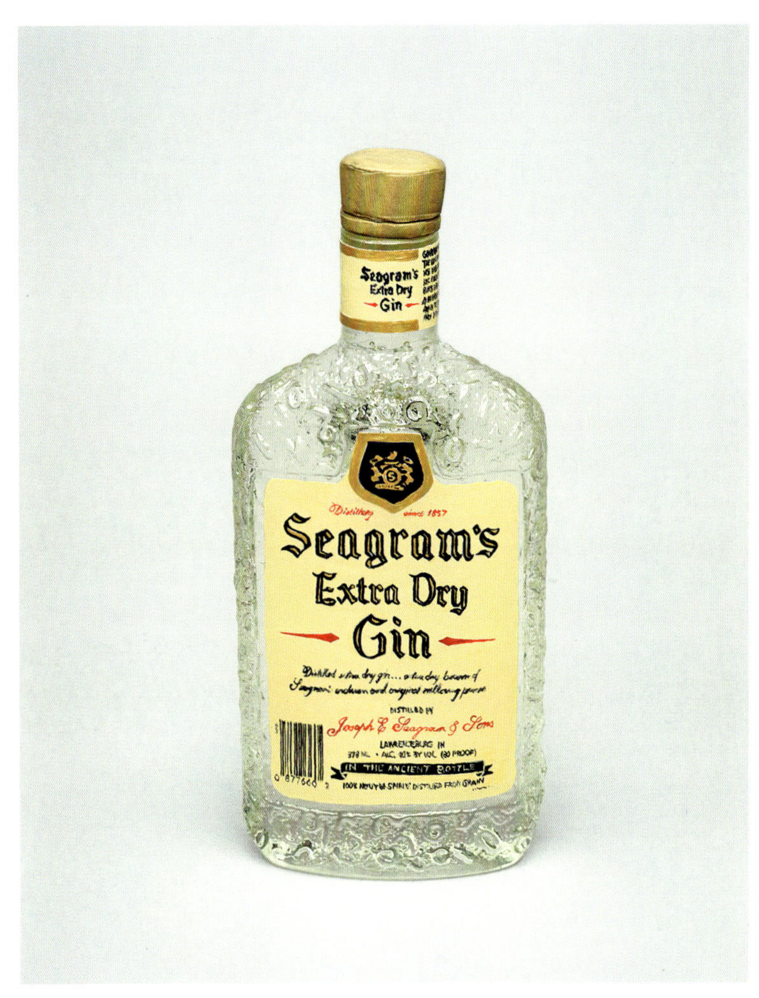
Seagram's
Extra Dry
Gin
Seagram's
Extra Dry
Gin
DISTILLED BY
IN THE ANCIENT BOTTLE

Daan van Golden, *Study H.M.*, 2004

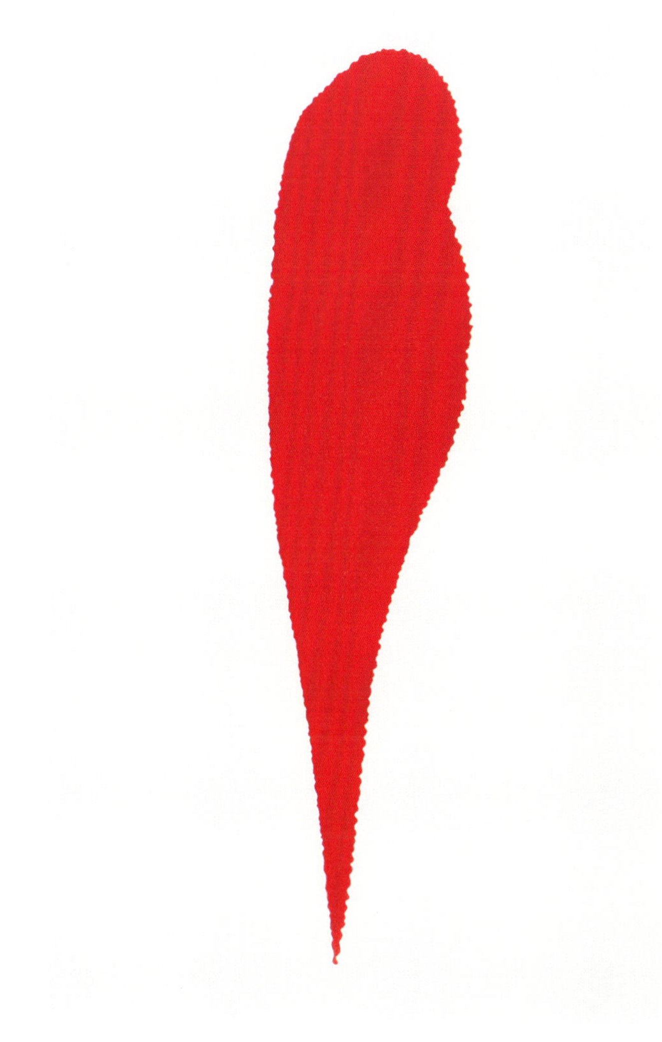

Felix Gonzalez-Torres, *"Untitled" (Paris)*, 1988

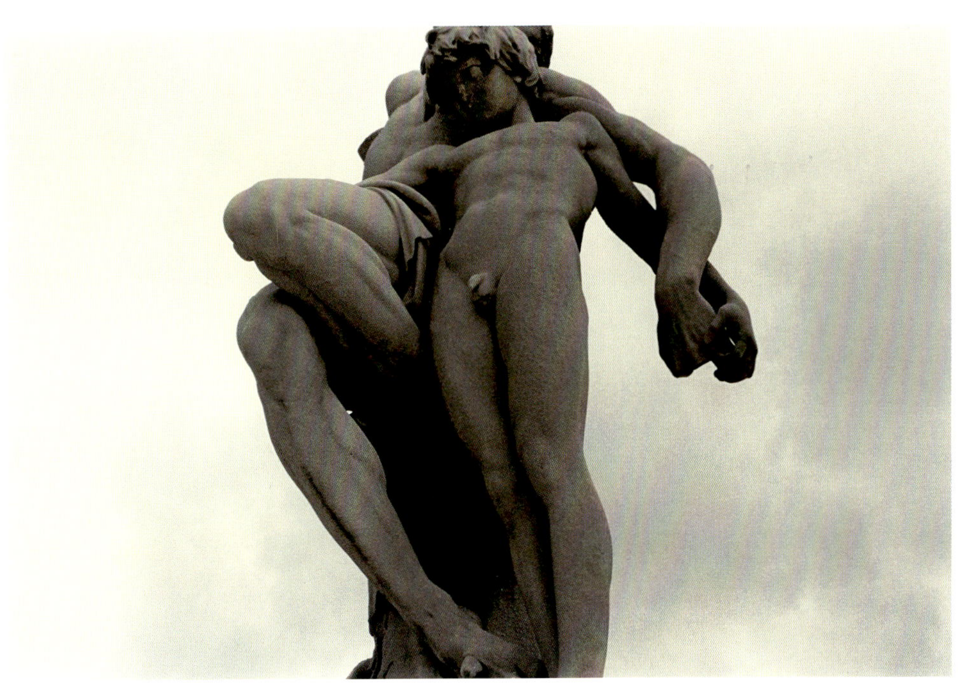

Felix Gonzalez-Torres, *"Untitled" (Portrait of Ross in LA)*, 1991

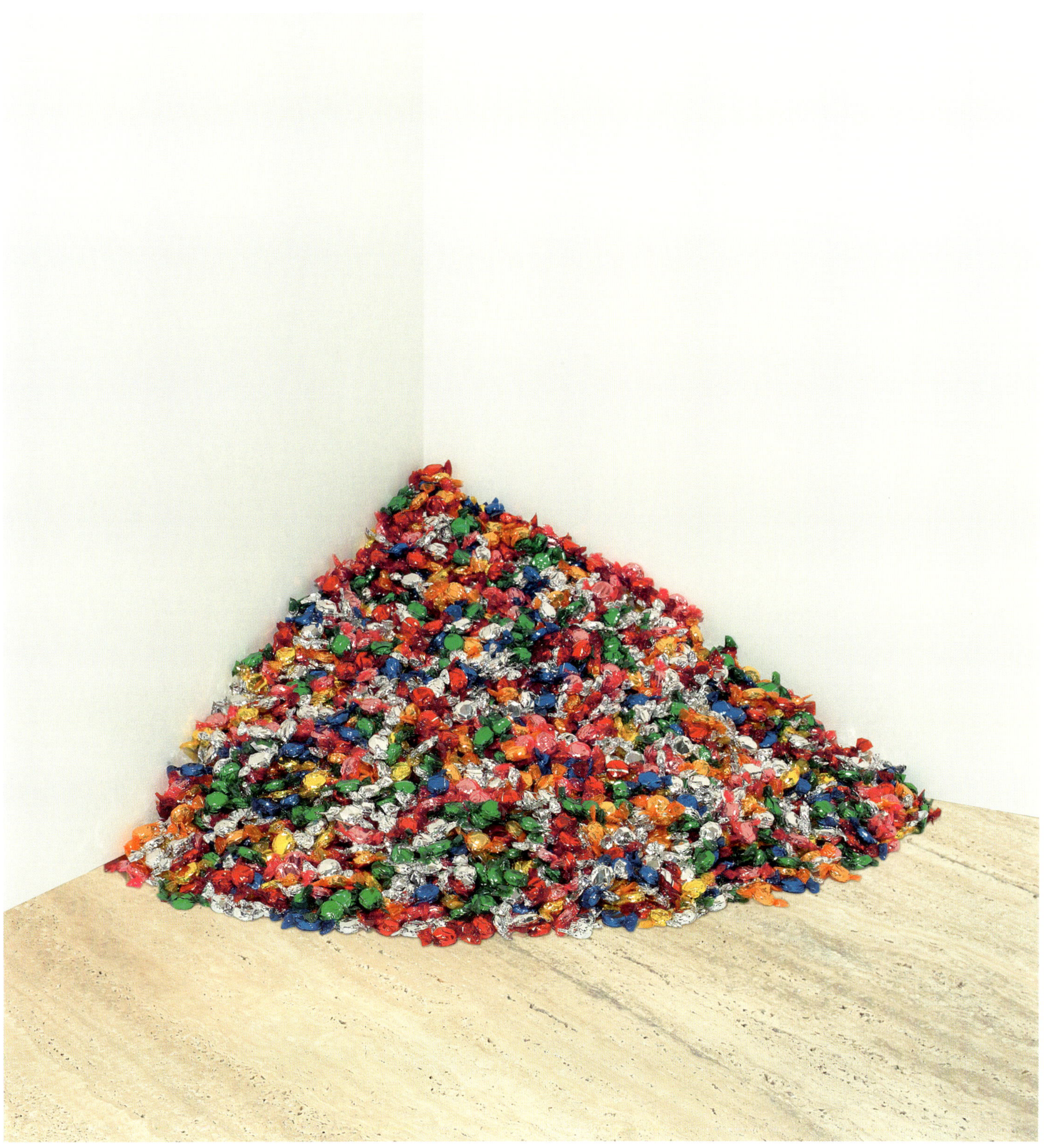

Mary Heilmann, *Green JA*, 2000

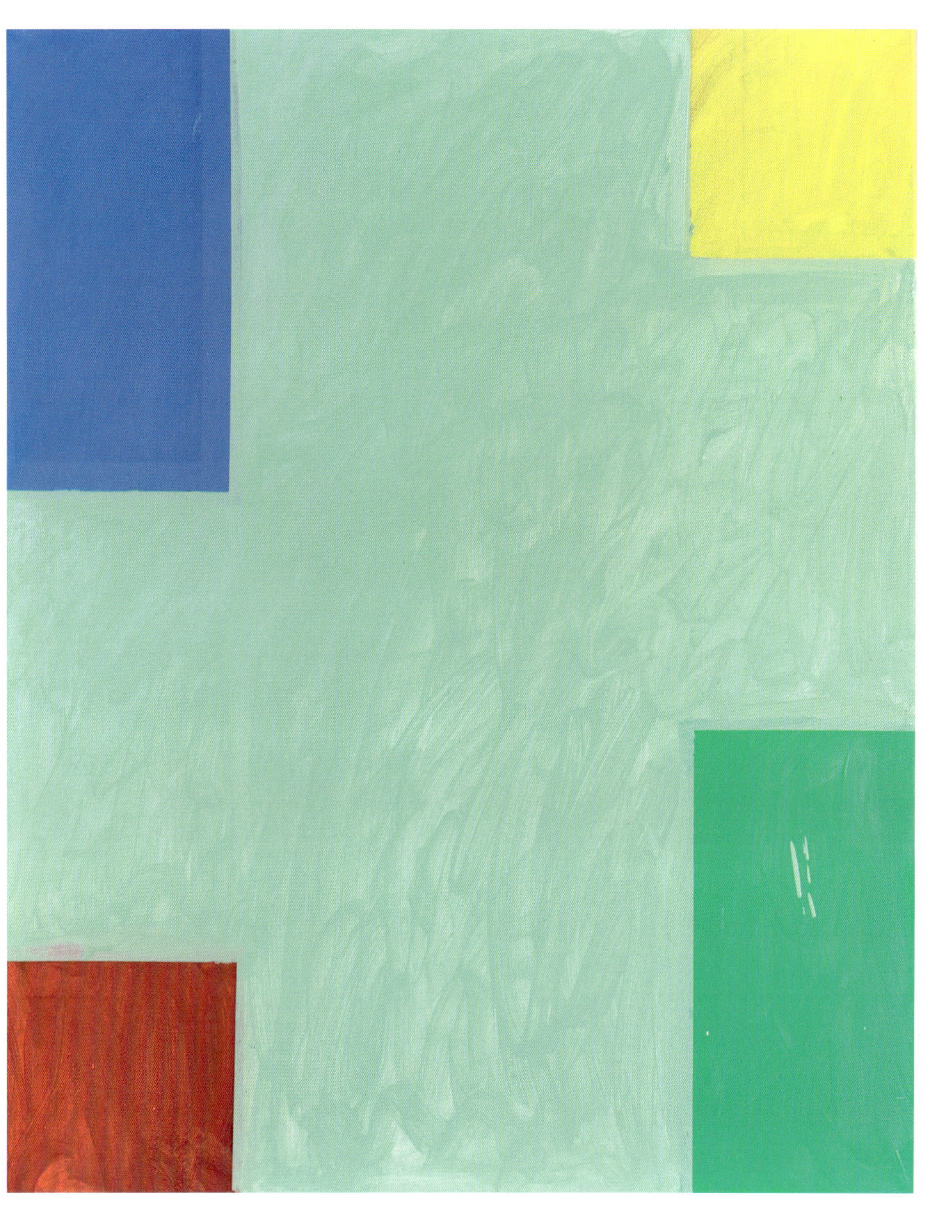

Arturo Herrera, *Let Me Go*, 2000

Jim Hodges, *Together/Between*, study for *Untitled (Portrait of Howard and Donna Stone)*, 1999

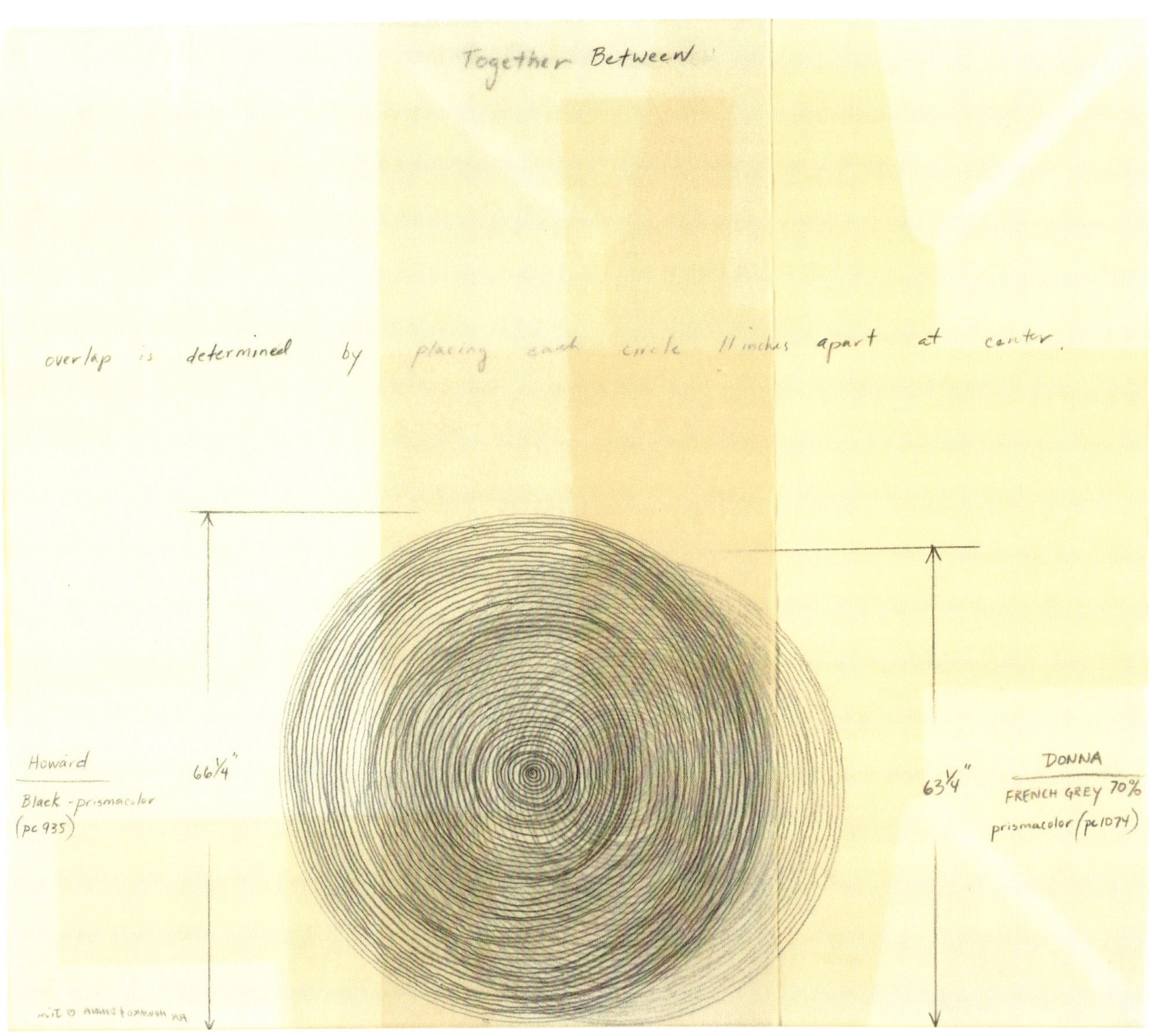
Together Between
overlap is determined by placing each circle 11 inches apart at center.
Howard
Black - prismacolor
(pc 935)
66 1/4"
63 1/4"
DONNA
FRENCH GREY 70%
prismacolor (pc1074)

Jim Hodges, *Revealed*, 2004

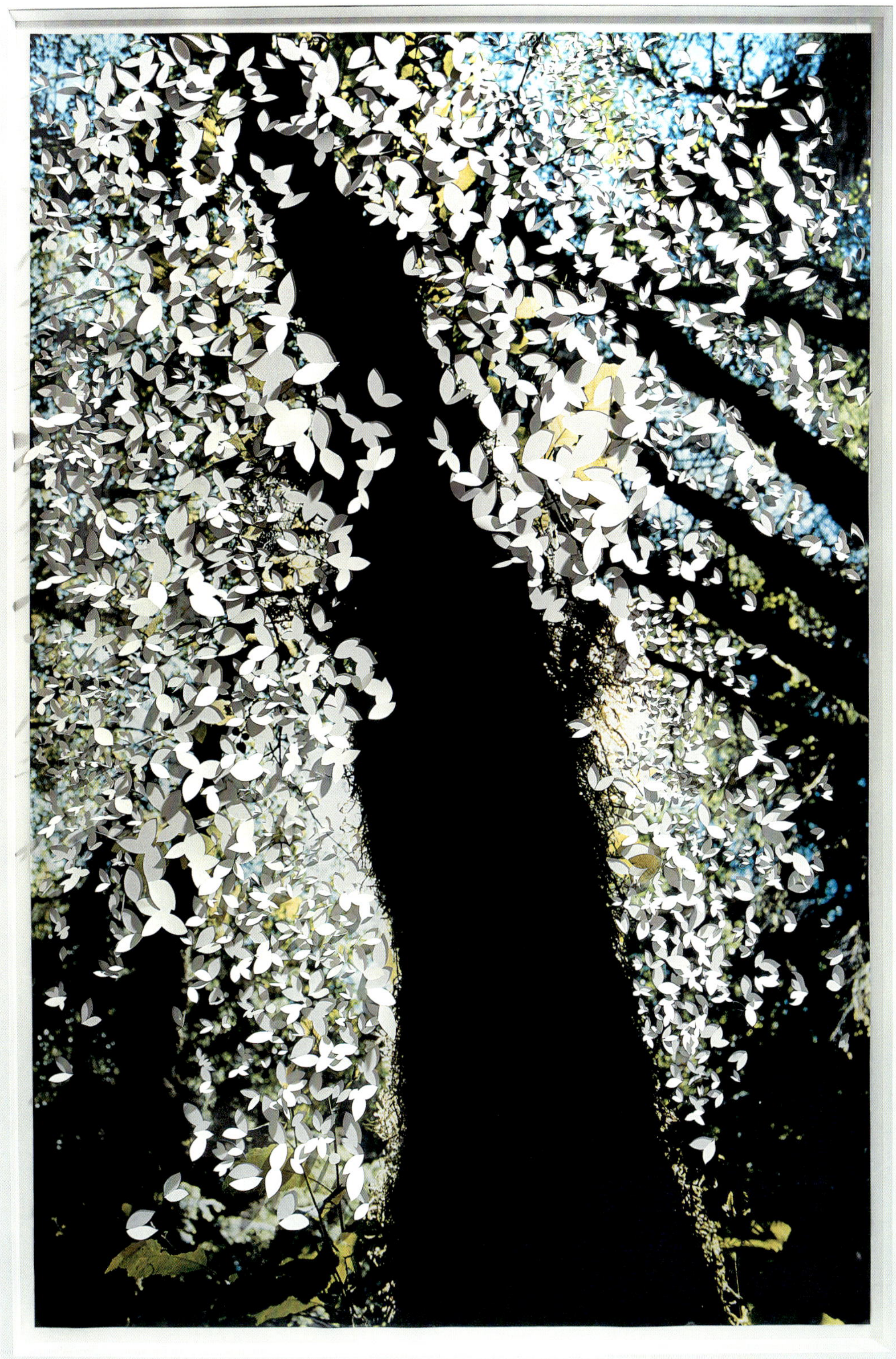

Roni Horn, *Deeps and Skies*, 1995–96

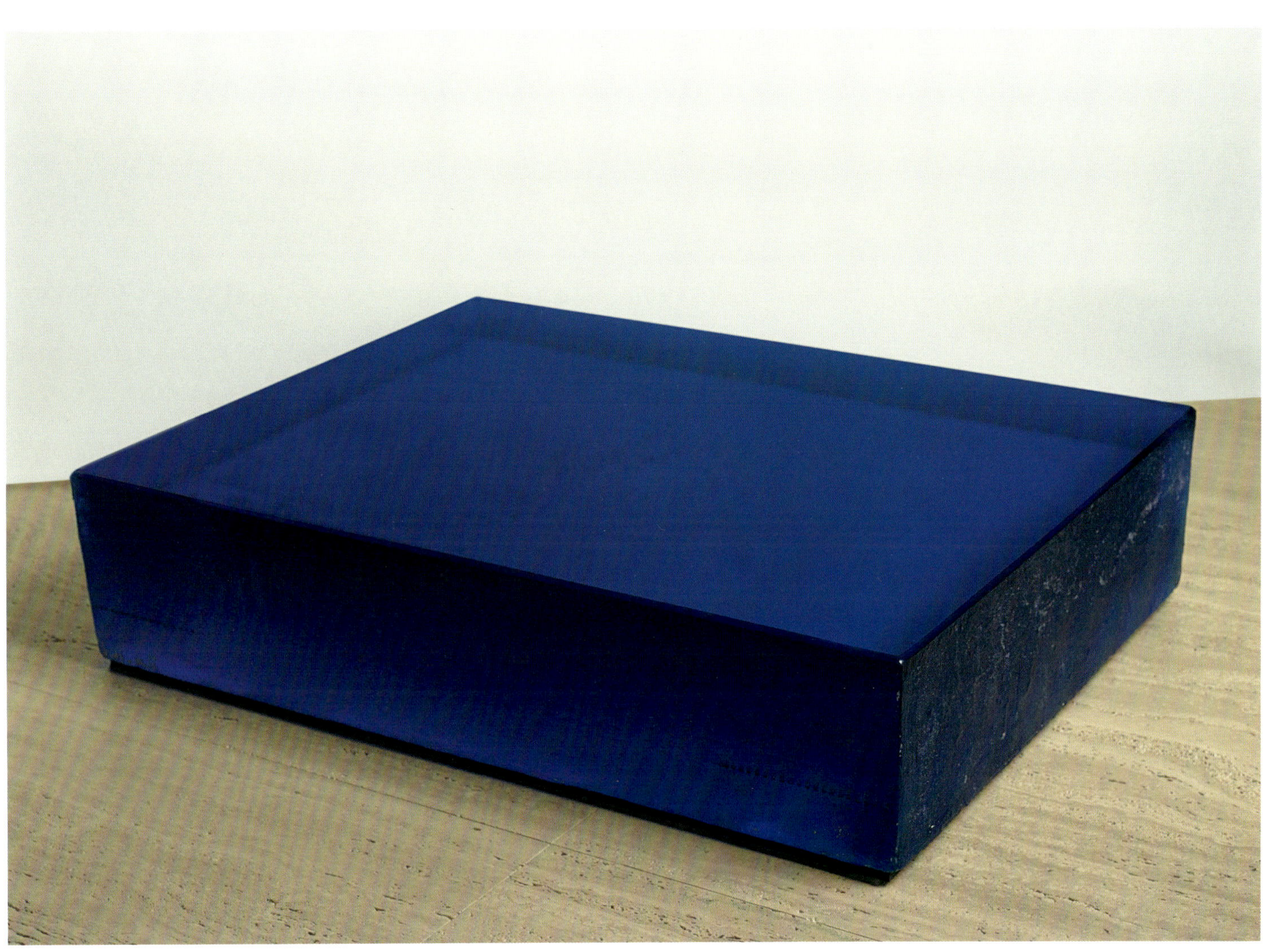

Pierre Huyghe, *The Housing Projects*, 1994/2001

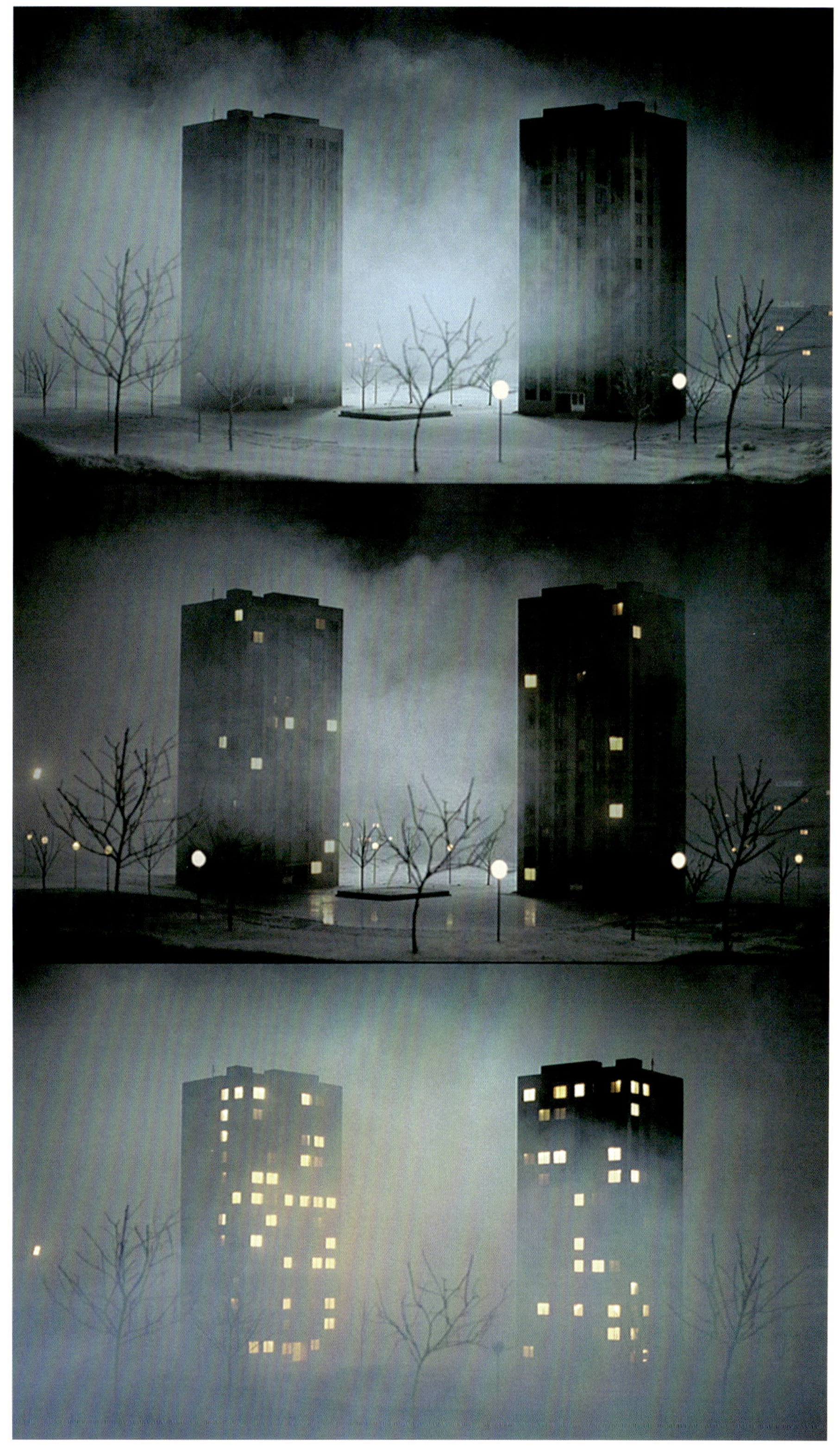

Ellsworth Kelly, *Red Diagonal*, 2007

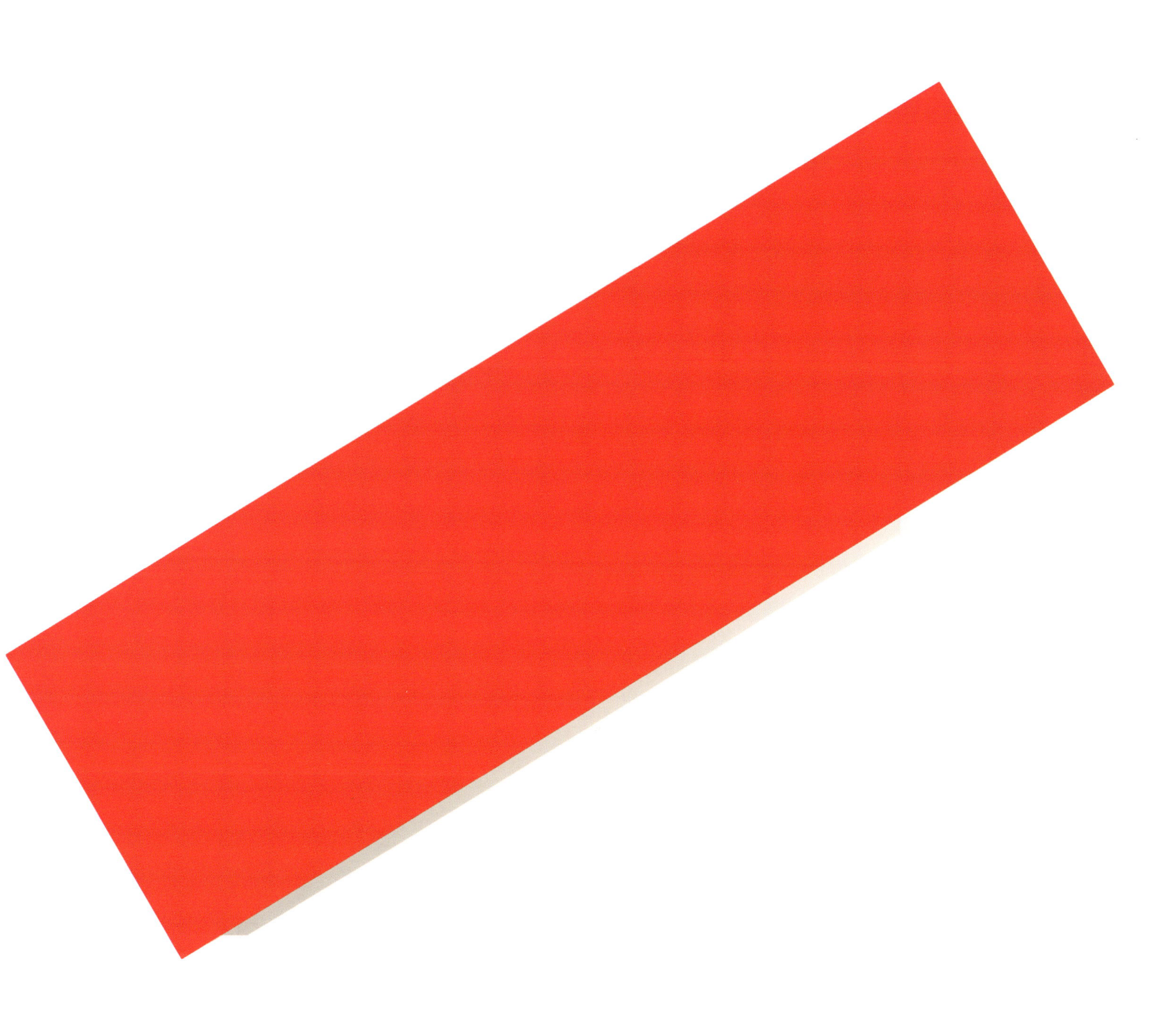

Raoul De Keyser, *Retour 3*, 1999

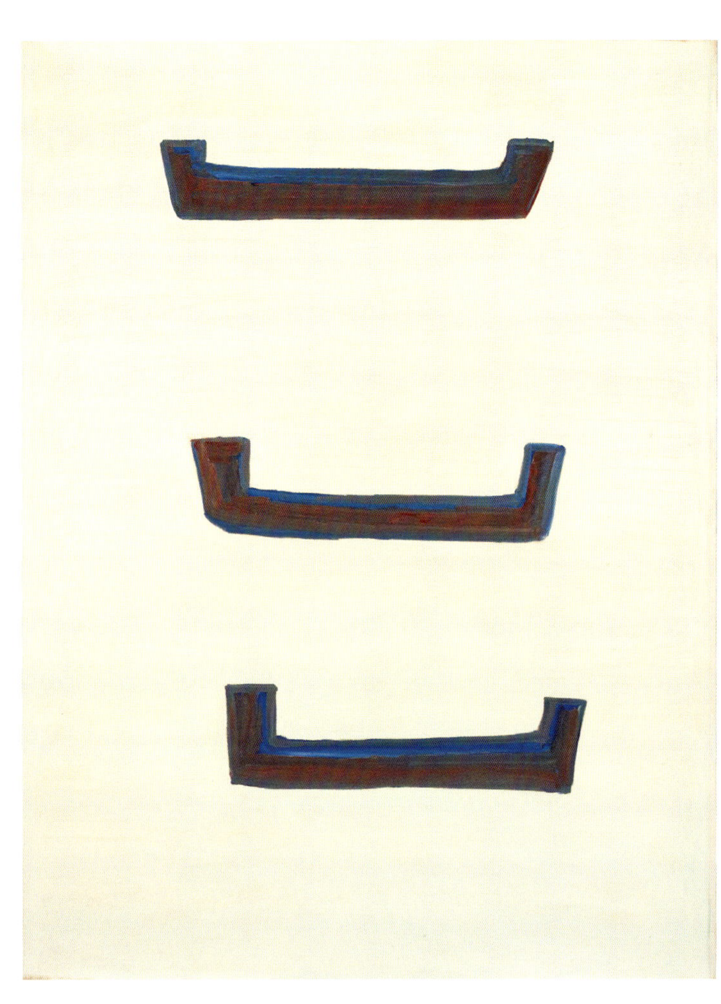

Byron Kim, *U.N. Building (Looking Downtown)*, 2008

Michael Krebber, *Beautiful Woman Beautifully Painted*, 2002

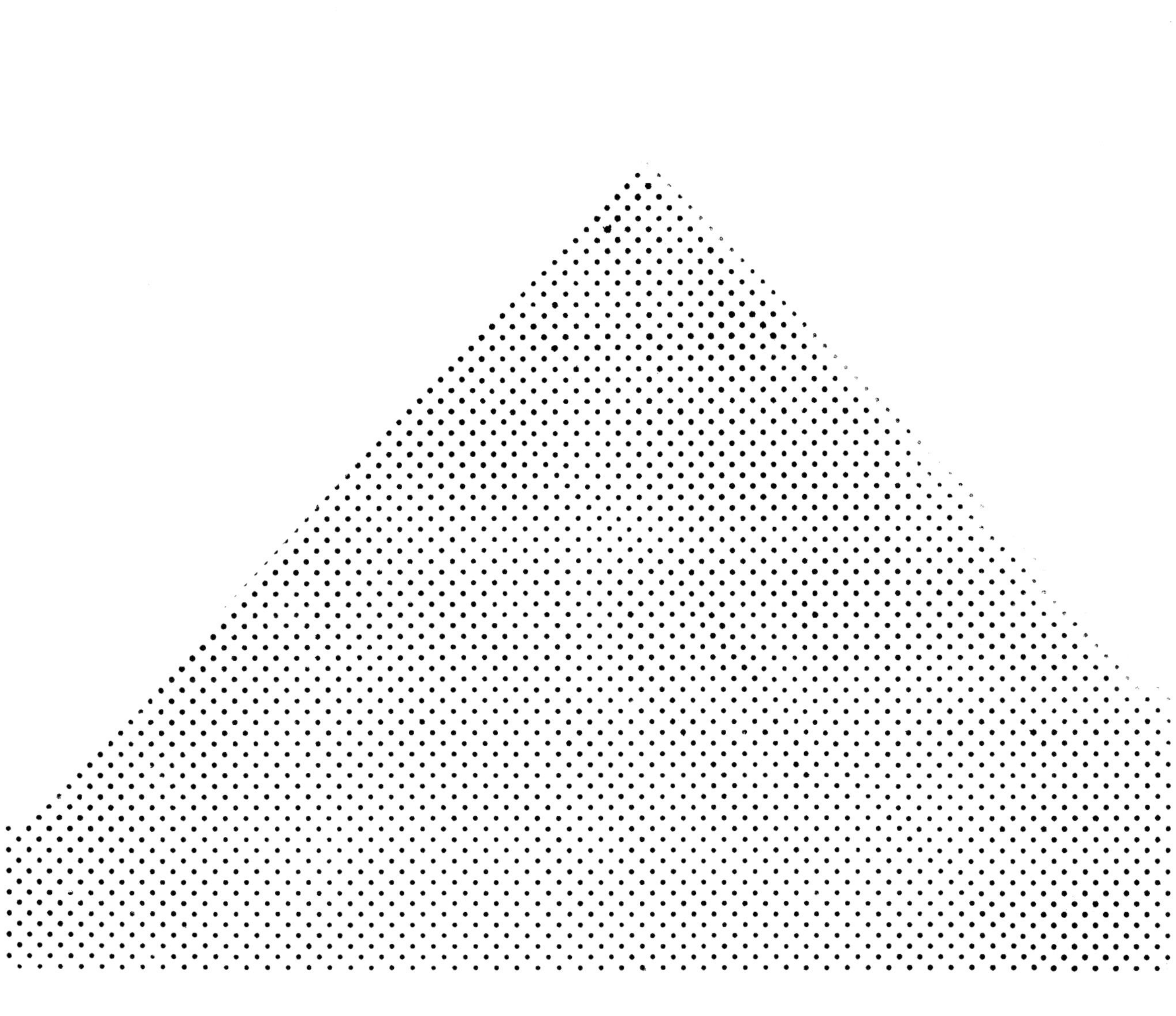

Judy Ledgerwood, *Red Pine*, 1990

Sol LeWitt, *Splotch #1*, 1999

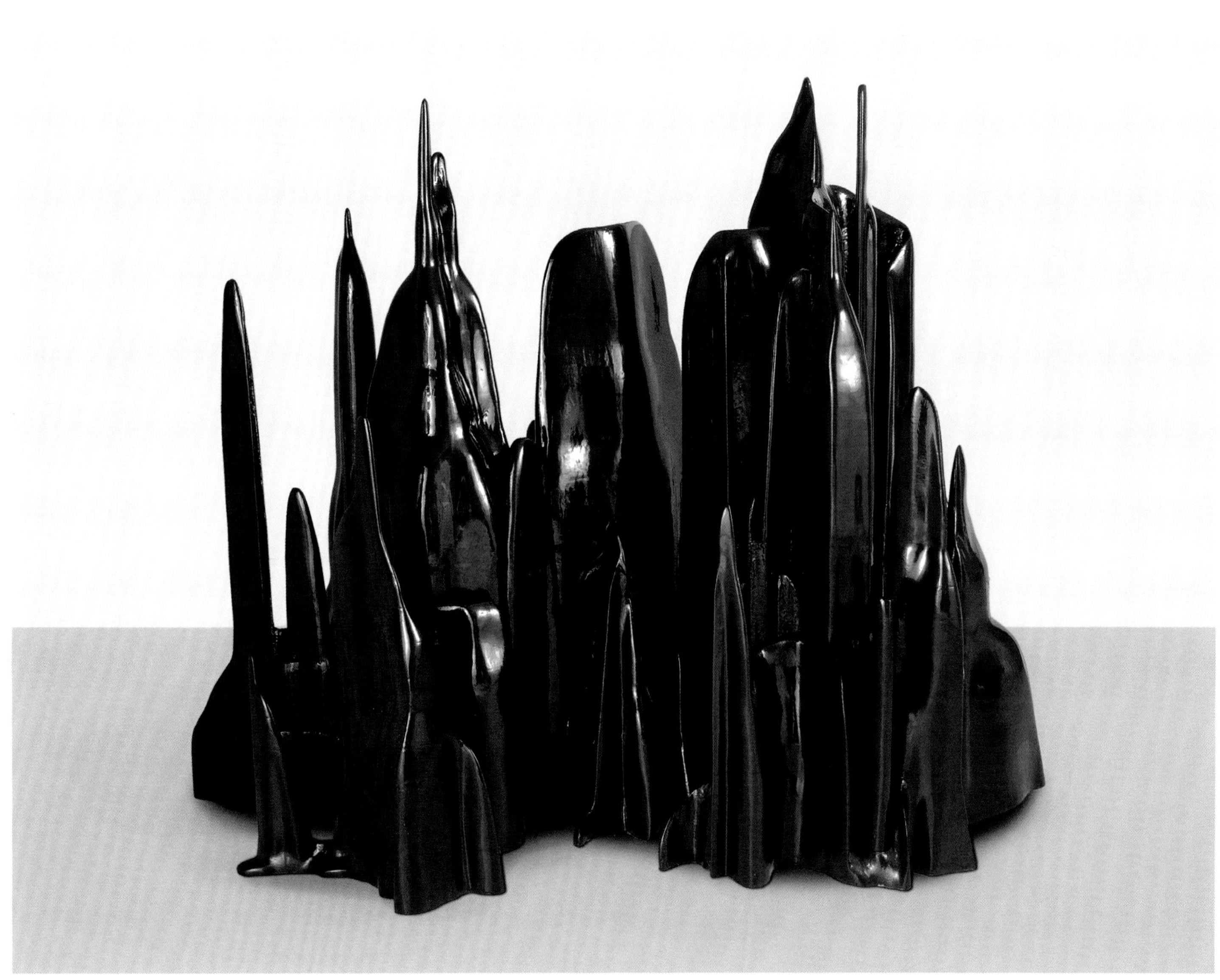

Sol LeWitt, Diagram for *Wall Drawing #1111: Circle with broken bands of color*, 2003

D I A G R A M

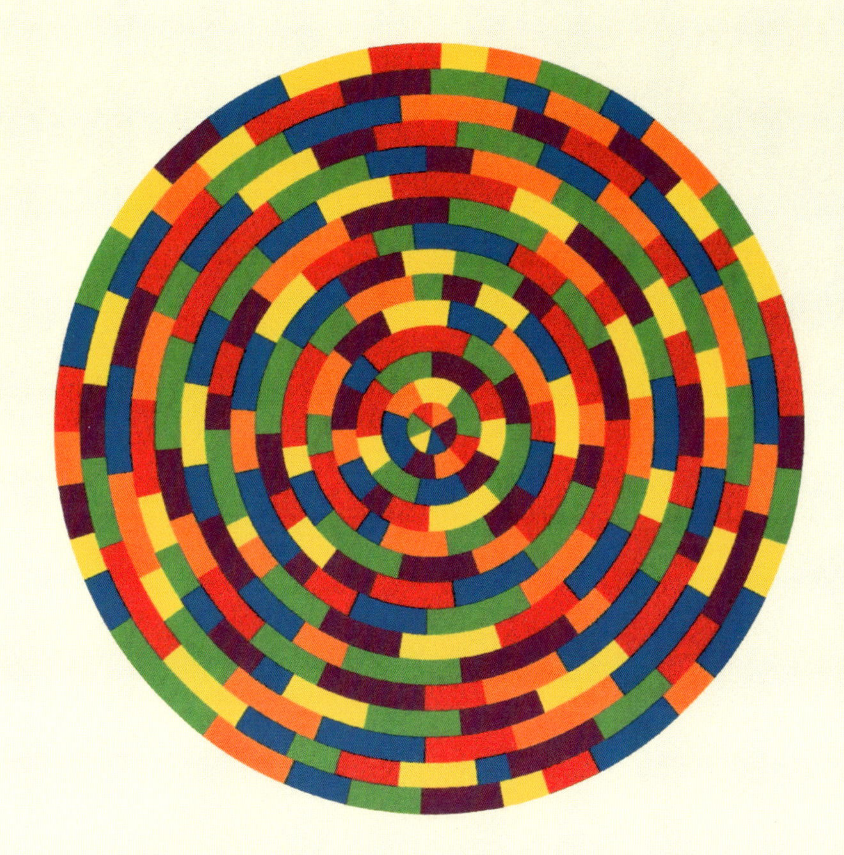

This is a diagram for the Sol LeWitt wall drawing number 1114. It should accompany the certificate if the wall drawing is sold or otherwise transferred but is not a certificate or a drawing.

Robert Mangold, *Distorted Circle within a Square (Grey)*, 1972

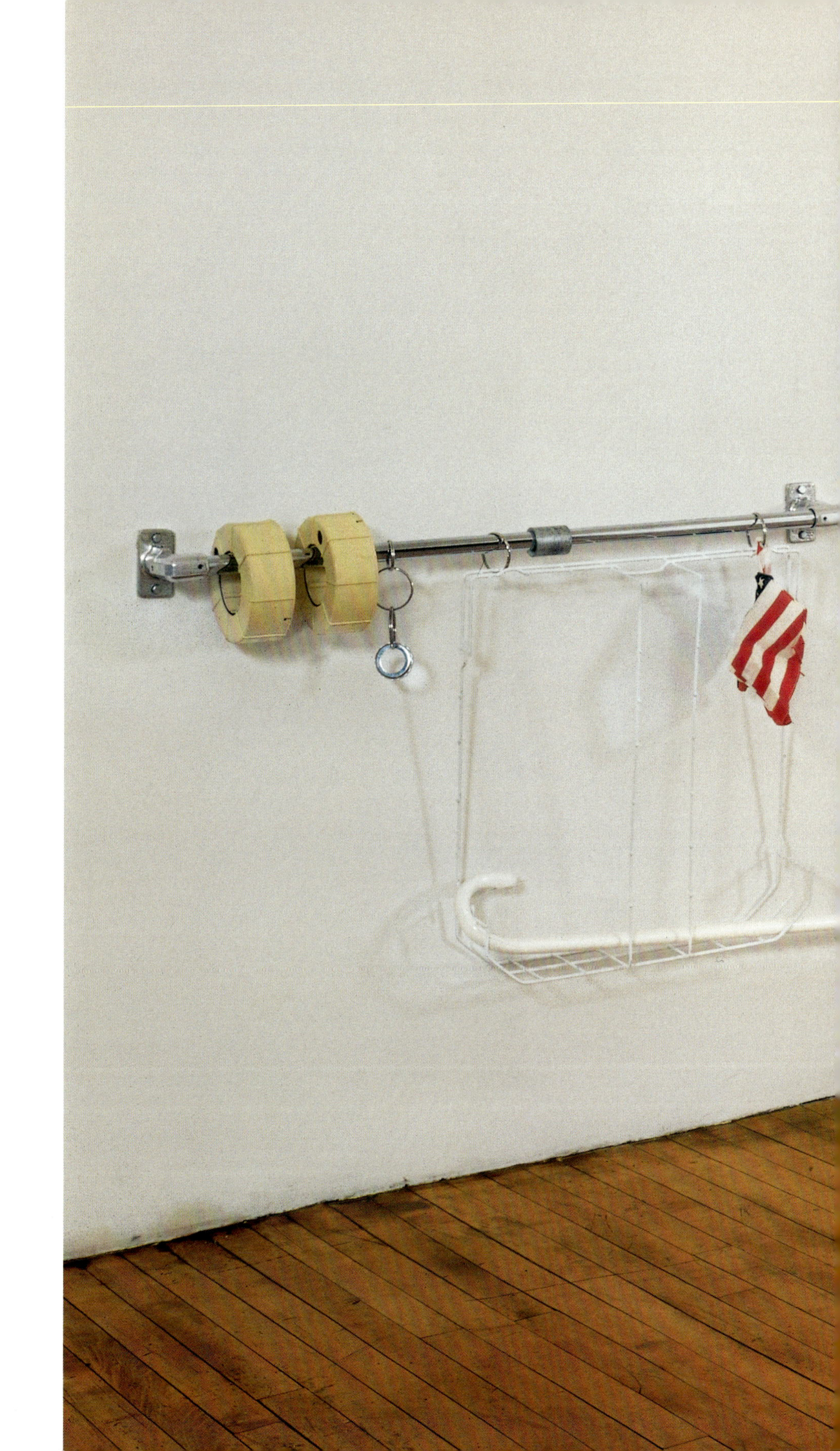

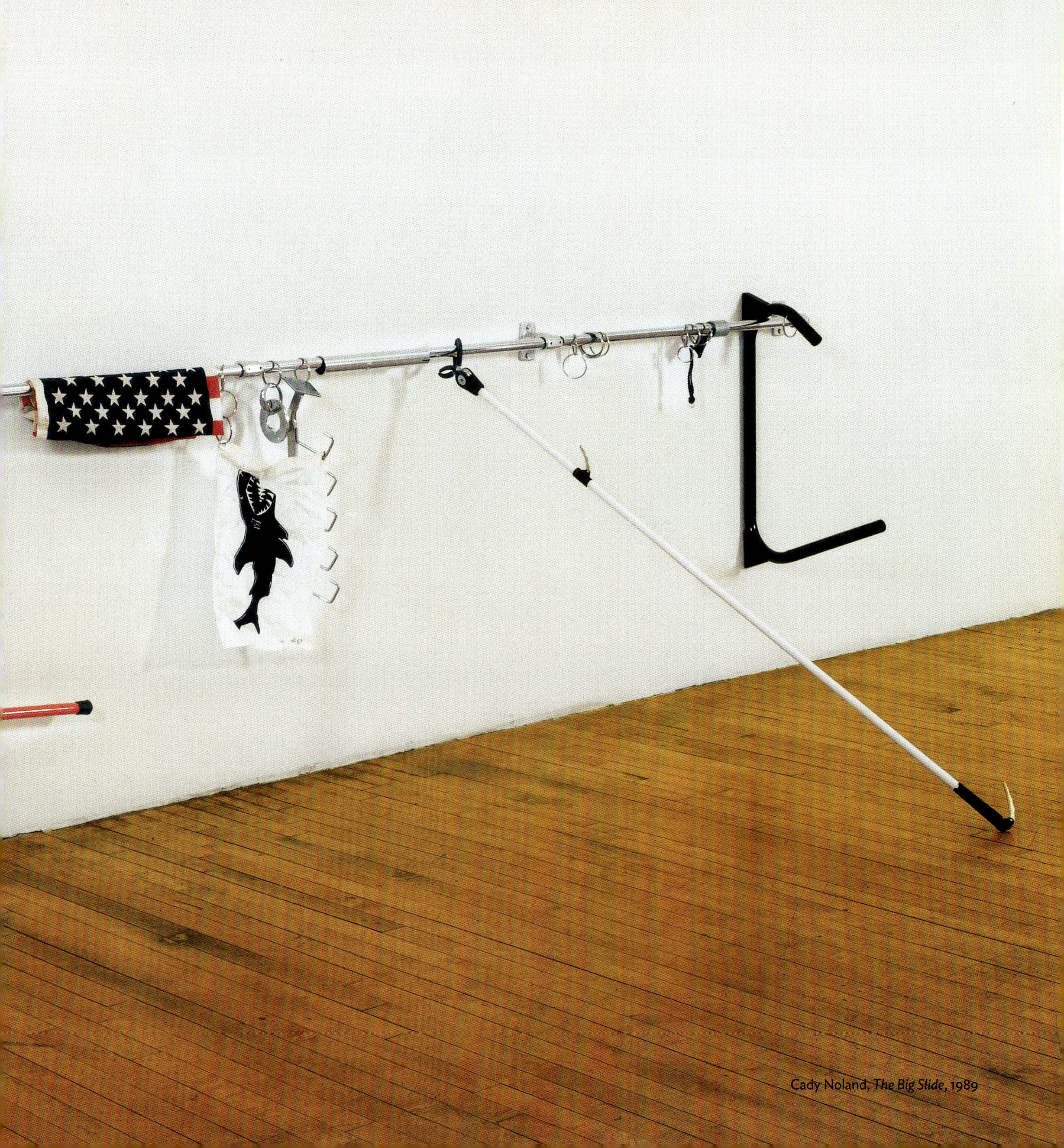

Cady Noland, *The Big Slide*, 1989

Cady Noland, *OOZEWALD*, 1989

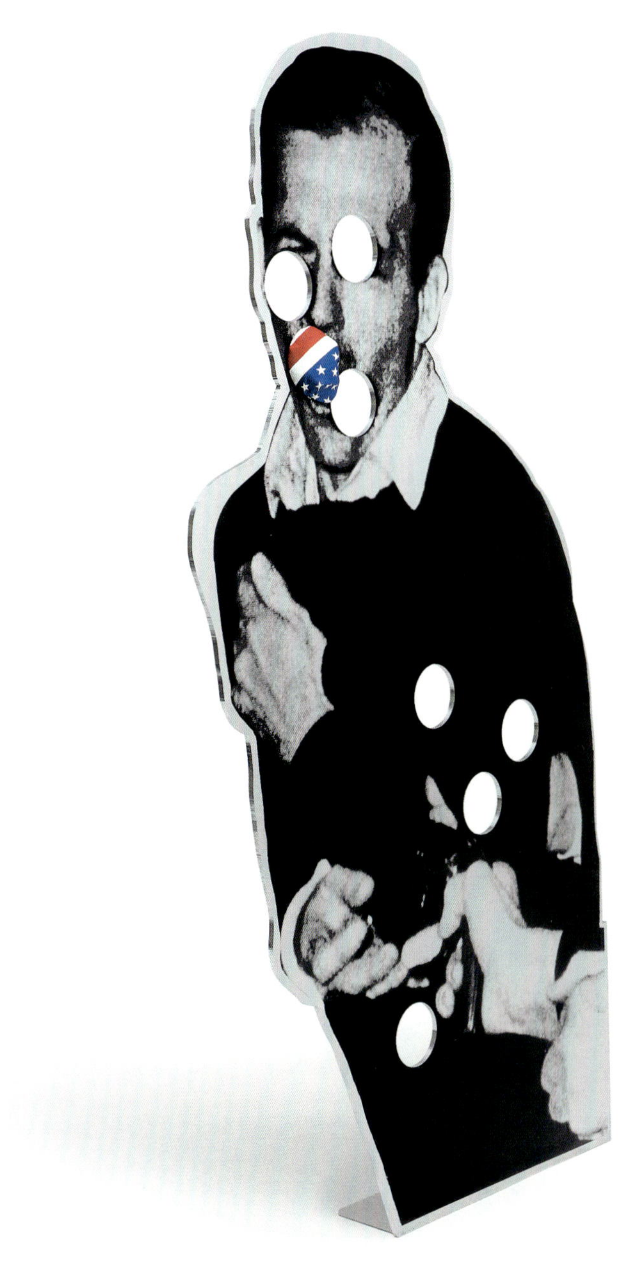

Gabriel Orozco, *Untitled*, 1998 *Eroded Suizekis 9*, 1999 *Palm*, 2001

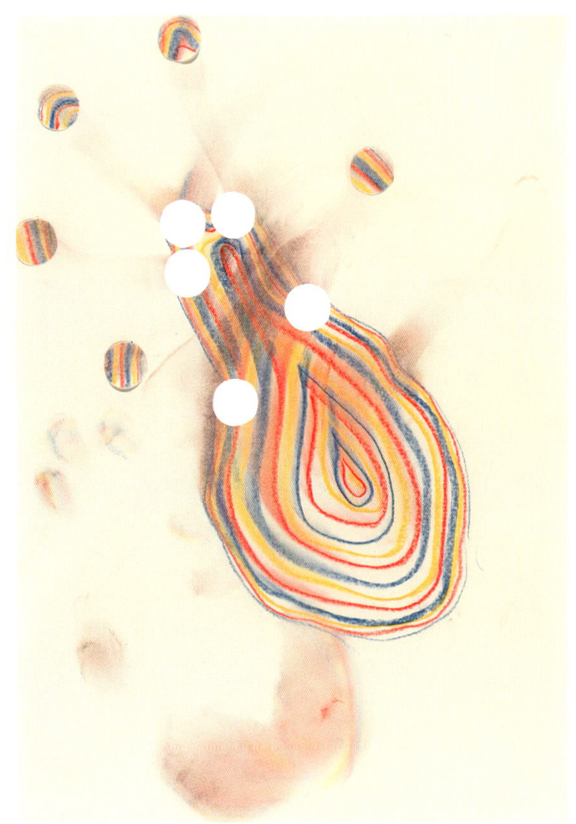

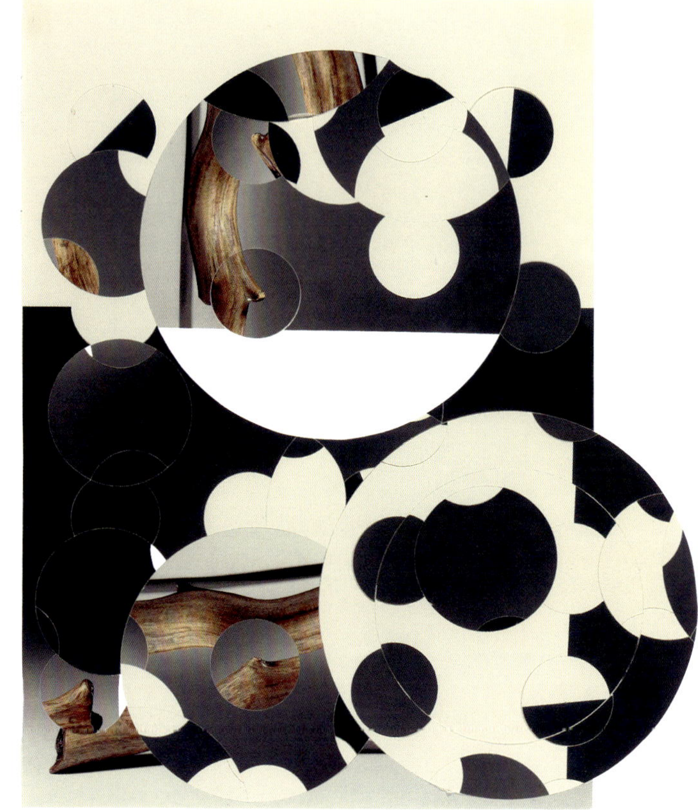

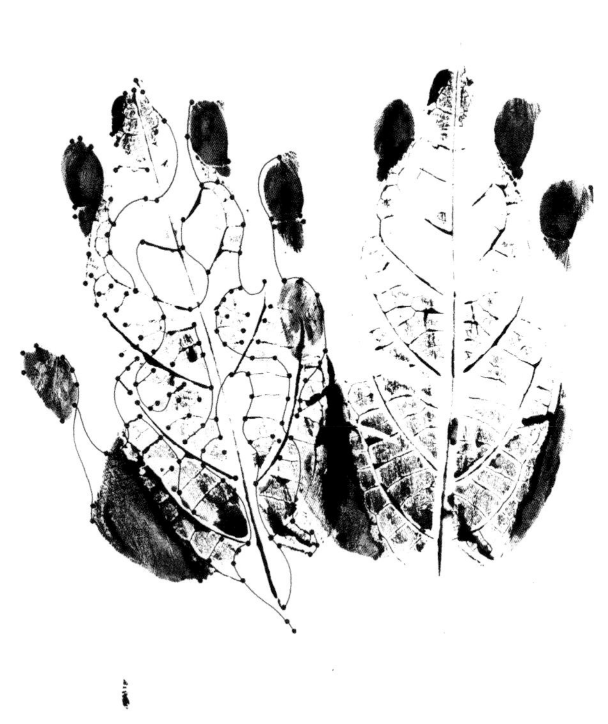

Gabriel Orozco, *Dent de Lion*, 1998

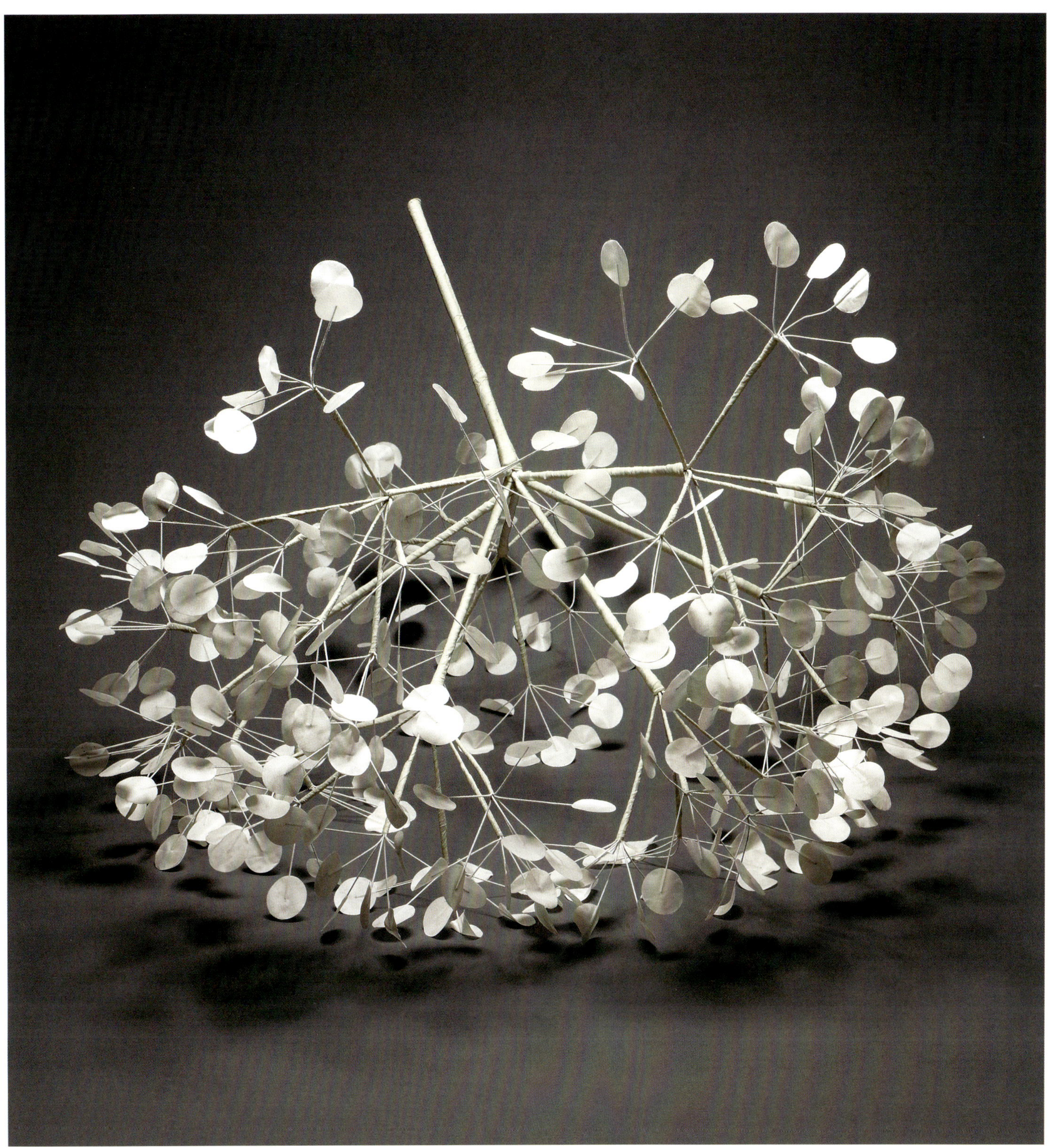

Gabriel Orozco, *Paper Foam Waves*, 1999

Gabriel Orozco, *Star Caps*, 2001

Total Perception, 2002

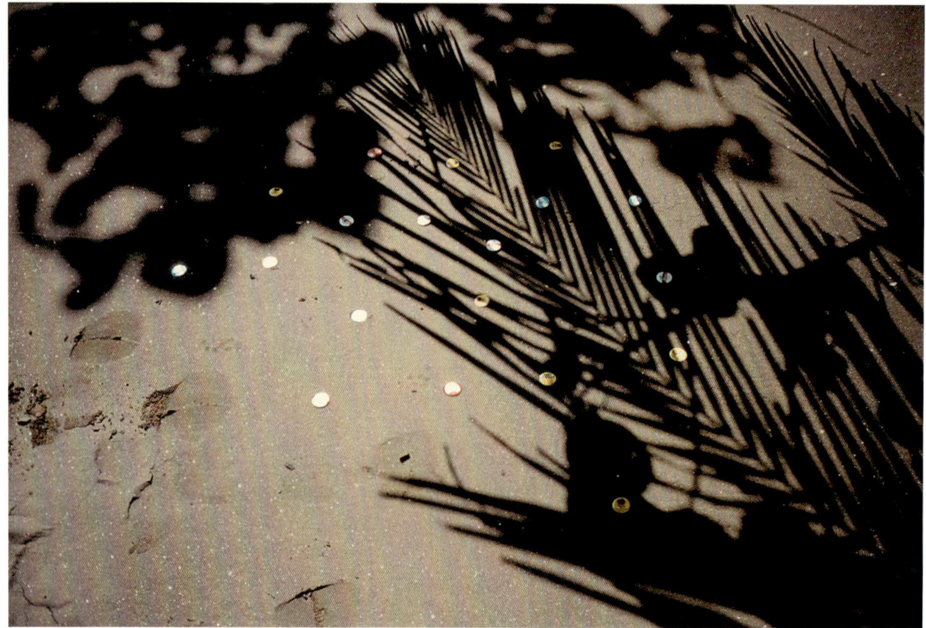

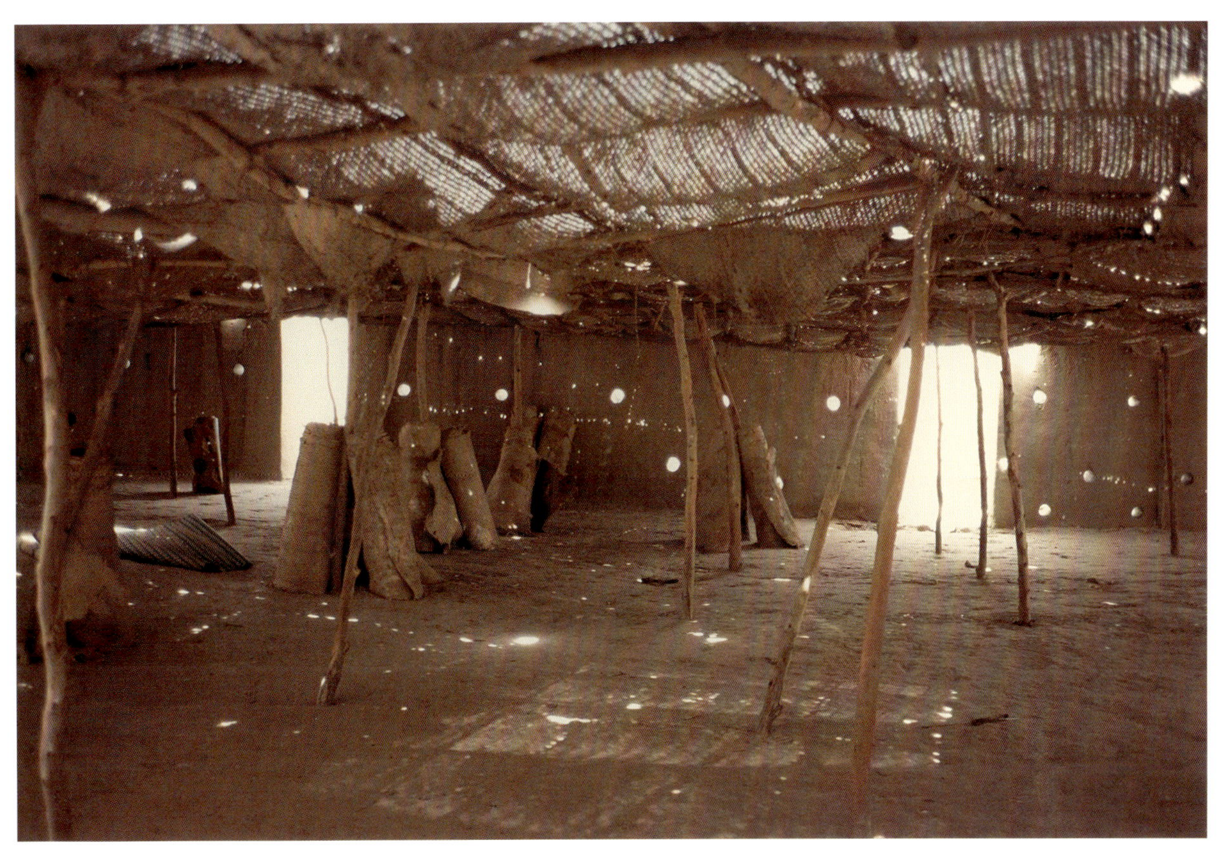

Gabriel Orozco, *Made in Belgium*, 1993

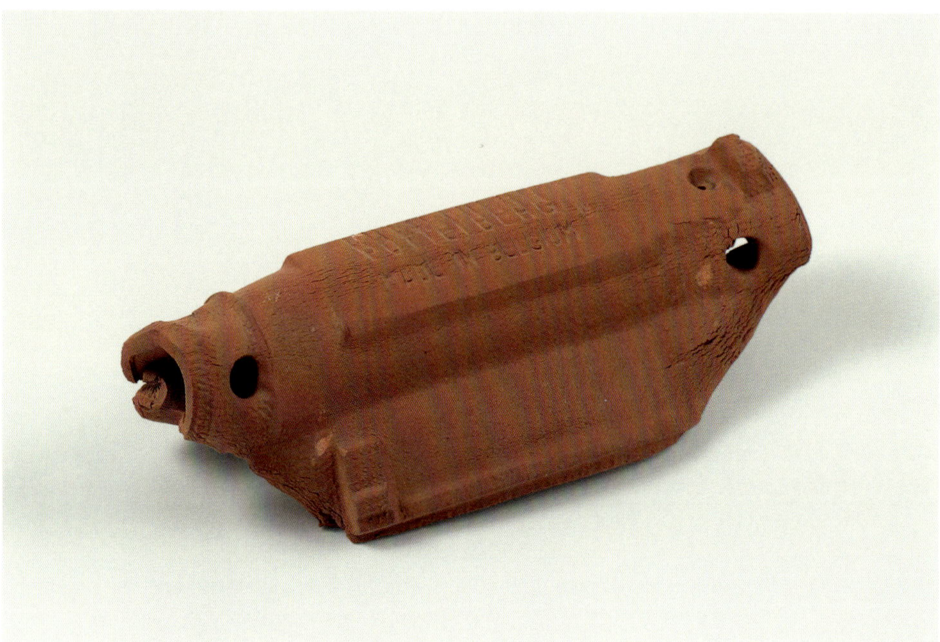

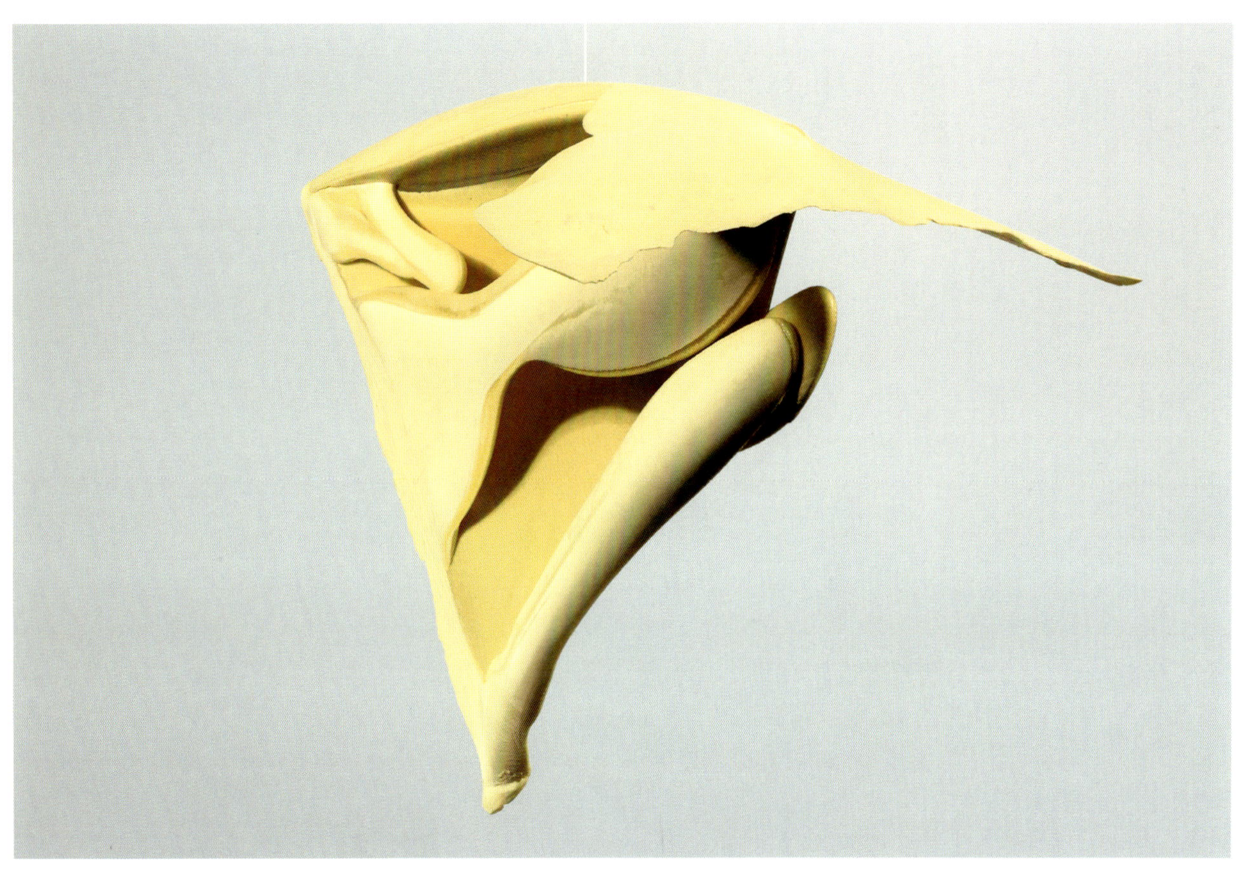

Michelangelo Pistoletto, *Girl Drawing*, 1979

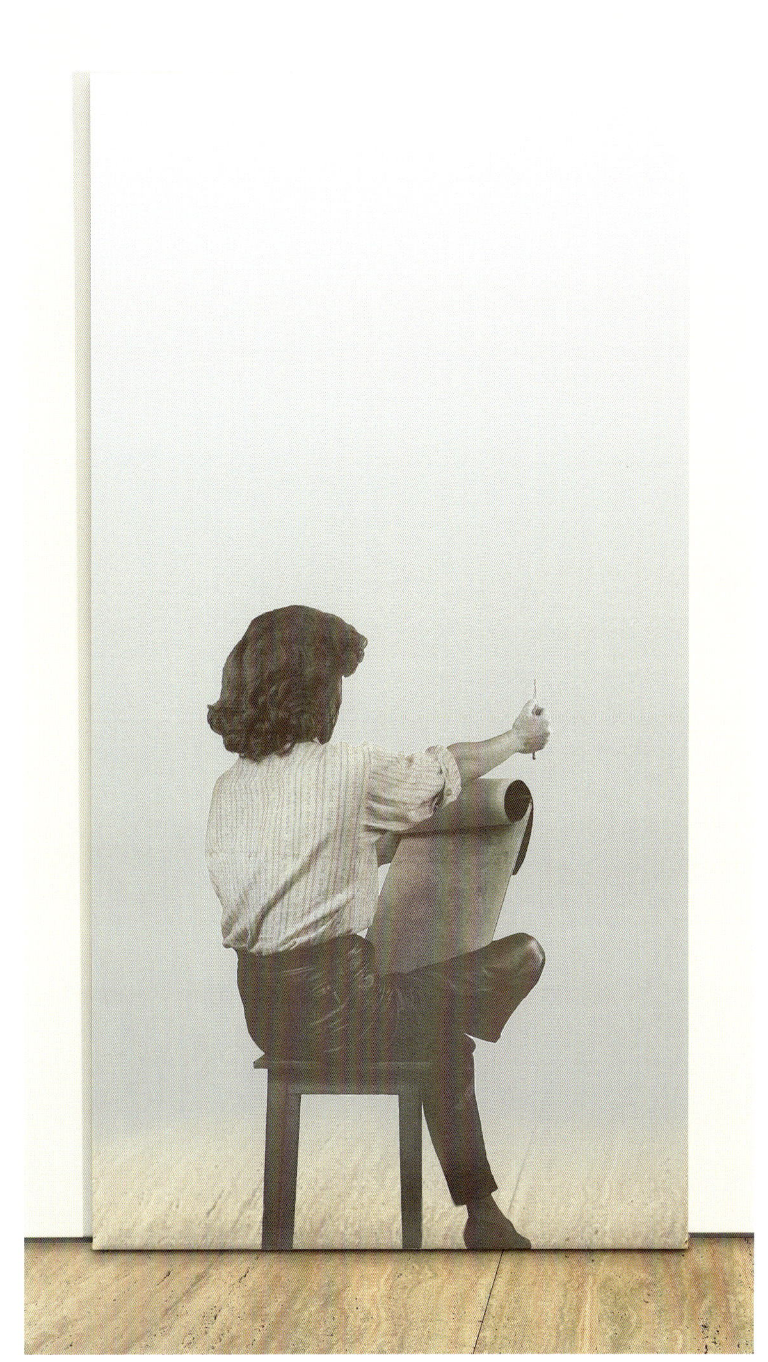

Sylvia Plimack Mangold, *The Maple Tree with Pine*, 2005

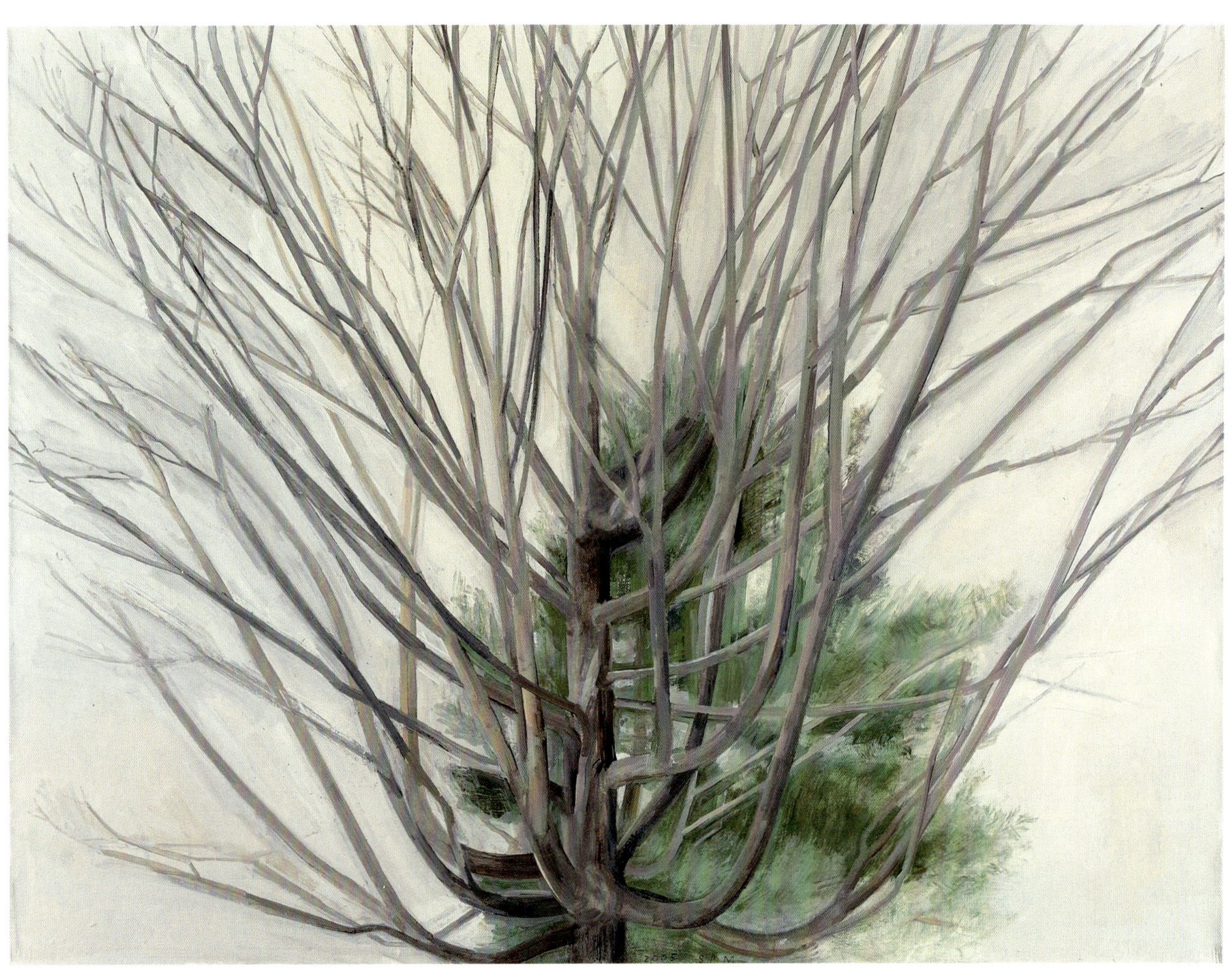

Gerhard Richter, *Gray*, 1973

Gerhard Richter, *Abstract Picture*, 2000

Robert Ryman, *Untitled*, 1961

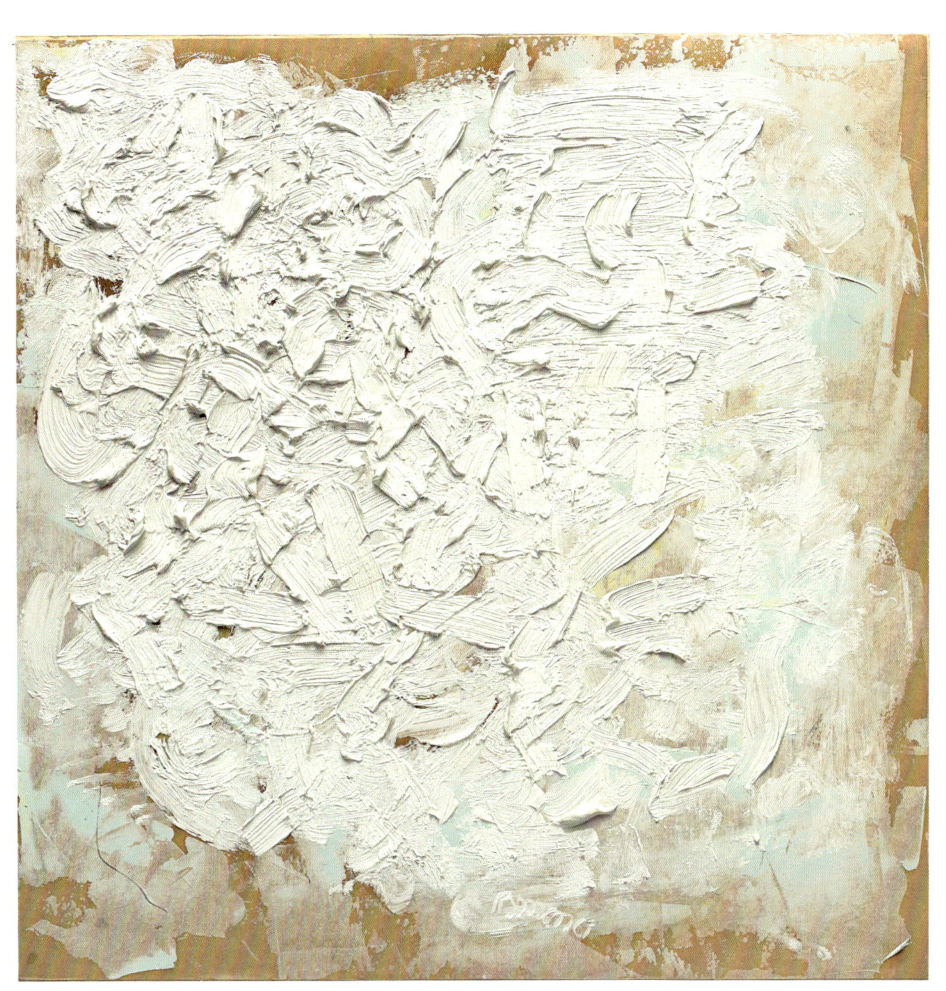

Fred Sandback, *Untitled, 1967*, 1967

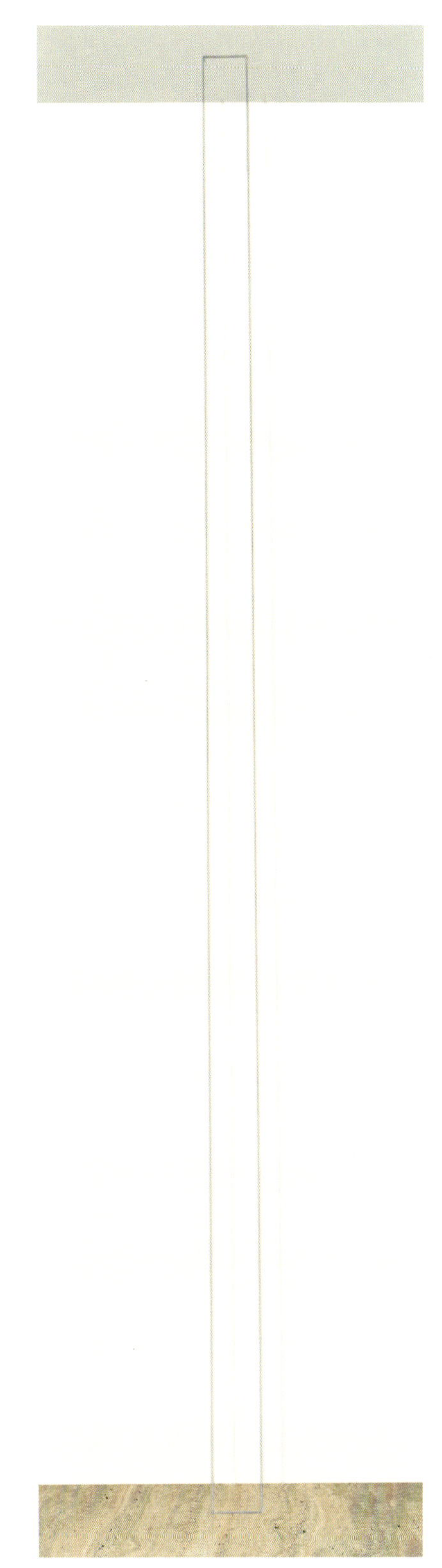

Thomas Struth, *Dallas Parking Lot, Dallas*, 2001

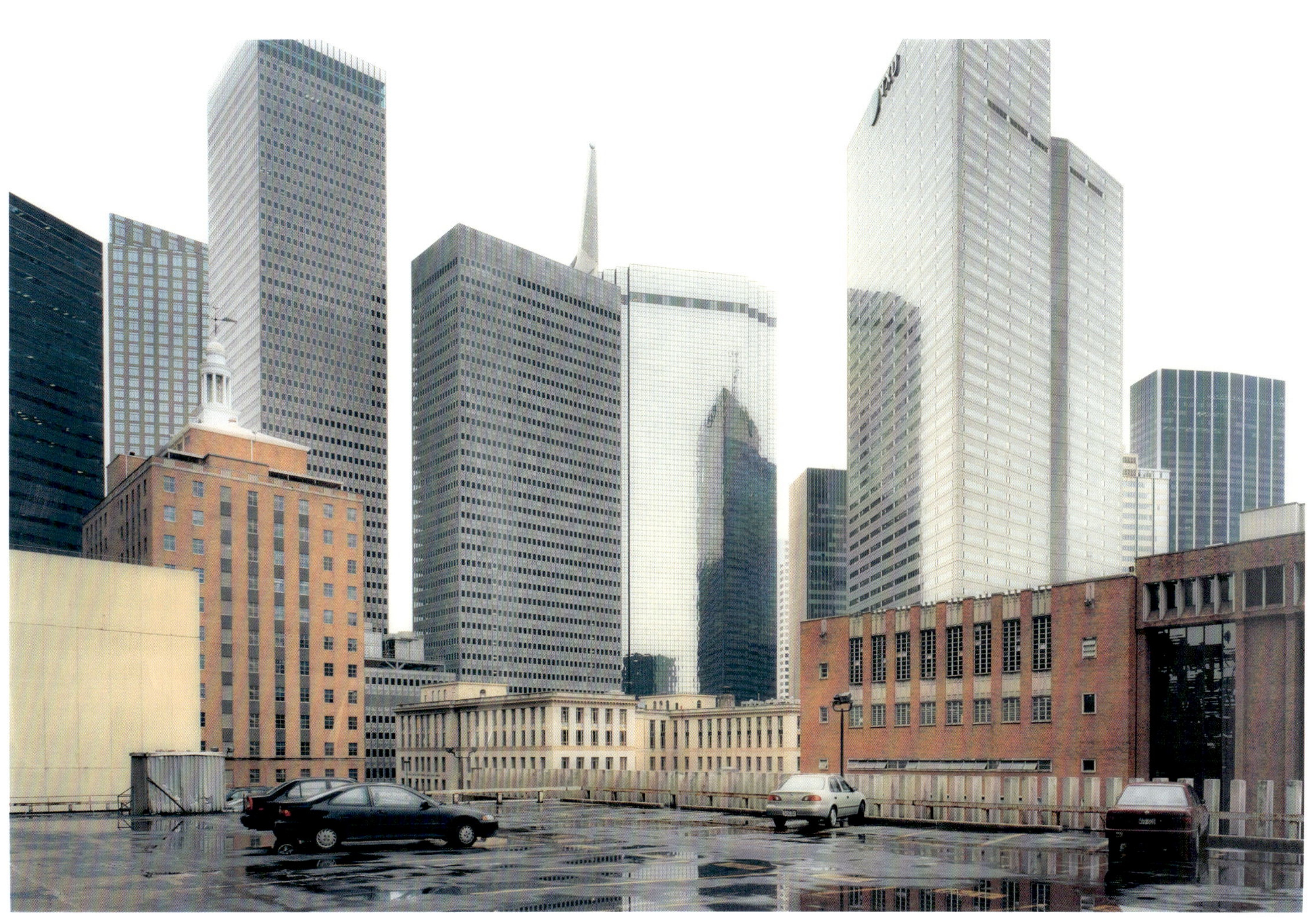

Tony Tasset, *Pumpkin*, 1998

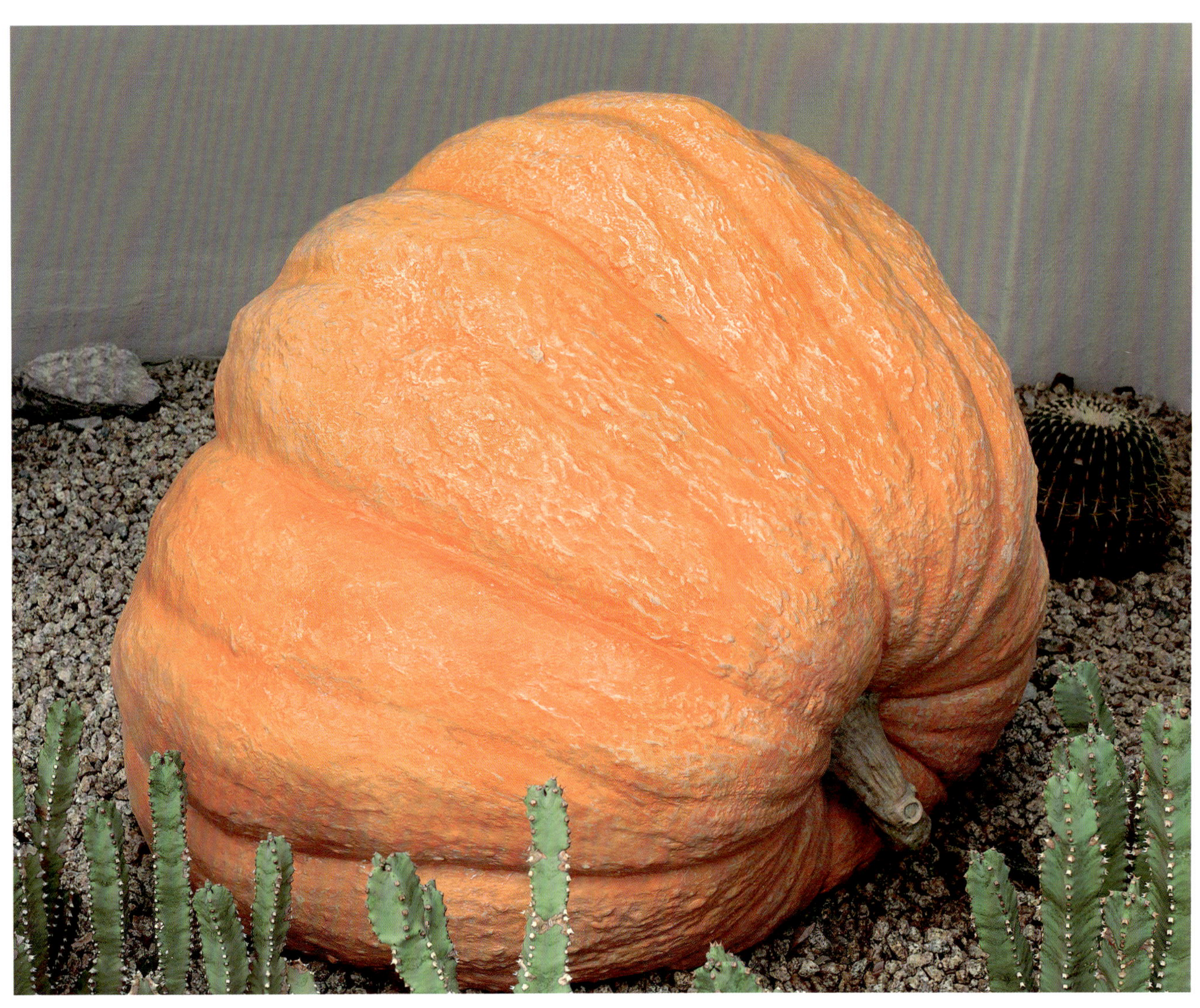

Rosemarie Trockel, *Untitled*, 1986

PRO

Richard Tuttle, *Twin River,* 1965

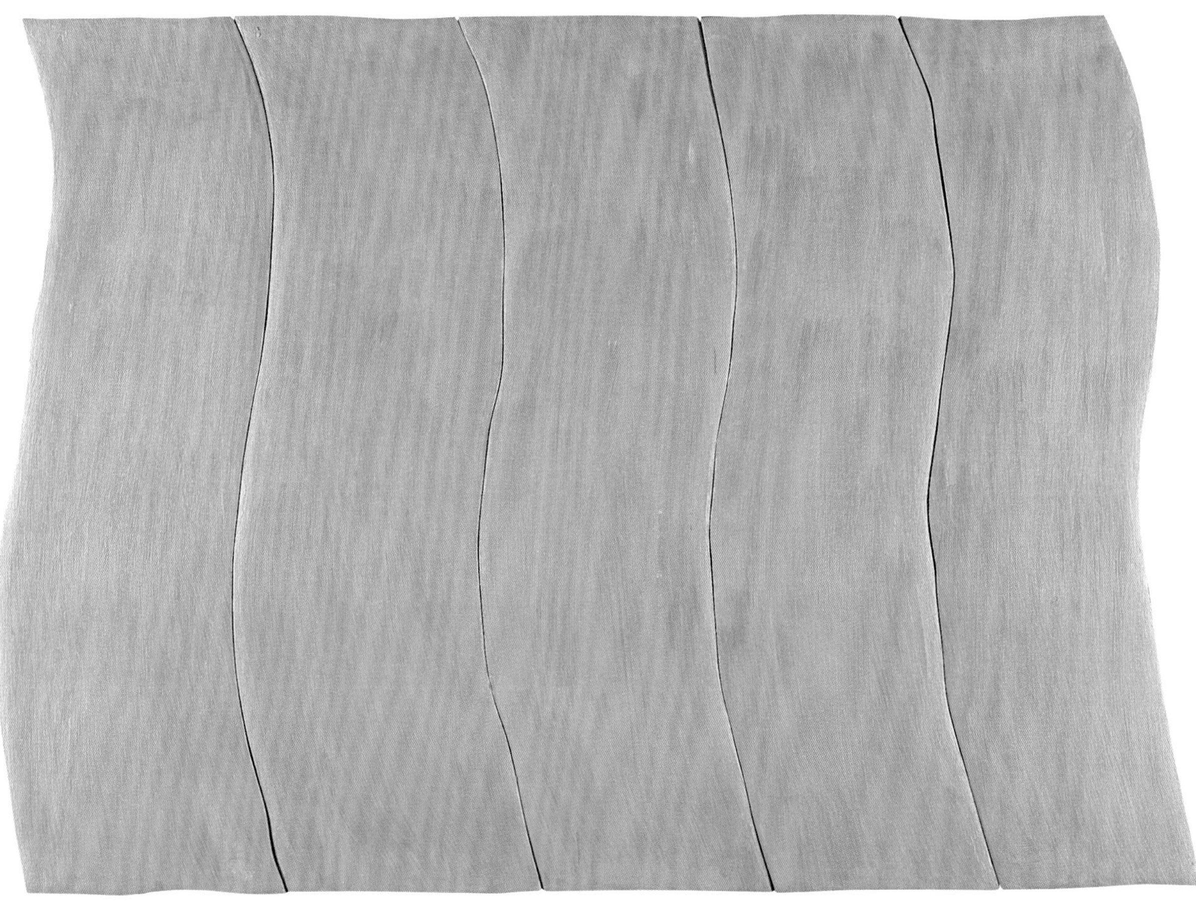

Luc Tuymans, *Shadow*, 1994

Jeff Wall, *Rainfilled Suitcase*, 2001

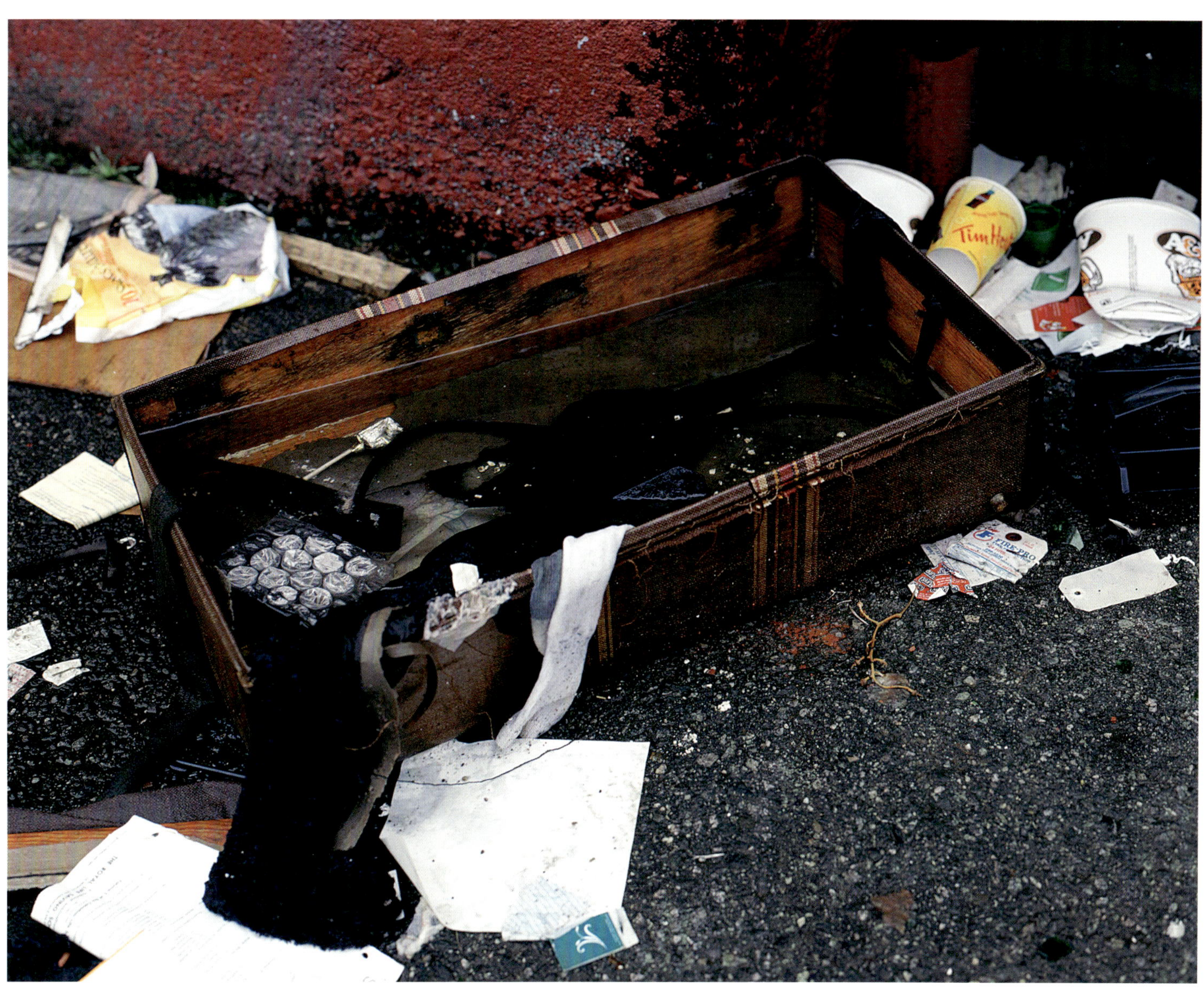

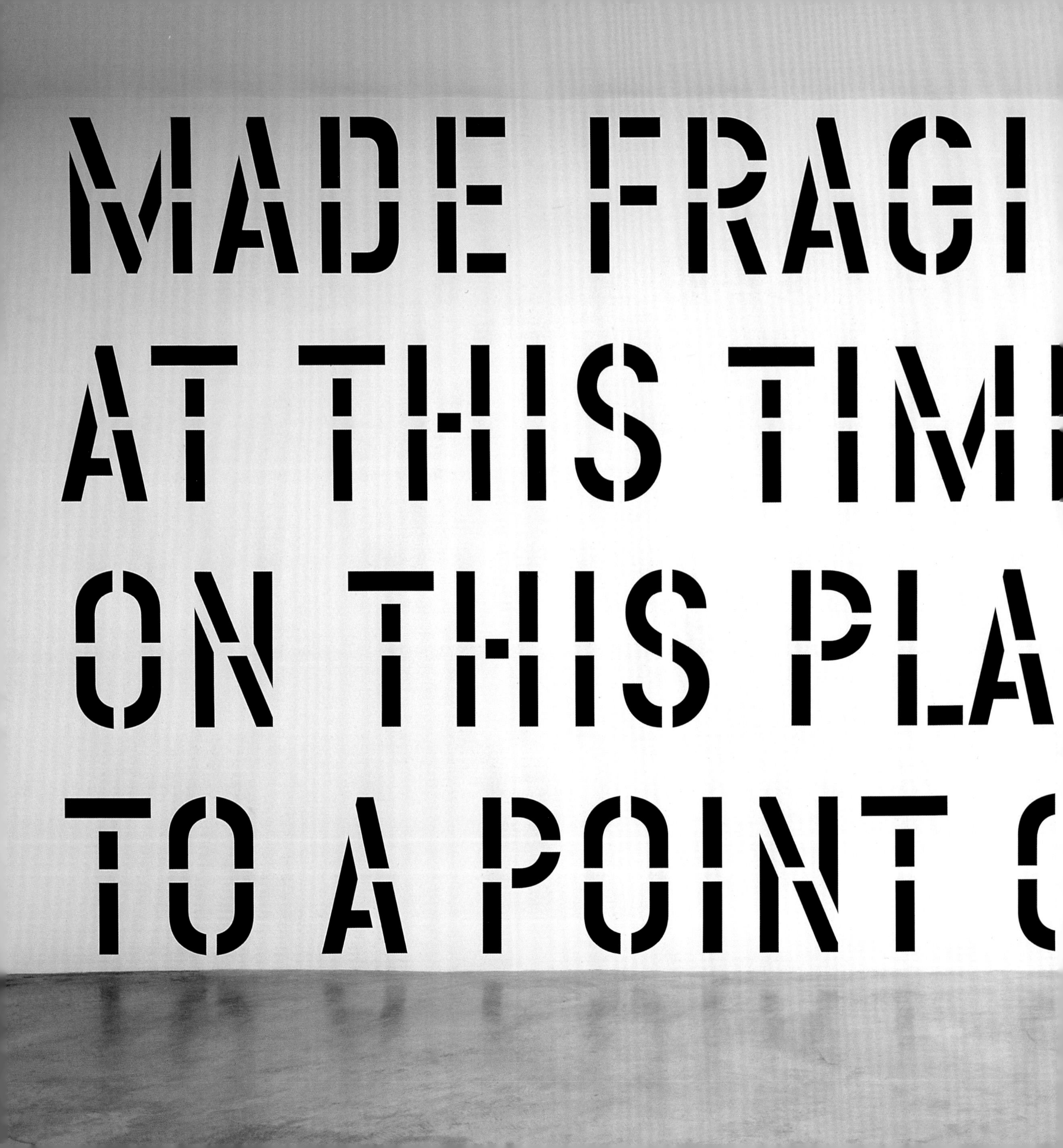

MADE FRAGI
AT THIS TIM
ON THIS PLA
TO A POINT

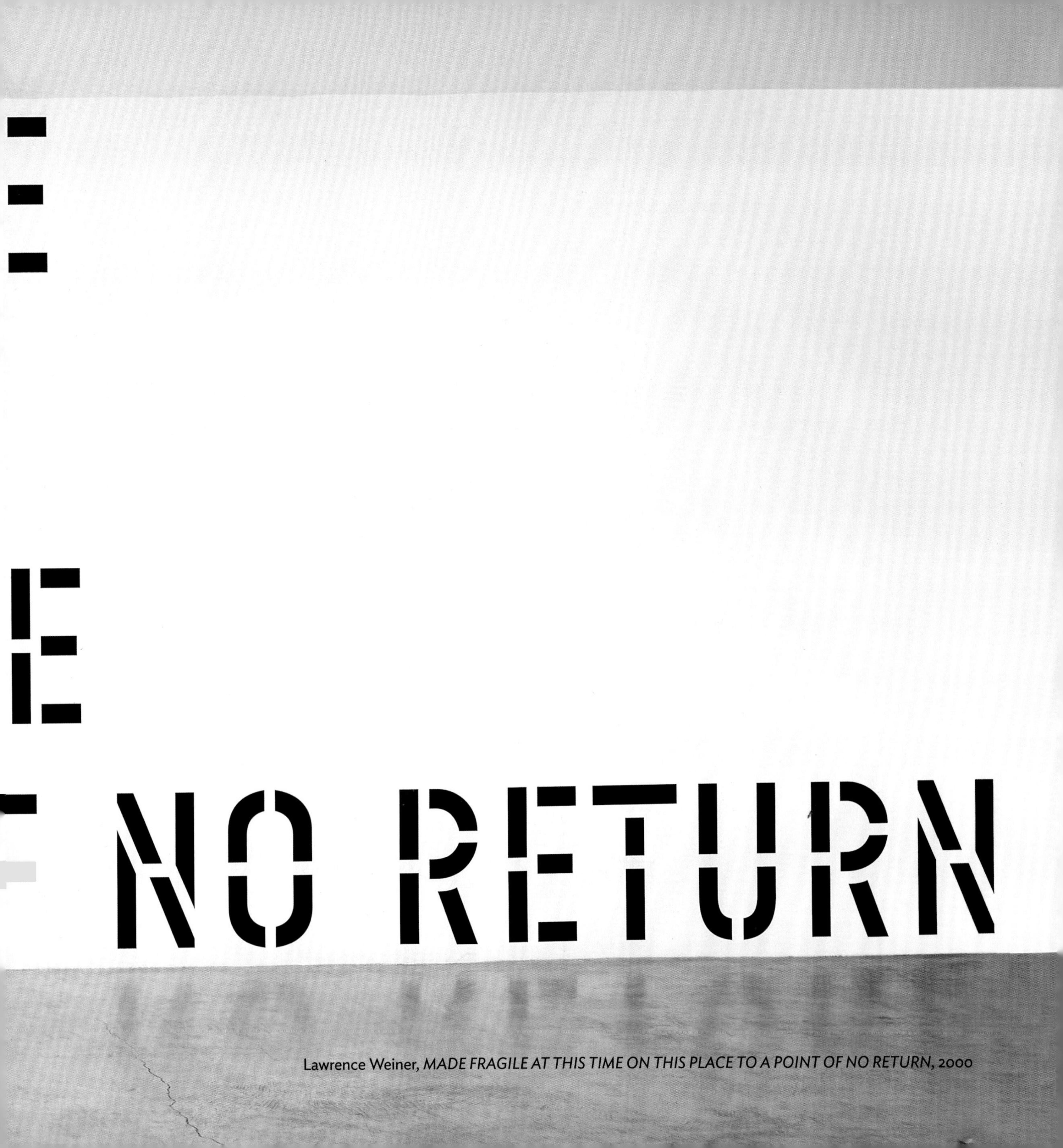

NO RETURN

Lawrence Weiner, *MADE FRAGILE AT THIS TIME ON THIS PLACE TO A POINT OF NO RETURN*, 2000

Franz West, *Duktus*, 1987

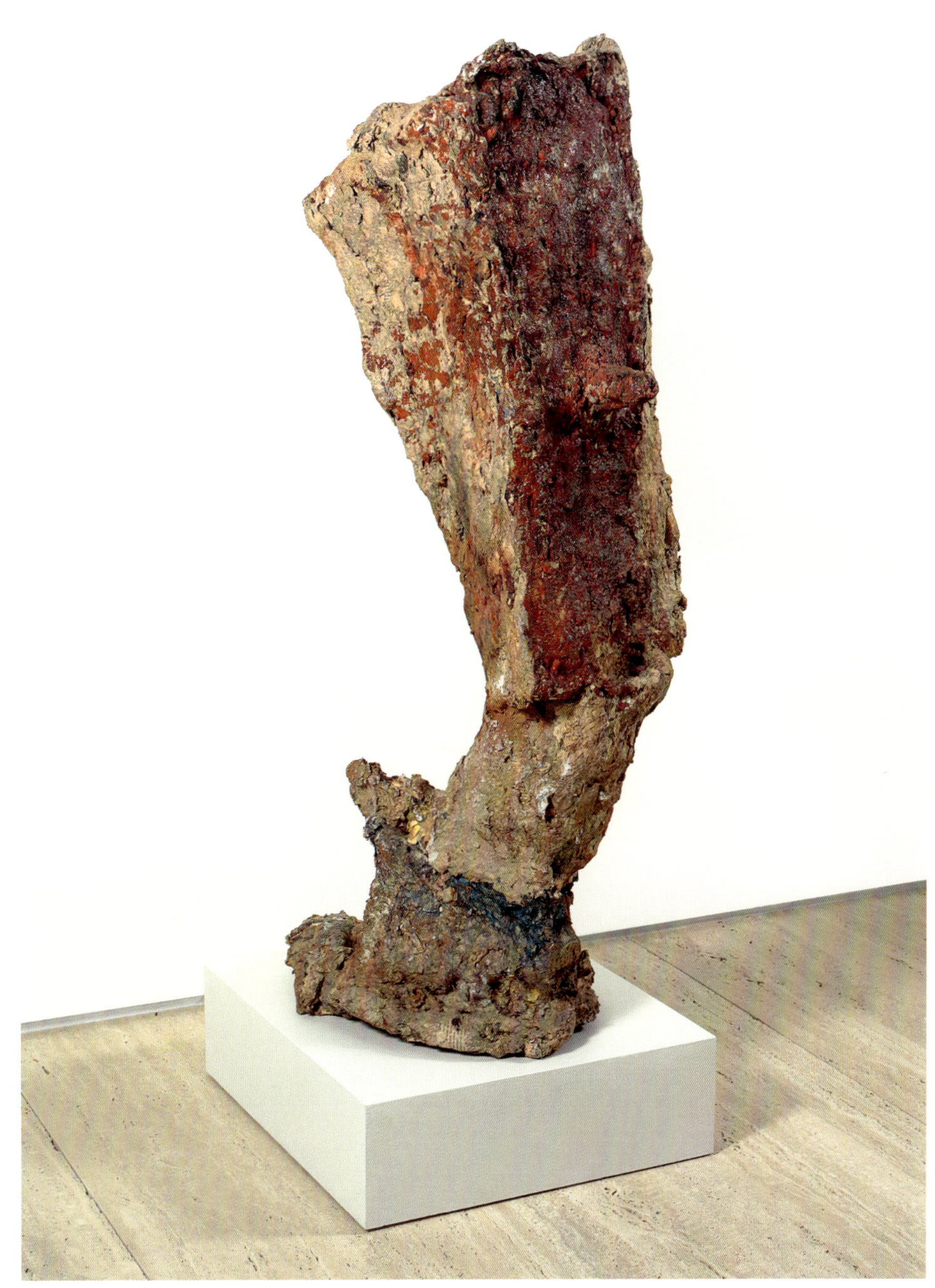

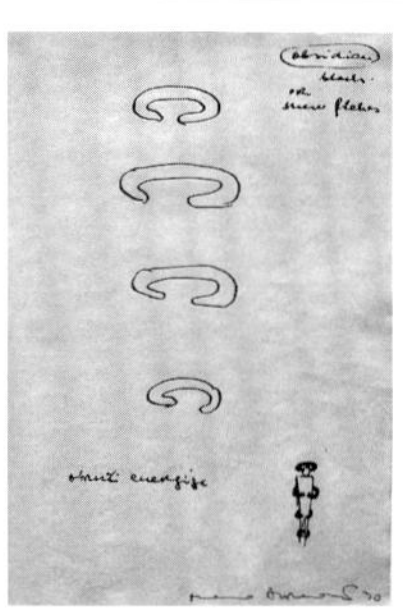

Marina Abramović
(Yugoslavian, born 1946)
Untitled, 1990
Black ink on paper
Sheet: 34.9 x 20.3 cm (13 ¾ x 8 in.)
Mount: 42.5 x 33.3 cm (16 ¾ x 13 ⅛ in.)

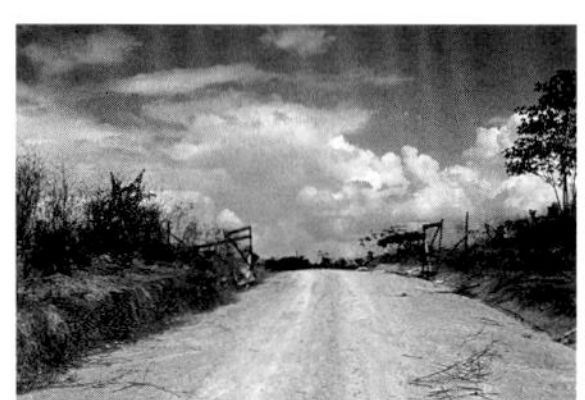

Doug Aitken
(American, born 1968)
monsoon, 1995
Color film, sound, transferred to digital video (monitor or projection) (edition of 5); 6:43 min. loop
Gift, 2007

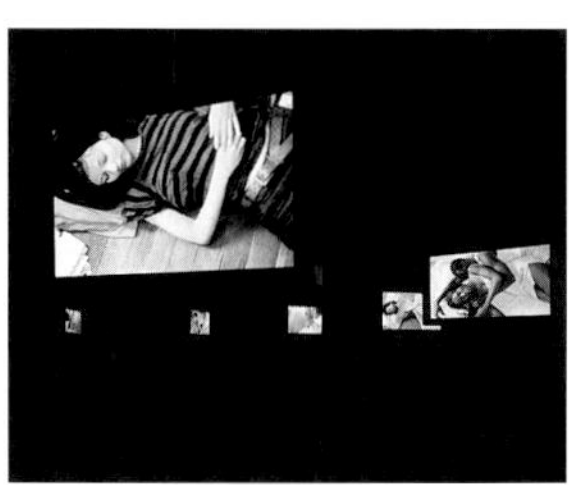

the moment, 2005
Eleven-channel digital video, sound (projected on plasma screens with mirrors) (edition of 4); 6:30 min. loop
Gift, 2007

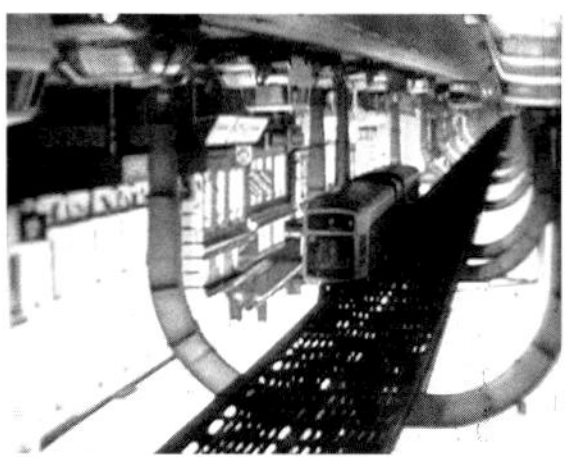

Darren Almond
(English, born 1971)
Schwebebahn, 1995
8mm black-and-white and color film, sound, transferred to digital video (projection) (edition of 5); 12 min. loop
Gift, 2007

Carl Andre
(American, born 1935)
Stillanovel Trial (No. 6), 1972
Typewriter ink on paper
29.5 x 20.8 cm (11 ⅝ x 8 3/16 in.)

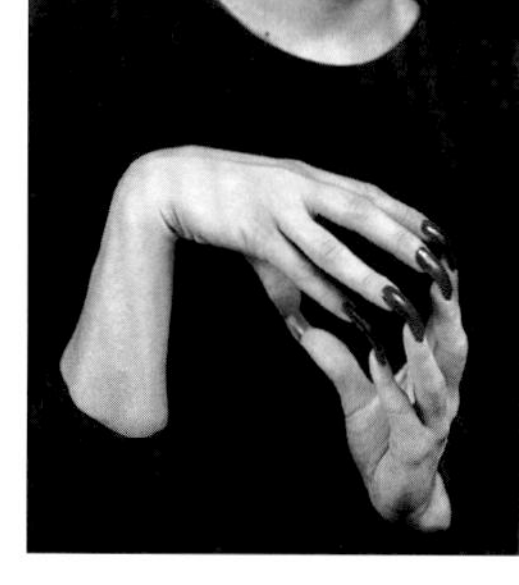

Janine Antoni
(American, born Bahamas 1964)
Ingrown, 1998
Chromogenic print (edition of 8)
46 x 41.4 cm (18 ⅛ x 16 ¼ in.)
Promised gift, 2010
See p. 30

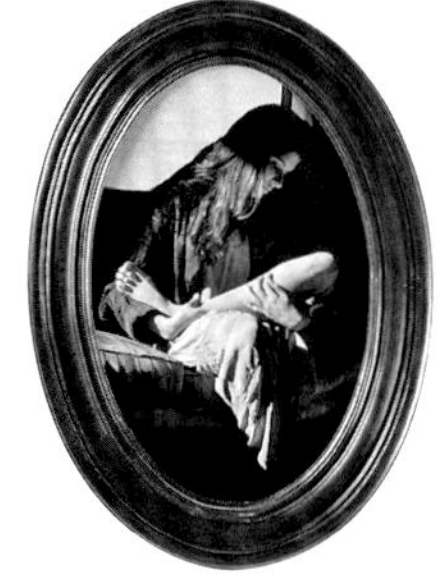

Coddle, 1999
Cibachrome print and hand-carved frame (edition of 10)
54.6 x 40.6 cm (21 ½ x 16 in.)
Promised gift, 2010
See p. 31

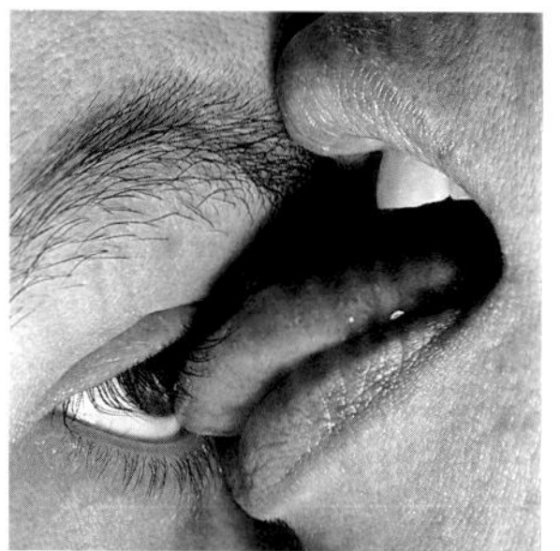

Mortar and Pestle, 1999
Chromogenic print
122 x 122 cm (48 x 48 in.)
Gift, 2002
See pp. 28–29

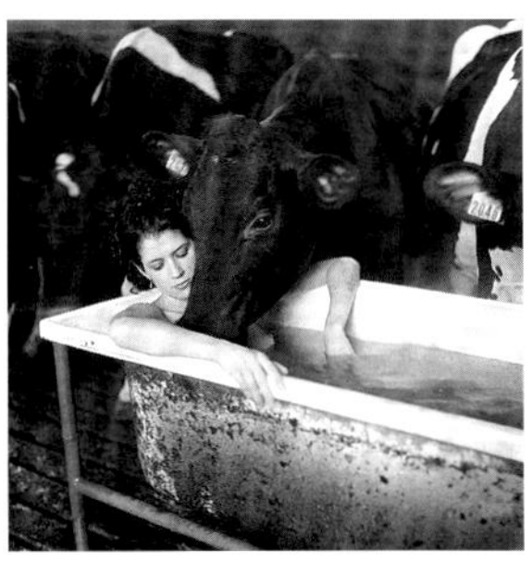

2038, 2000
Chromogenic print (edition of 10)
50.8 x 50.8 cm (20 x 20 in.)
Promised gift, 2010
See pp. 32–33

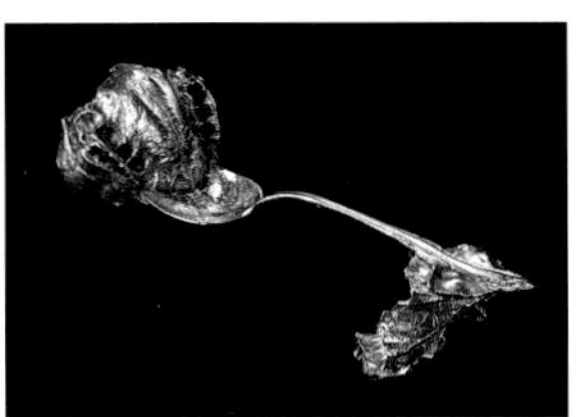

Umbilical, 2000
Sterling silver cast of family silverware and negative impression of artist's mouth and mother's hand (edition of 35)
7.6 x 20.3 x 7.6 cm (3 x 8 x 3 in.)

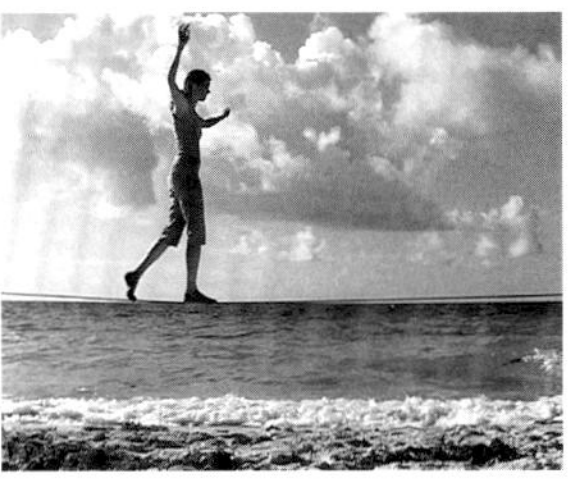

Touch, 2002
Color video, sound (projection) (edition of 5); 9:37 min. loop
Gift, 2007

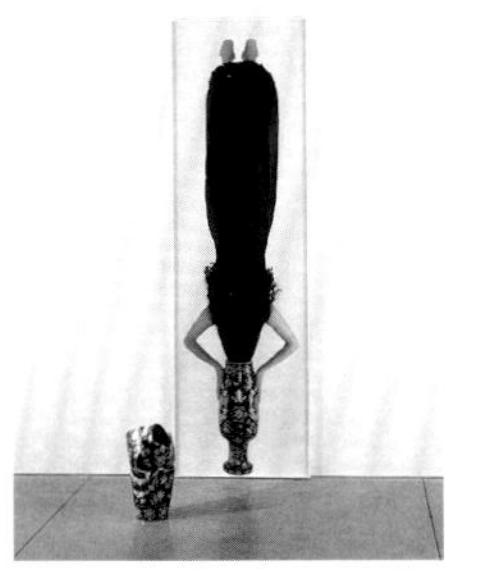

Caryatid (cobalt blue glazed porcelain with gold ceramic ornamentation), 2003
Chromogenic print and broken vessel
Print: 243.2 x 75.6 cm (95 ¾ x 29 ¾ in.)
Vessel: 25.4 x 30.5 x 40.6 cm (10 x 12 x 16 in.)
Promised gift, 2010
See p. 34

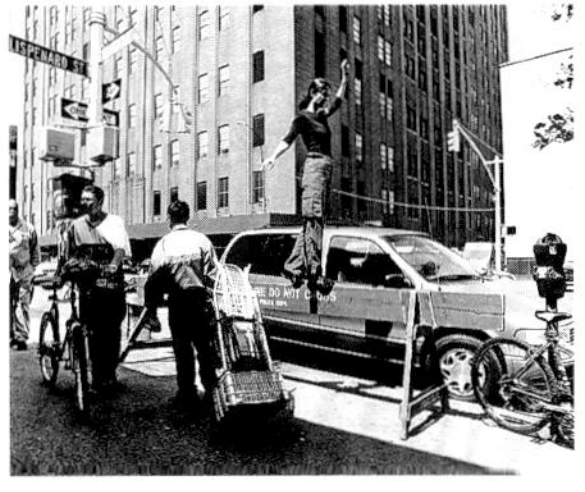

Tangent, 2003
Chromogenic print (edition of 10)
76.2 x 101.6 cm (30 x 40 in.)
Promised gift, 2010
See p. 35

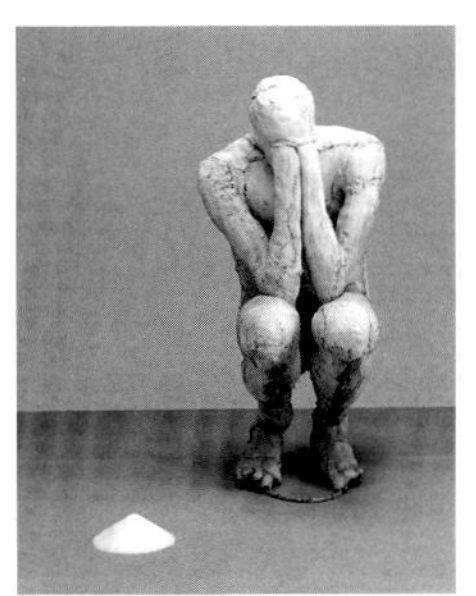

Miroslaw Balka
(Polish, born 1958)
Salt Seller, 1988
Wood, jute, salt, and steel
Figure: 106.7 x 55.9 x 35.6 cm (42 x 22 x 14 in.)
Gift, 2000

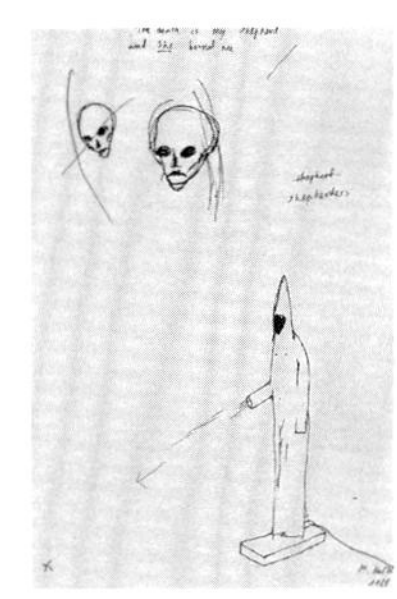

Untitled (Death Is My Shepherdess), 1989
Crayon and black pen on paper
27.9 x 20.5 cm (11 x 8 ¹⁄₁₆ in.)

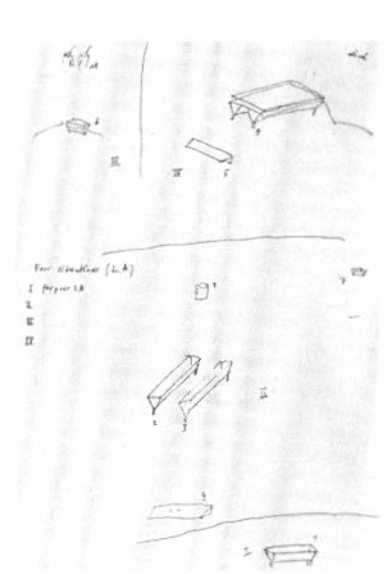

Untitled, 1993
Pen on paper
27.9 x 20.5 cm (11 x 8 ¹⁄₁₆ in.)

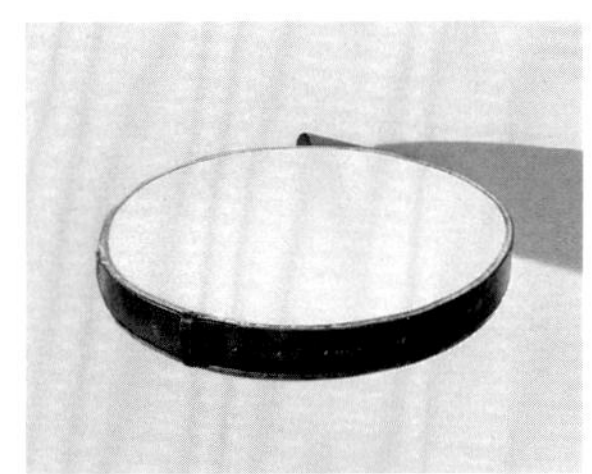

. . . and I was here, 2003
Tray of salt at exact diameter and height of artist's belt, when worn
78.7 x 83.8 x 43.2 cm (31 x 33 x 17 in.)

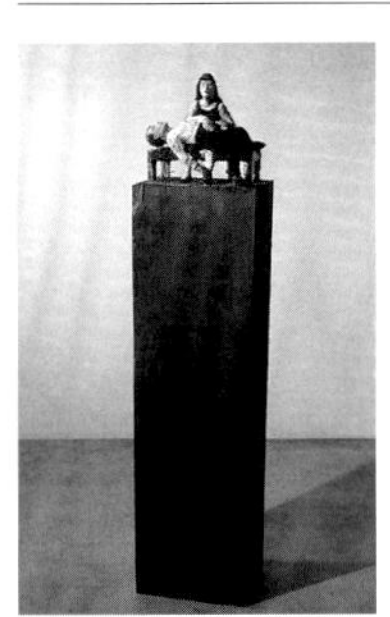

Stephan Balkenhol
(German, born 1957)
Woman with Man in Agony, 1996
Wawa wood and wood stain
151.1 x 33.7 x 24.1 cm (59 ½ x 13 ¼ x 9 ½ in.)

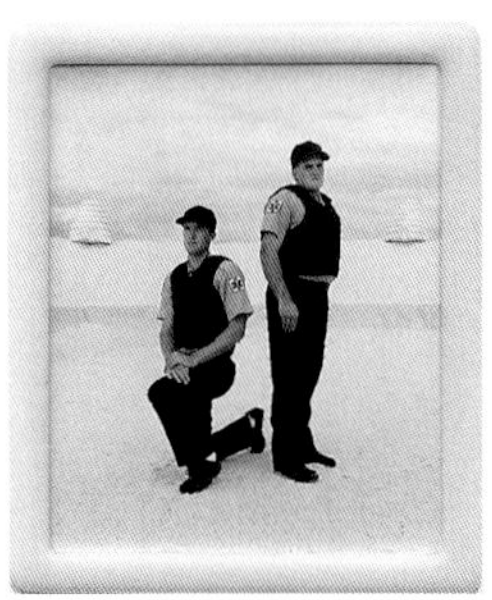

Matthew Barney
(American, born 1967)
Cremaster 2: Deseret, 1999
Four chromogenic prints in acrylic frames (edition of 3)
Panels 1, 4: 69.2 x 59.1 cm (27 ¼ x 23 ¼ in.)
Panel 2: 69.2 x 84.5 cm (27 ¼ x 33 ¼ in.)
Panel 3: 69.2 x 191.1 cm (27 ¼ x 75 ¼ in.)
Gift, 2002
Shown: Panel 1

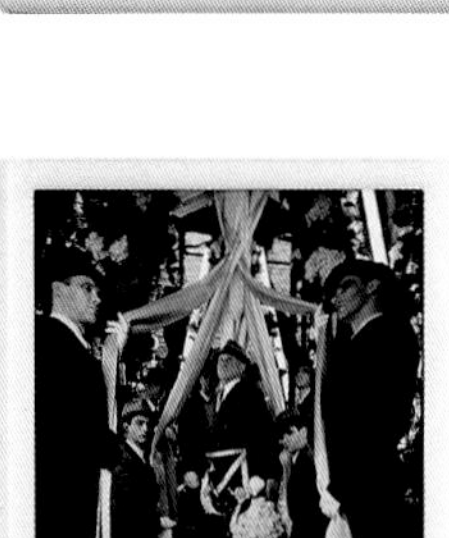

Cremaster 3: The Dance of Hiram Abiff, 2002
Four chromogenic prints in acrylic frames (edition of 3)
Panels 1, 2, 4: 107.6 x 86.4 cm (42 ⅜ x 34 in.)
Panel 3: 137.2 x 111.8 cm (54 x 44 in.)
Promised gift, 2009
Shown: Panel 2

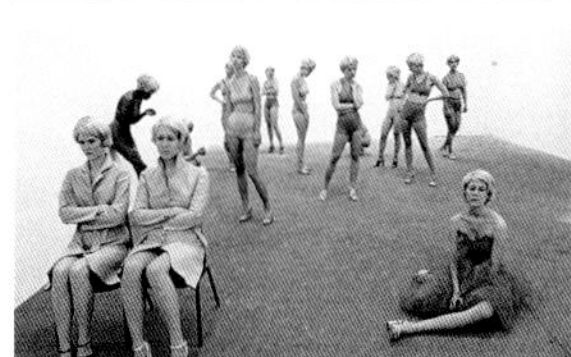

Vanessa Beecroft
(Italian, born 1969)
Piano Americano, 1996
Color video and sound (projection) (edition of 8); 30 min. loop
Gift, 2007

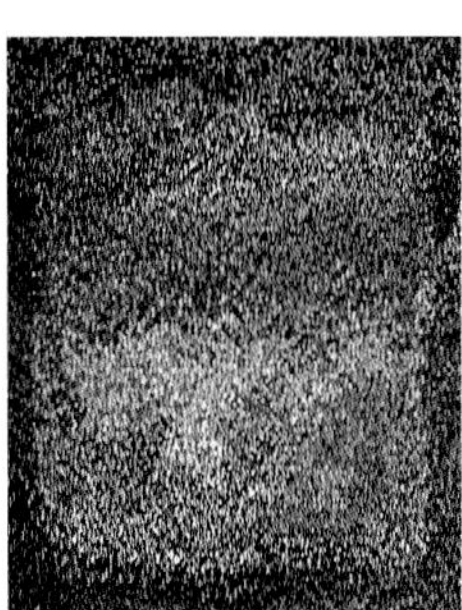

Marie Krane Bergman
(American, born 1962)
Tulip, 1999
Acrylic on canvas
152.4 x 127 cm (60 x 50 in.)

Part of One Year (May), 2003
Acrylic on canvas
177.8 x 177.8 cm (70 x 70 in.)

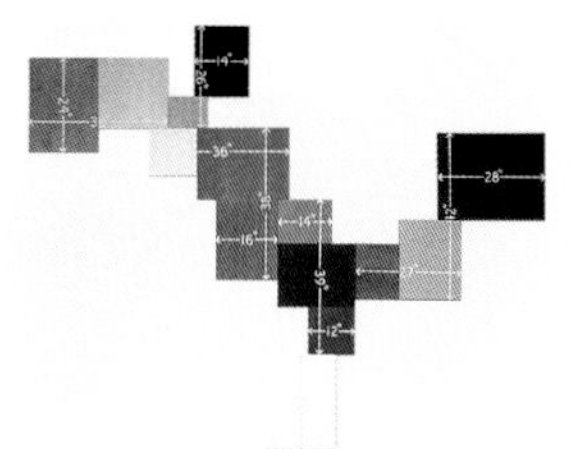

Mel Bochner
(American, born 1940)
Either/If/Or/Both (And), 1999
Acrylic and oil on canvas (14 panels)
274.3 x 340.4 cm (108 x 134 in.)

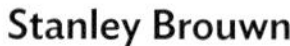

Stanley Brouwn
In accordance with the wishes of the artist, no details of his life and work shall be published.

One of two works is a promised gift, 2010.

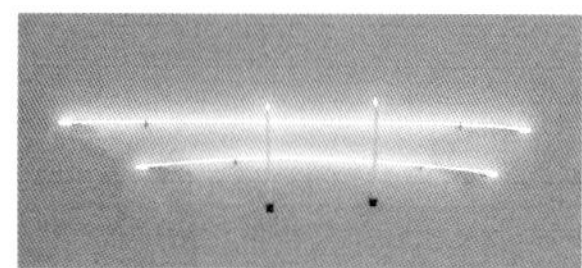

Pier Paolo Calzolari
(Italian, born 1943)
Untitled, 1970
Neon, transformer, metal candleholders, and candles (edition of 3)
34 x 130 cm (13 ⅜ x 51 3/16 in.)

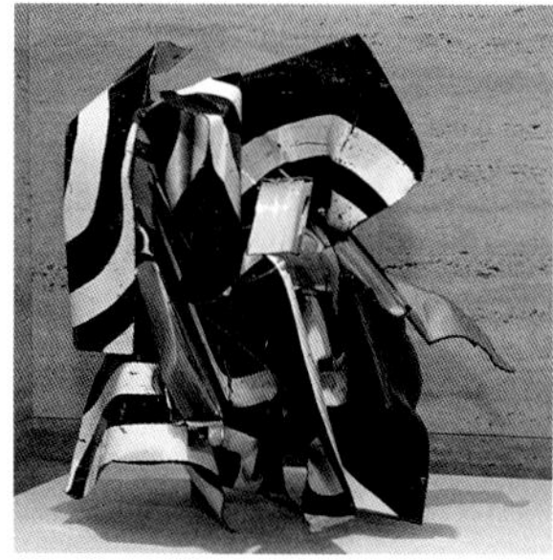

John Chamberlain
(American, born 1927)
White Monkey, 2007
Painted and chromed steel
45.7 x 48.3 x 45.7 cm (18 x 19 x 18 in.)

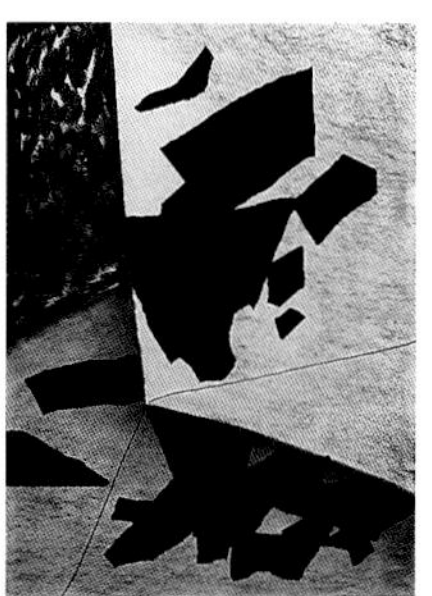

Paul Chan
(American, born Hong Kong 1973)
Pythagoras Was Wrong (for 6th Light), 2007
Mixed media on paper
76.2 x 57.2 cm (30 x 22 ½ in.)

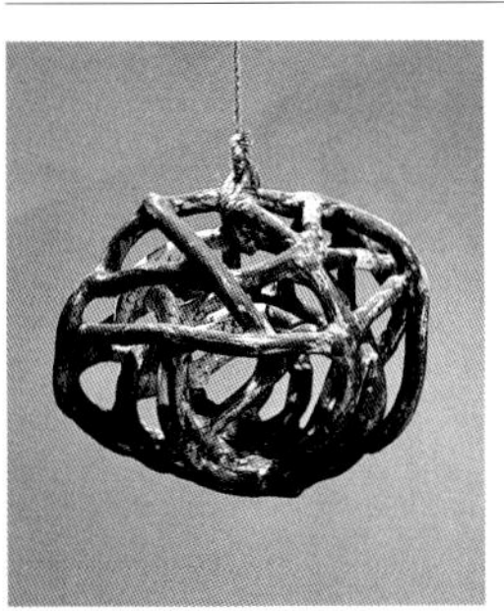

Anne Chu
(American, born 1959)
Hanging Rock (two), 2007
Ceramic with glaze
38.1 x 43.2 x 40.6 cm (15 x 17 x 16 in.)

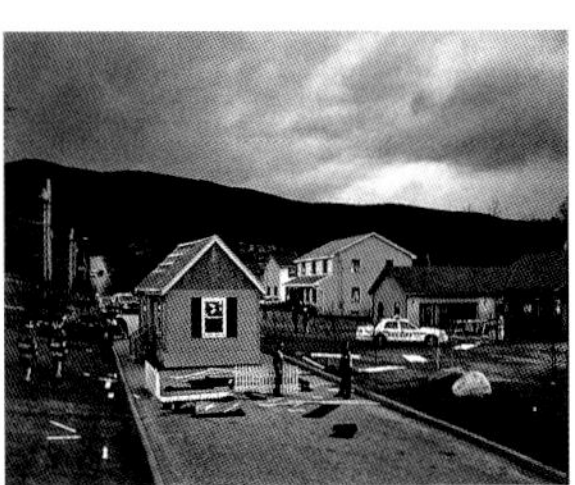

Gregory Crewdson
(American, born 1962)
Untitled, 2002
Digital chromogenic print
(edition of 10)
121.9 x 152.4 cm (48 x 60 in.)

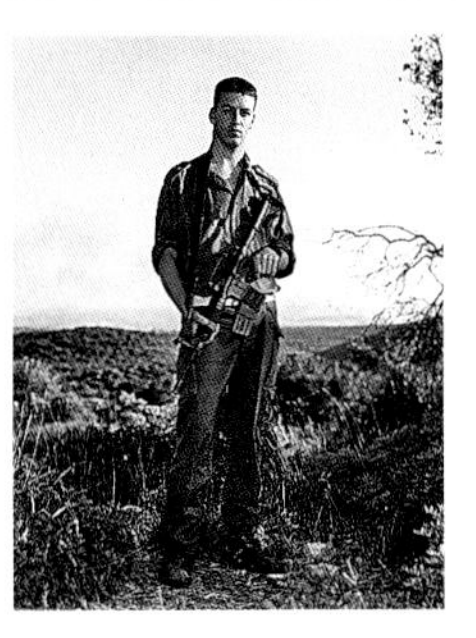

Rineke Dijkstra
(Dutch, born 1959)
Amit, Golani Brigade, Orev Unit, Elyacim, Israel, May 26, 1999, 1999
Chromogenic print (edition of 10)
180.3 x 147 cm (71 x 58 in.)
Gift, 2002

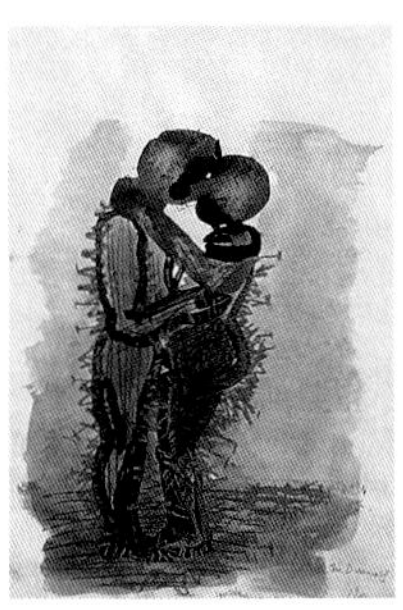

Marlene Dumas
(South African, born 1953)
Needles and Pins, 1989
India ink, gouache, and pastel on paper
55.2 x 41.3 cm (21 ¾ x 16 ¼ in.)

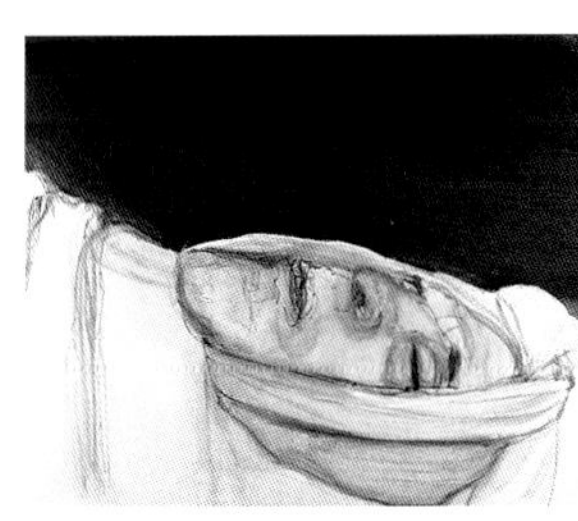

The Deceased, 2002
Oil on canvas
110 x 130 cm (43 5/16 x 51 3/16 in.)
See pp. 38–39

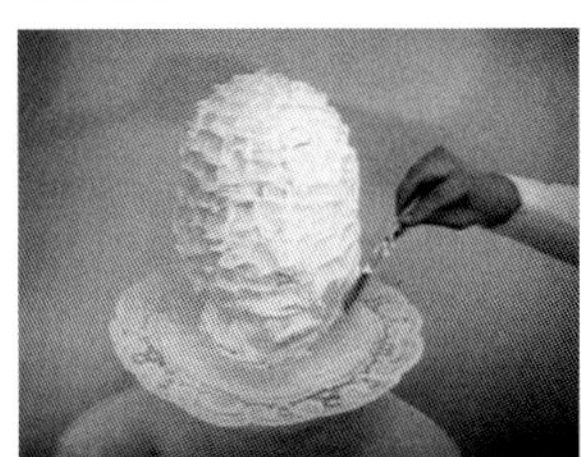

Jeanne Dunning
(American, born 1960)
Icing, 1996
Color video, sound (projection)
(edition of 6); 30 min. loop
Gift, 2007

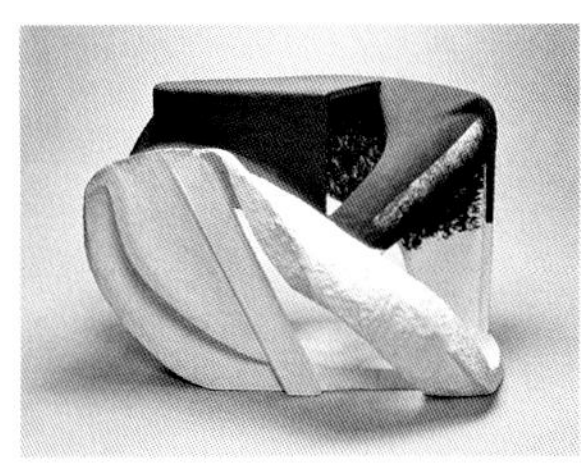

Vincent Fecteau
(American, born 1969)
Untitled, 2008
Papier-mâché and acrylic paint
50 x 72 x 48 cm (19 11/16 x 28 3/8 x 18 7/8 in.)
Promised gift, 2009
See pp. 40–41

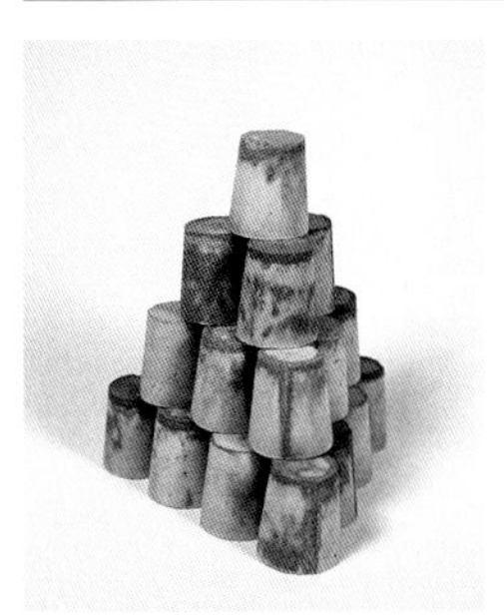

Tony Feher
(American, born 1956)
Permanent Sand Castle, 1993
Cast sand mix
33 x 30.5 x 30.5 cm (13 x 12 x 12 in.)

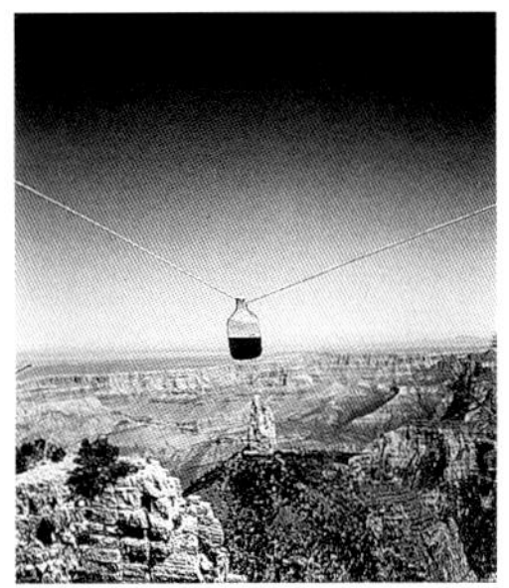

North Rim, 1994/2001
Chromogenic print (edition of 25)
21.6 x 19.1 cm (8 ½ x 7 ½ in.)

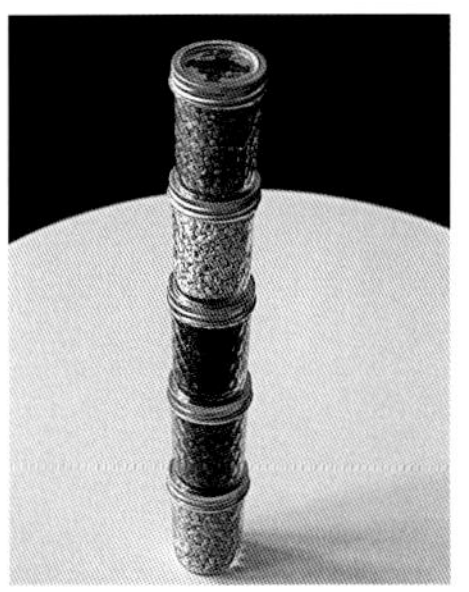

Albuquerque, 1997
Five Ball jars with Mason bands and decorative dome lids (edition of 13)
Each: 7 x 10.2 cm (2 ¾ x 4 in.)

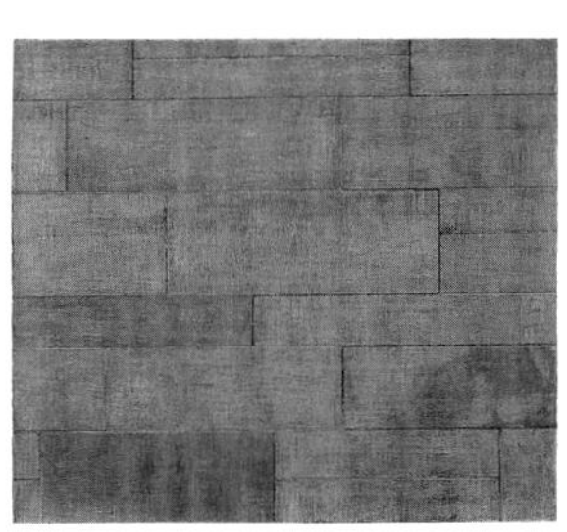

Julia Fish
(American, born 1950)
5811 South Ellis, 1995
Oil on canvas
61 x 71.1 cm (24 x 28 in.)
Promised gift, 2010
See pp. 42–43

Frost II, 1996
Oil on canvas
68.6 x 61 cm (27 x 24 in.)
See pp. 44–45

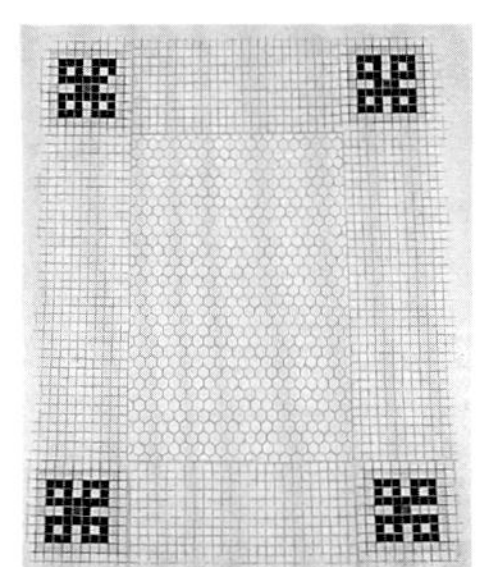

Entry-plan with four corners, 2000
Oil on canvas
125.1 x 102.2 cm (49 ¼ x 40 ¼ in.)

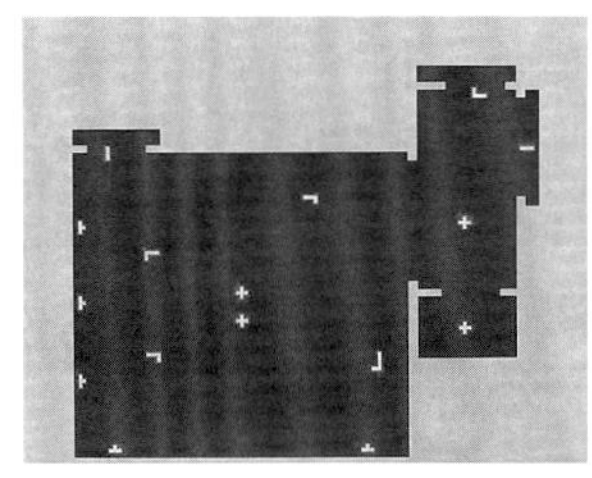

Living Room: NorthEast, with lights, action, 2003–05
Oil on canvas
82.6 x 108 cm (32 ½ x 42 ½ in.)
See pp. 46–47

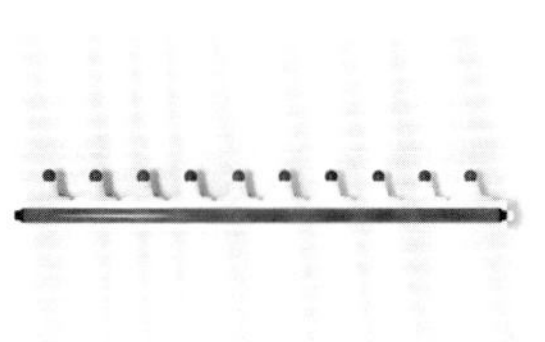

Dan Flavin
(American, 1933–1996)
one of May 27, 1963, 1963
Red fluorescent and incandescent light on acrylic and Masonite and pine
20 x 122 x 16.5 cm (8 x 48 x 6 ½ in.)
Promised gift, 2010
See pp. 48–49

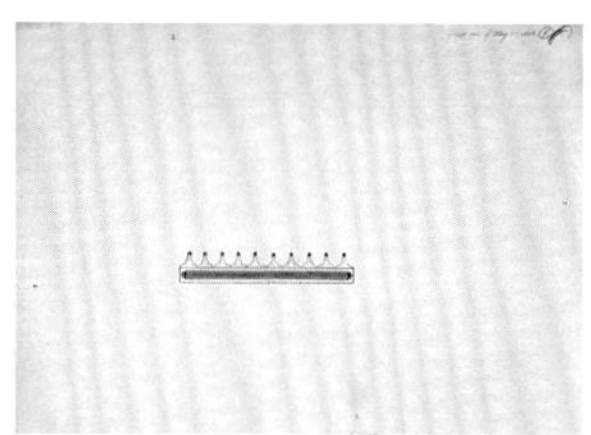

Drawing for "one of May 27, 1963," 1964
Red pencil on double-ply board
29.2 x 29.2 cm (11 ½ x 11 ½ in.)
Promised gift, 2010

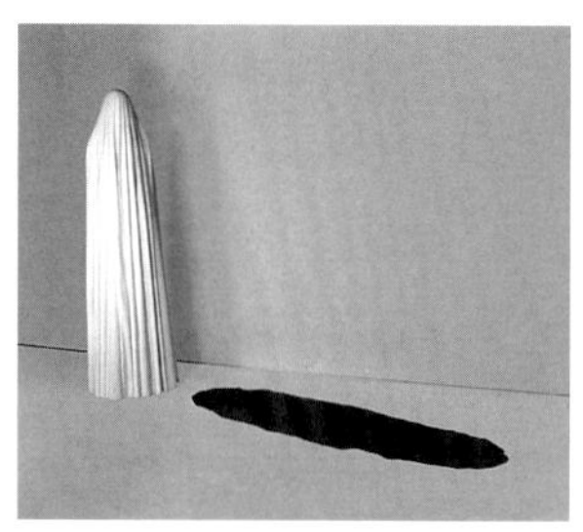

Katharina Fritsch
(German, born 1956)
Ghost and Pool of Blood, 1988
Polyester and Plexiglas (edition of 3)
Ghost: 200 x 59.7 x 61 cm
(78 ¾ x 23 ½ x 24 in.)
Pool: 0.6 x 57.2 x 209.6 cm
(¼ x 22 ½ x 82 ½ in.)
Promised gift, 2010
See pp. 50–51

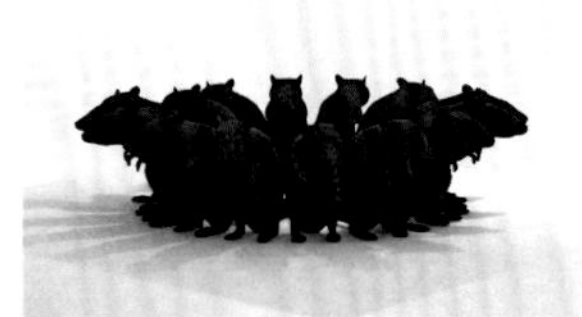

Rat King Model, 1991/98
Polyester and paint (edition of 8)
15 x 58 cm (5 ⅞ x 22 ⅞ in.)
Promised gift, 2010

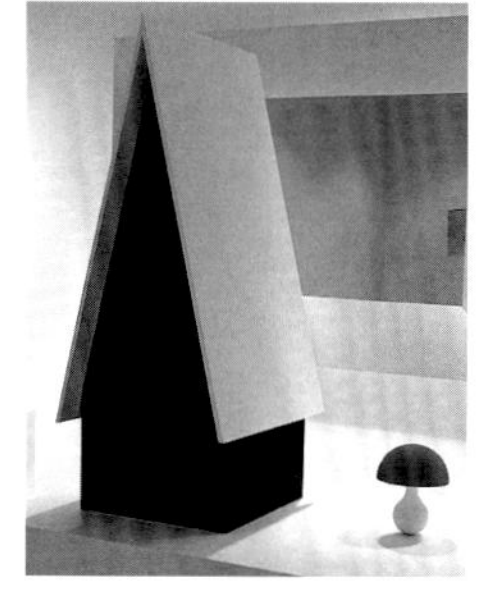

Witch's House and Mushroom, 1999
Wood, polyester, and paint (edition of 8)
House: 80 x 40 x 40 cm
(31 ½ x 15 ¾ x 15 ¾ in.)
Mushroom: 15 x 12 cm (5 ⅞ x 4 ¹⁄₁₆ in.)
Promised gift, 2010

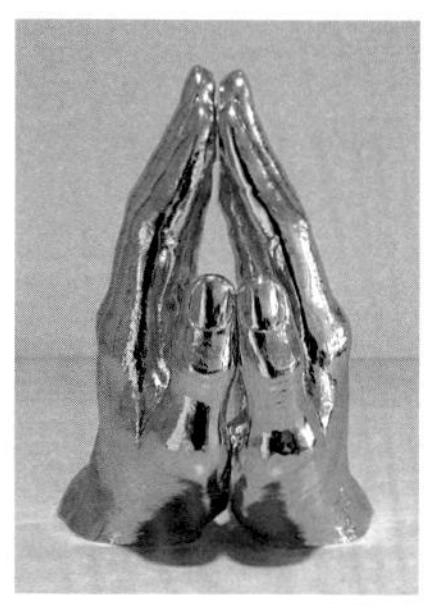

Praying Hands, 2003/04
Cast and painted polyester (edition of 16)
19.7 x 14.6 x 13 cm (7 ¾ x 5 ¾ x 5 ⅛ in.)

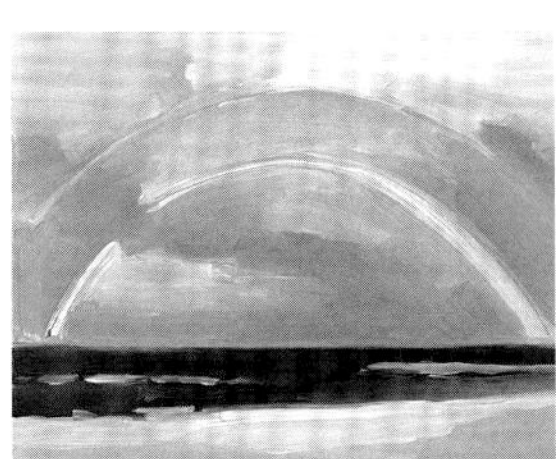

Maureen Gallace
(American, born 1960)
Summer Rainbow, Cape Cod, 2006
Oil on panel
22.9 x 30.5 cm (9 x 12 in.)
See pp. 52–53

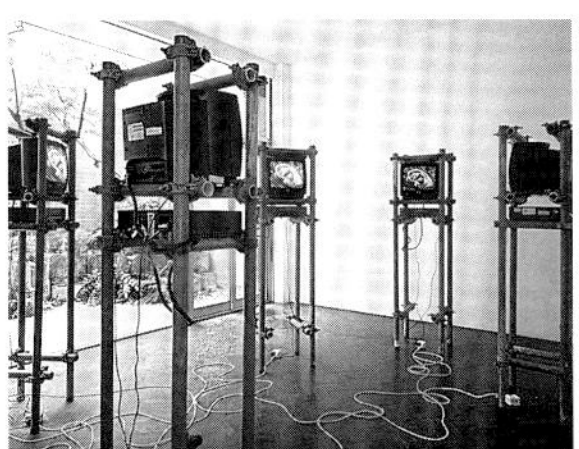

Kendell Geers
(South African, born 1968)
Tears for Eros, 1999
Color video, sound (five monitors), metal scaffolding
Dimensions variable
Purchased with the Donna and Howard Stone New Media Fund, 2000

Gaylen Gerber
(American, born 1955)
Support, oil on *Support/Moon*, Gaylen Gerber with Adrian Schiess, 2003
Oil, enamel, and polyurethane foam on canvas
50 x 60 cm (19 ⅝ x 23 ⅝ in.)

Untitled, n.d.
Oil on canvas
96.5 x 96.5 cm (38 x 38 in.)
Promised gift, 2010

Untitled, n.d.
Oil on canvas
96.5 x 96.5 cm (38 x 38 in.)
Promised gift, 2010

Untitled, n.d.
Graphite on paper, Plexiglas frame
69.1 x 69.1 cm (27 3/16 x 27 3/16 in.)

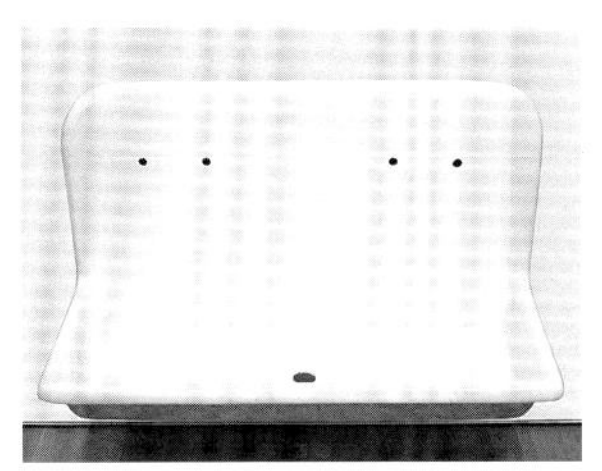

Robert Gober
(American, born 1954)
Double Sink, 1984
Plaster, wood, steel, wire lath, and semi-gloss enamel paint
91.4 x 162.6 x 71.1 cm (36 x 64 x 28 in.)
Promised gift, 2010
See pp. 54–55

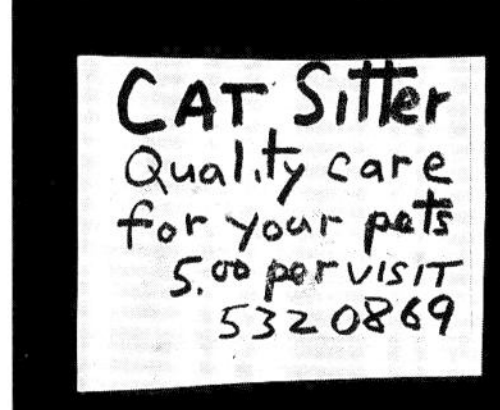

Untitled, 2000–01
Intaglio print (edition of 15)
6.7 x 8.7 cm (2 ⅝ x 3 7/16 in.)
Promised gift, 2008

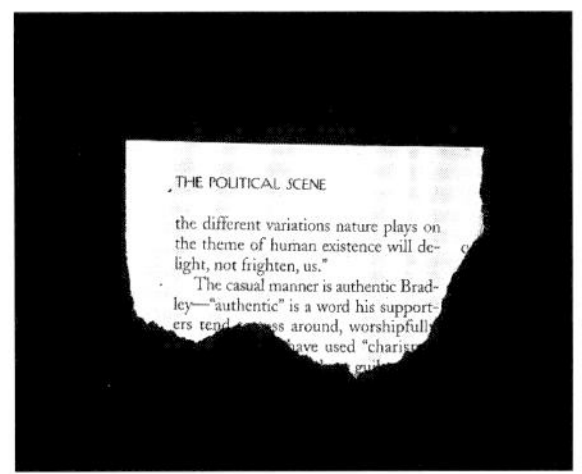

THE POLITICAL SCENE

the different variations nature plays on the theme of human existence will delight, not frighten, us."

The casual manner is authentic Bradley—"authentic" is a word his supporters tend ... around, worshipfull... ...ave used "charis...

Untitled, 2000–01
Intaglio print (edition of 15)
4.8 x 7.6 cm (1 ⅞ x 3 in.)
Promised gift, 2008

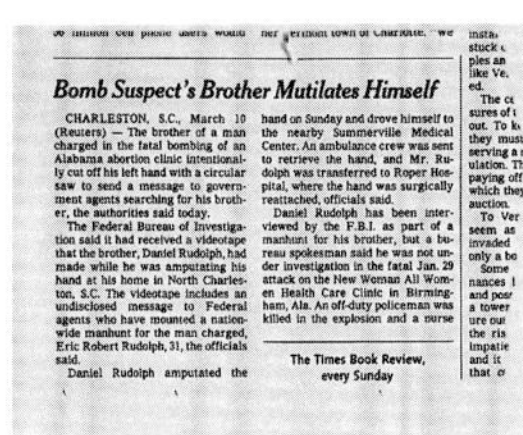

Bomb Suspect's Brother Mutilates Himself

CHARLESTON, S.C., March 10 (Reuters) — The brother of a man charged in the fatal bombing of an Alabama abortion clinic intentionally cut off his left hand with a circular saw to send a message to government agents searching for his brother, the authorities said today.

The Federal Bureau of Investigation said it had received a videotape that the brother, Daniel Rudolph, had made while he was amputating his hand at his home in North Charleston, S.C. The videotape includes an undisclosed message to Federal agents who have mounted a nationwide manhunt for the man charged, Eric Robert Rudolph, 31, the officials said.

Daniel Rudolph amputated the hand on Sunday and drove himself to the nearby Summerville Medical Center. An ambulance crew was sent to retrieve the hand, and Mr. Rudolph was transferred to Roper Hospital, where the hand was surgically reattached, officials said.

Daniel Rudolph has been interviewed by the F.B.I. as part of a manhunt for his brother, but a bureau spokesman said he was not under investigation in the fatal Jan. 29 attack on the New Woman All Women Health Care Clinic in Birmingham, Ala. An off-duty policeman was killed in the explosion and a nurse

The Times Book Review, every Sunday

Untitled, 2000–01
Intaglio print (edition of 15)
10.5 x 13 cm (4 ⅛ x 5 1/16 in.)
Promised gift, 2008

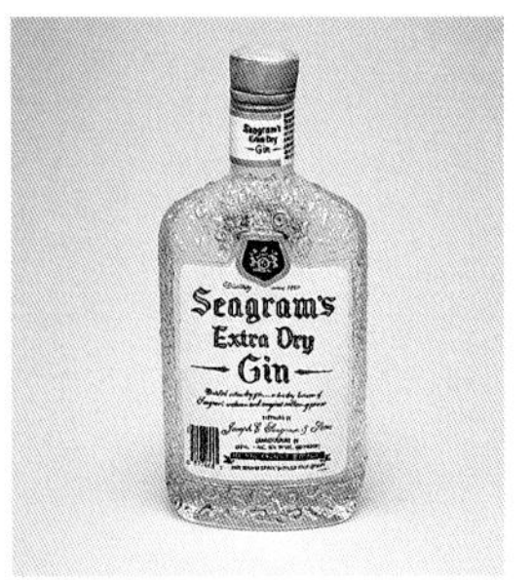

Untitled, 2000–01
Cast hot glass, paper, paint, and cast plastic (edition of 4)
23.5 x 10.2 x 3.8 cm (9 1/4 x 4 x 1 1/2 in.)
See pp. 56–57

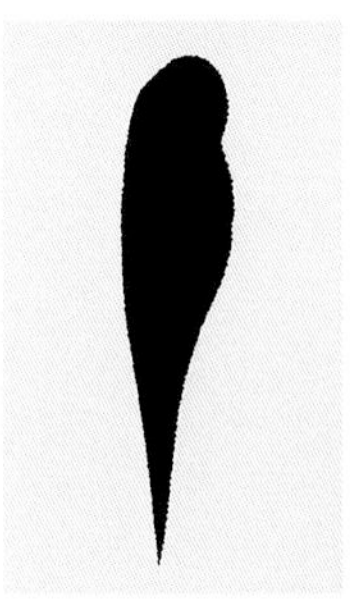

Daan van Golden
(Dutch, born 1936)
Study H.M., 2004
Oil on canvas
145 x 90 cm (57 1/16 x 35 7/16 in.)
Promised gift, 2010
See pp. 58–59

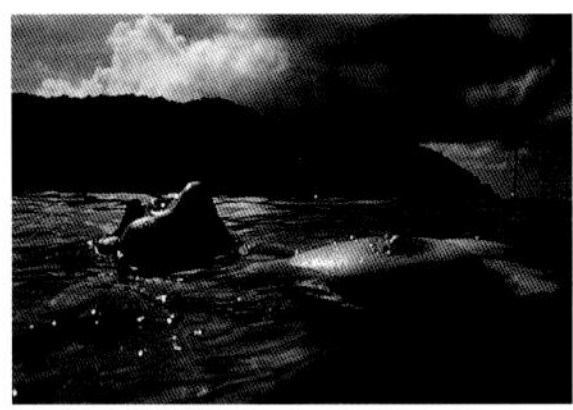

Nan Goldin
(American, born 1953)
Valerie Floating in the Sea, Mayeaux, 2001
Cibachrome print (edition of 15)
76.2 x 101.6 cm (30 x 40 in.)

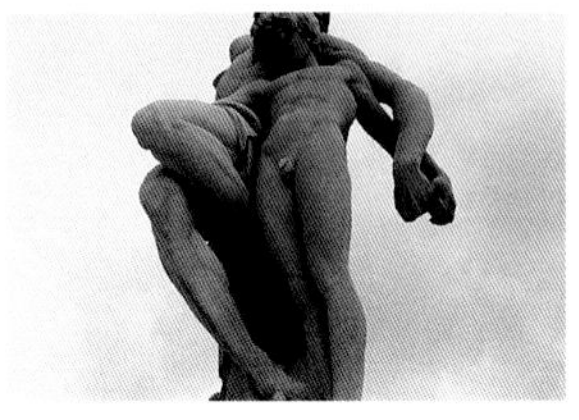

Felix Gonzalez-Torres
(Cuban, 1957–1996)
"Untitled" (Paris), 1988
Chromogenic print
32.1 x 48.6 cm (12 5/8 x 19 1/8 in.)
Promised gift, 2010
See pp. 60–61

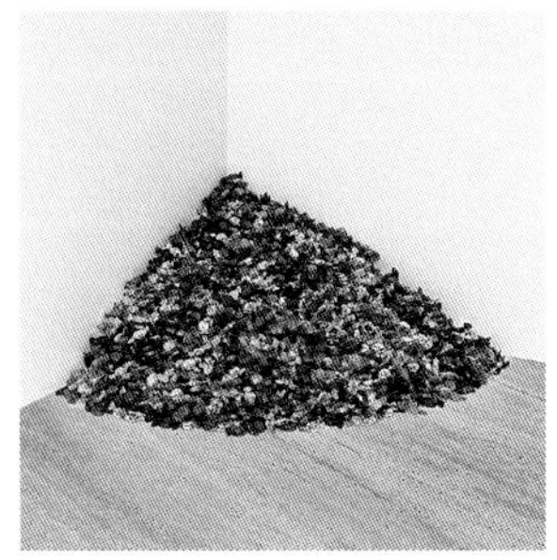

"Untitled" (Portrait of Ross in LA), 1991
175 pounds of Fruit Flasher candy
Dimensions variable
Promised gift, 2010
See pp. 62–63

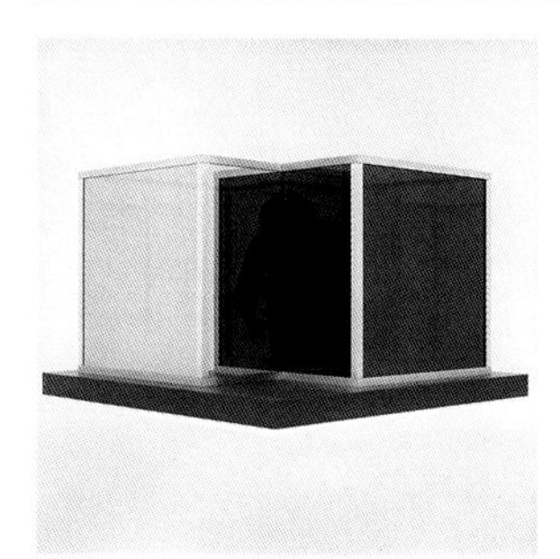

Dan Graham
(American, born 1942)
Two Way Mirror Joined Cubes, 1996
Mirror and aluminum
91.4 x 91.4 x 58.4 cm (36 x 36 x 23 in.)

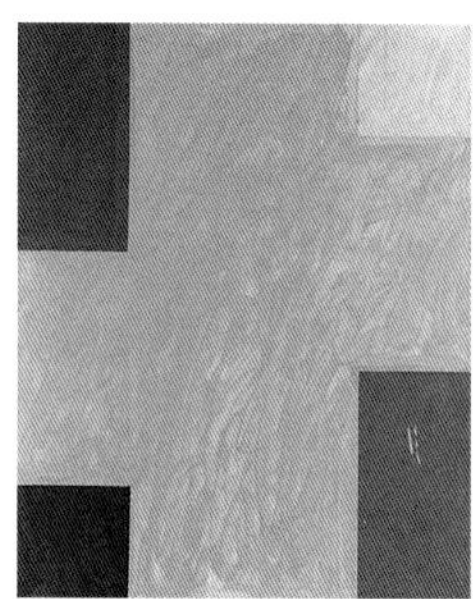

Mary Heilmann
(American, born 1940)
Green JA, 2000
Oil on canvas
101.6 x 81.9 cm (40 x 32 1/4 in.)
See pp. 64–65

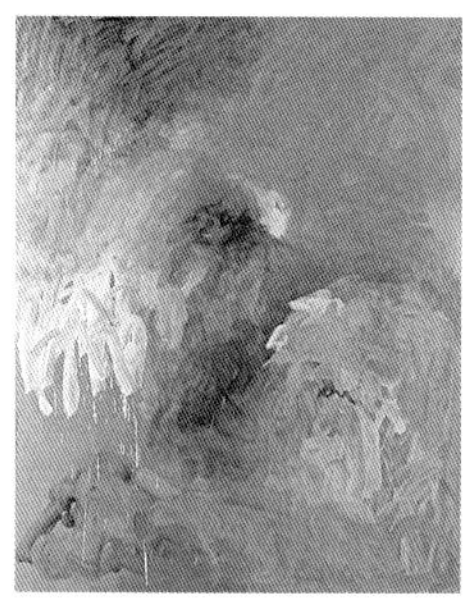

Heaven, 2004
Oil on canvas
190.5 x 152.4 cm (75 x 60 in.)
Promised gift, 2009

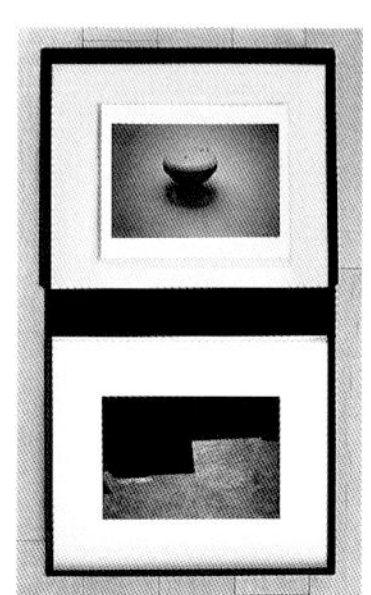

Arturo Herrera
(Venezuelan, born 1959)
The Passing of the Pig, 1995
Six gelatin silver prints in portfolio (edition of 5)
32.4 x 39.4 cm (12 3/4 x 15 1/2 in.)
Shown: Detail

Untitled, 1997
Toned silver print (edition of 7)
40.6 x 50.8 cm (16 x 20 in.)

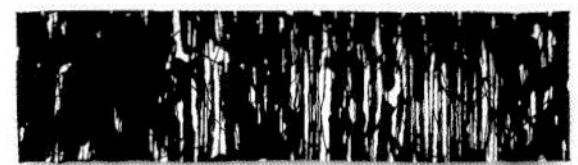

Let Me Go, 2000
Wool felt
165.1 x 640.1 cm (65 x 252 in.)
Promised gift, 2010
See pp. 66–67

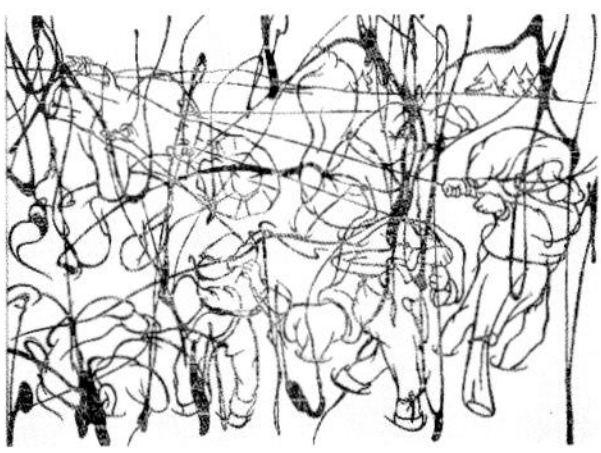

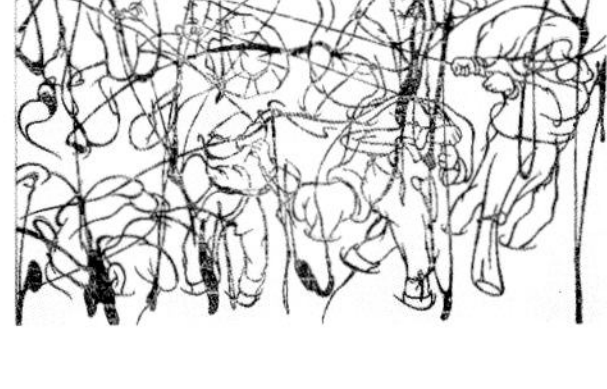

Untitled, 2003
Printed paper cutout mounted on paper
168.9 x 229.9 cm (66 ½ x 90 ½ in.)

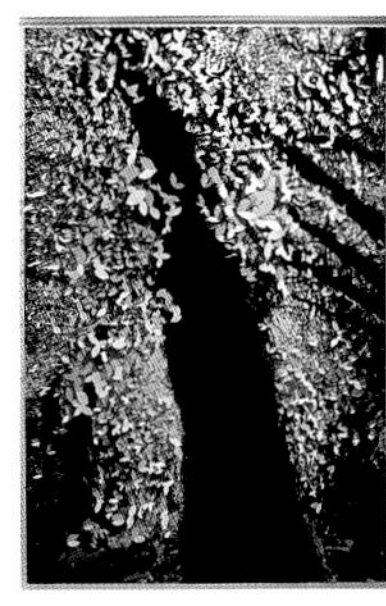

Revealed, 2004
Cut chromogenic print
242.6 x 163.8 x 10.2 cm
(95 ½ x 64 ½ x 4 in.)
Promised gift, 2010
See pp. 70–71

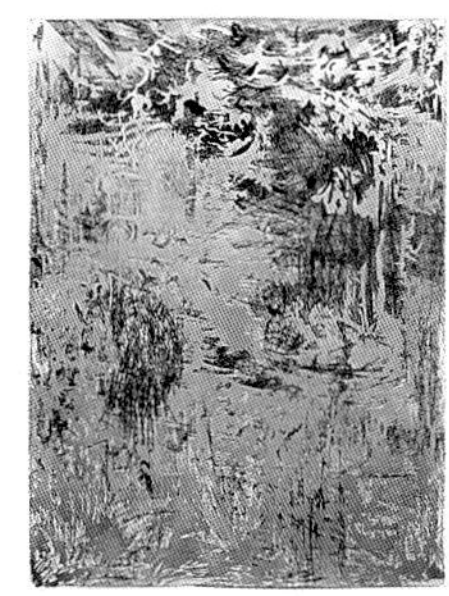

Untitled (Study for Gray), 2009
Charcoal and twenty-four-carat gold on paper
127 x 96.5 cm (50 x 30 in.)

Roger Hiorns
(English, born 1975)
Before the Rain, 2003
Glass, Plexiglas, painted wood, tape, card paper, and copper sulphate (two elements)
90 x 112 x 75 cm (35 ⅜ x 44 ⅛ x 29 ½ in.)
55 x 134 x 83 cm (21 ⅝ x 52 ¾ x 32 ⅝ in.)

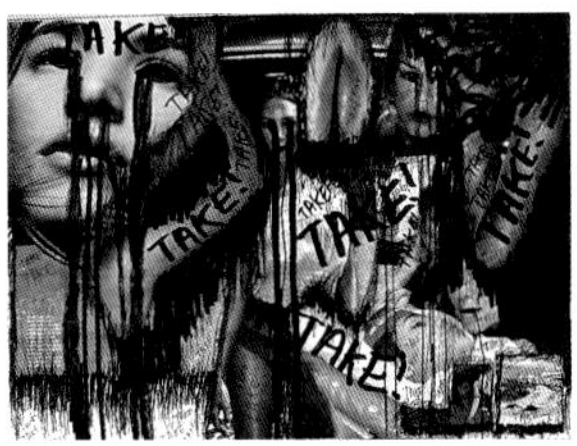

Thomas Hirschhorn
(Swiss, born 1957)
Series-KS-18, 24, 26, and *43*, 2002
Collage, pen, marker, and cellophane
KS-18: 35.6 x 44.5 cm (14 x 17 ½ in.)
KS-24: 33.7 x 45.7 cm (13 ¼ x 18 in.)
KS-26: 34.6 x 44.5 cm (13 ⅝ x 17 ½ in.)
KS-43: 33.3 x 47.6 cm (13 ⅛ x 18 ¾ in.)
Shown: *KS-24*

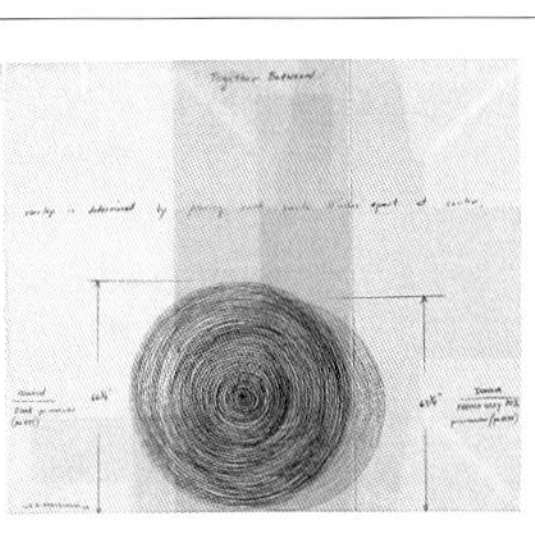

Jim Hodges
(American, born 1957)
Untitled (Portrait of Howard and Donna Stone), 1999
Prismacolor pencil on wall
Dimensions variable
See pp. 68–69
Shown: Study entitled *Together/ Between*

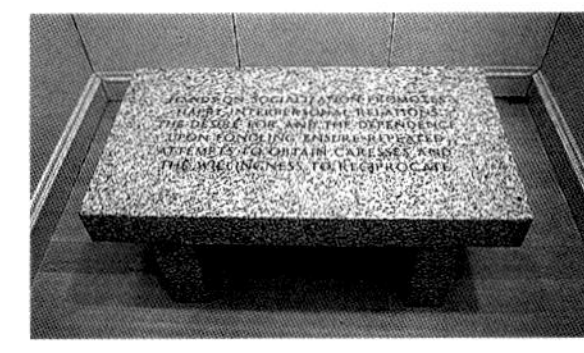

Jenny Holzer
(American, born 1950)
Untitled (Selection from the Living Series), 1989
Granite (edition of 3)
43.2 x 91.4 x 45.7 cm (17 x 36 x 18 in.)

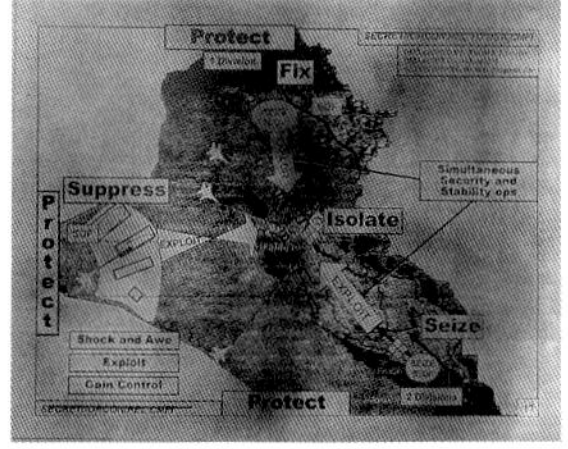

Protect Protect Deep Purple, 2007
From the series *Map*
Oil on linen
200.7 x 259.7 cm (79 x 102 ¼ in.)

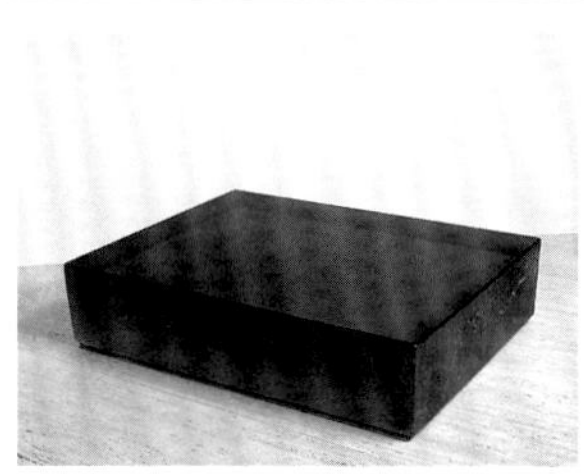

Roni Horn
(American, born 1955)
Deeps and Skies, 1995–96
Solid cast glass
21.3 x 103.2 x 76.8 cm
(8 3/8 x 40 5/8 x 30 1/4 in.)
Promised gift, 2010
See pp. 72–73

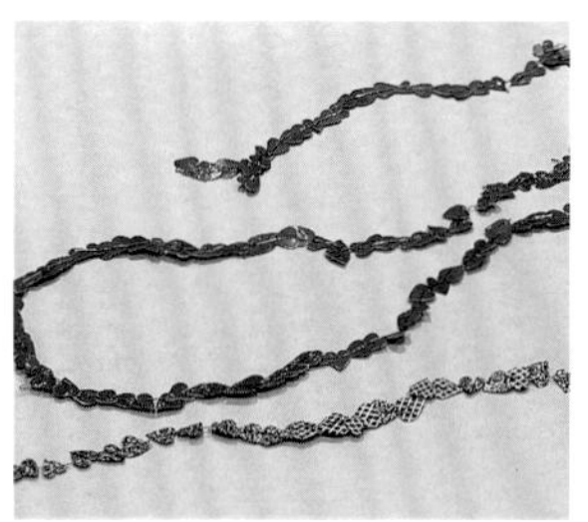

Jessica Hutchins
(American, born 1971)
Untitled (Hearts), 1999
Playing card fragments and staples
Dimensions variable

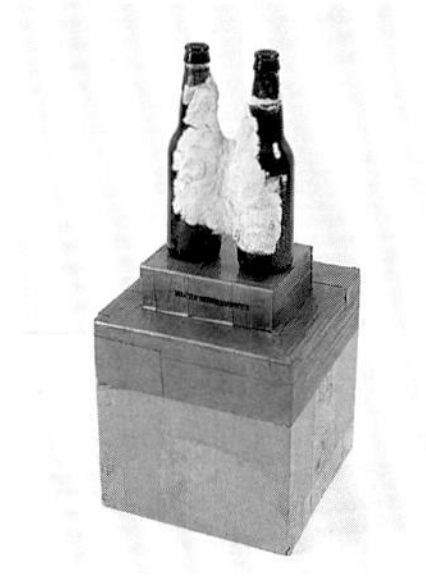

Young Lovers and Their Time, 1999
Bottles, paper-mâché collage, and cardboard box with tape
43.2 x 30.5 x 30.5 cm (17 x 12 x 12 in.)

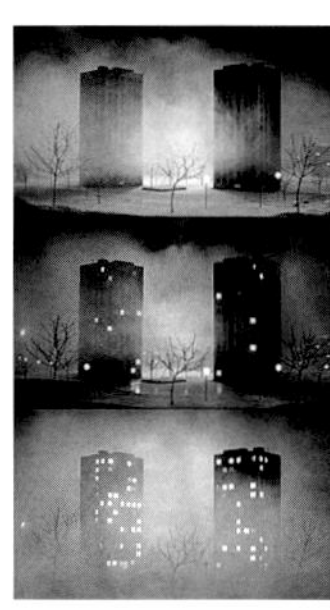

Pierre Huyghe
(French, born 1962)
The Housing Projects, 1994/2001
VistaVison film, sound, transferred to digital video (projection on screen) (edition of 5); 7:51 min. loop
Gift, 2007
See pp. 74–75

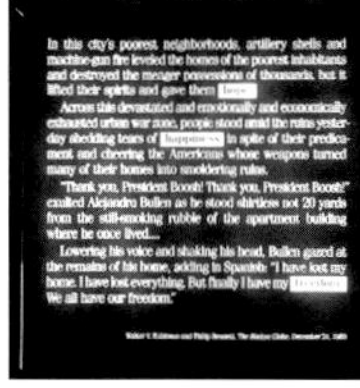

Alfredo Jaar
(Chilean, born 1956)
Hope, Happiness, Freedom, 1990
Photo transparency in light box
52.1 x 52.1 x 13.3 cm
(20 1/2 x 20 1/2 x 5 1/4 in.)

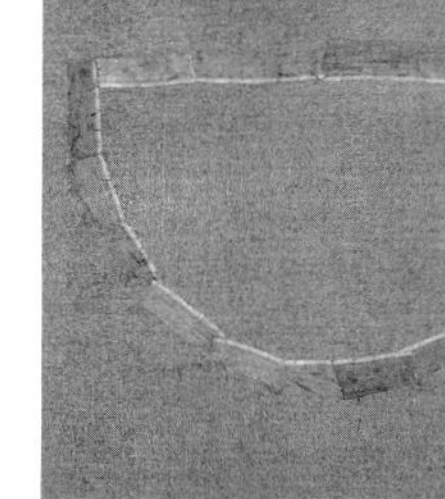

Sergej Jensen
(Danish, born 1973)
Untitled (Censored), 2003
Linen on linen
73.7 x 76.2 cm (29 x 30 in.)

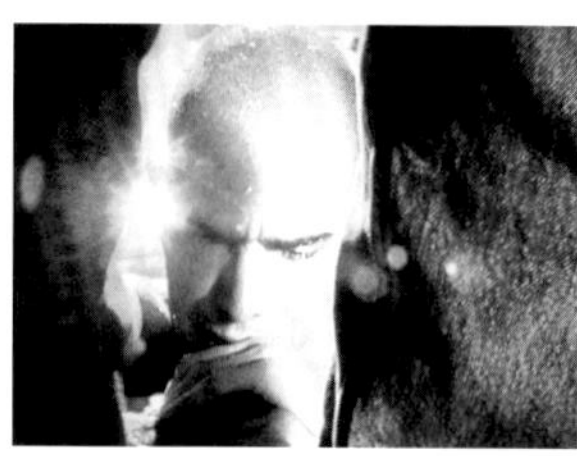

Isaac Julien
(English, born 1960)
Choreography and movement by Javier De Frutos
The Long Road to Mazatlán, 2000
16mm black-and-white and color film, sound, transferred to three-channel digital video (rear projection on screen); 18 min. loop
Gift, 2007

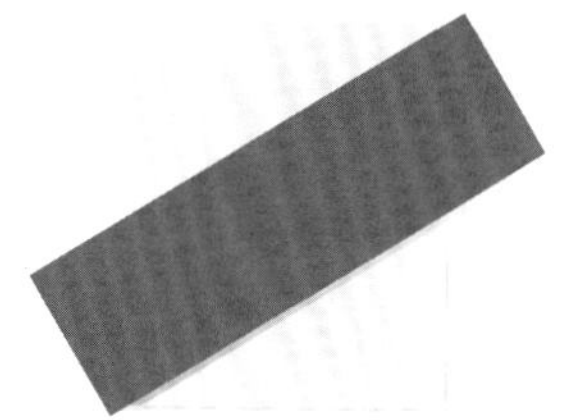

Ellsworth Kelly
(American, born 1923)
Red Diagonal, 2007
Oil on canvas (two joined panels)
214 x 277.8 x 6.7 cm
(84 1/4 x 109 3/8 x 2 5/8 in.)
Promised gift, 2008
See pp. 76–77

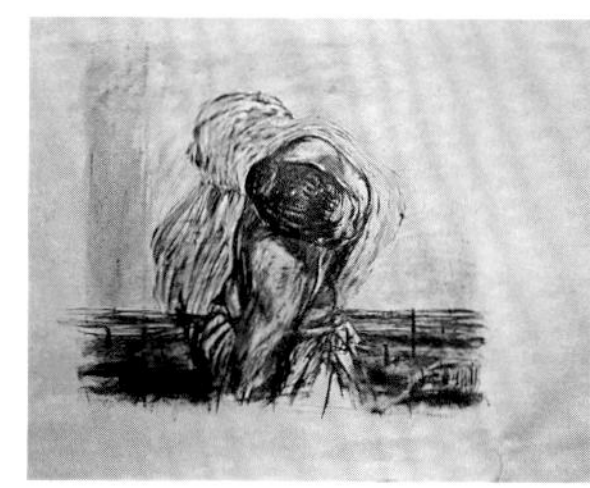

William Kentridge
(South African, born 1955)
Drawing from Felix in Exile, 1994
Charcoal and pastel on paper
120 x 150 cm (47 1/4 x 59 1/16 in.)

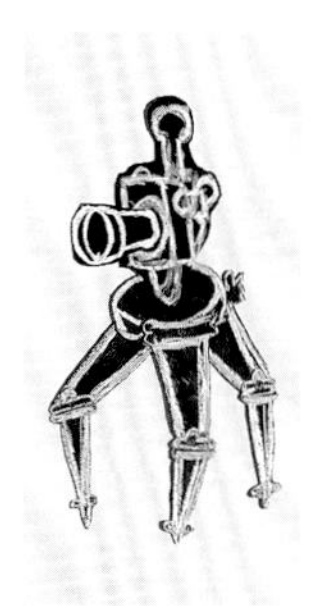

A Gross Violation (Fragments from Ubu Tells the Truth), 1996
Chalk on paper
Dimensions variable
Shown: Detail

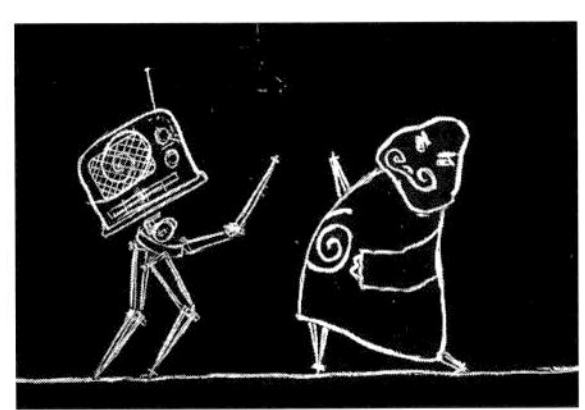

Ubu Tells the Truth, 1997
35mm color film, sound, transferred to digital video (projection) (edition of 4); 8 min.
Gift, 2007

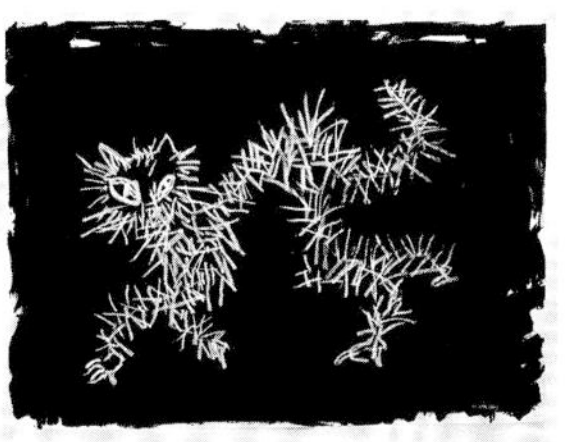

Cat, 1998
Chalk on painted paper
112.4 x 148 cm (44 1/4 x 58 1/4 in.)

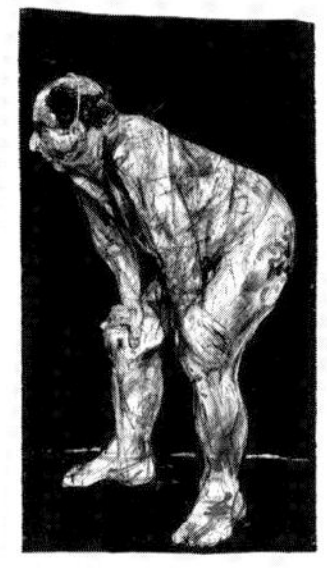

Ubu Drawing (Listening Man), 1998
Charcoal, gouache, and pastel on paper
191.8 x 108 cm (75 1/2 x 42 1/2 in.)

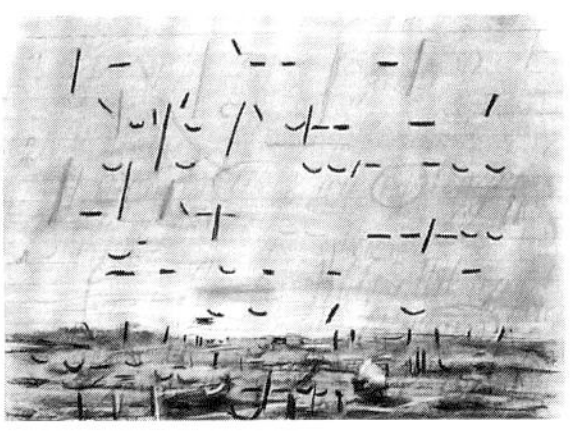

Drawing from "Zeno Writing" (Landscape, text fragments), 2002
Charcoal and red crayon on ivory wove paper
80 x 121 cm (31 1/2 x 47 5/8 in.)
Partial and promised gift, 2004

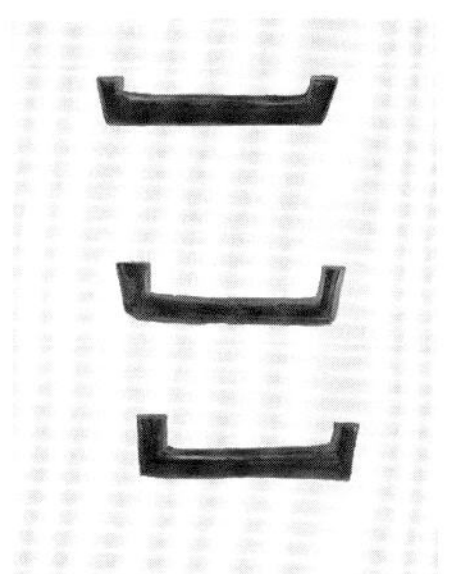

Raoul De Keyser
(Belgian, born 1930)
Retour 3, 1999
Oil on canvas
165.1 x 117.8 cm (65 x 46 3/8 in.)
Promised gift, 2010
See pp. 78–79

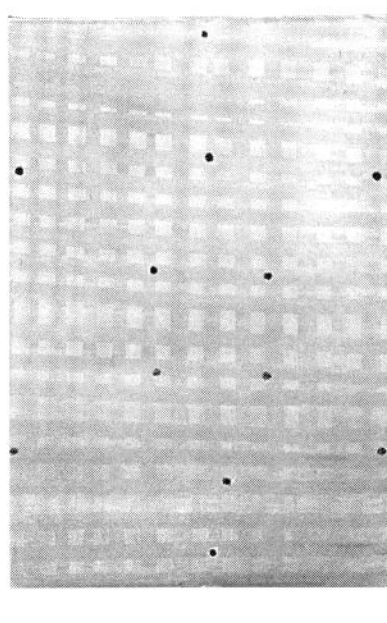

Come on, play it again nr. 9, 2001
Oil on canvas
71 x 50 cm (27 15/16 x 19 11/16 in.)

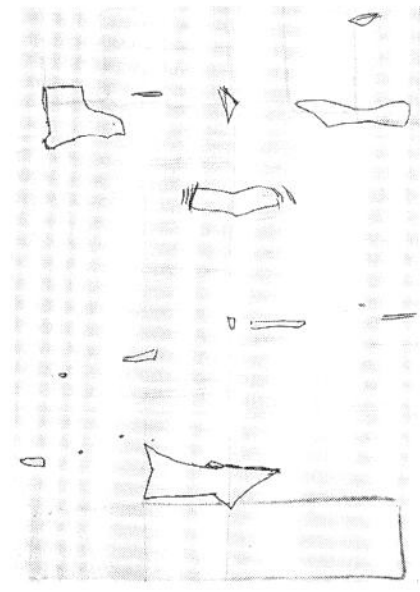

Reserve, 2003
Oil on canvas
90 x 65 cm (35 3/8 x 25 5/8 in.)

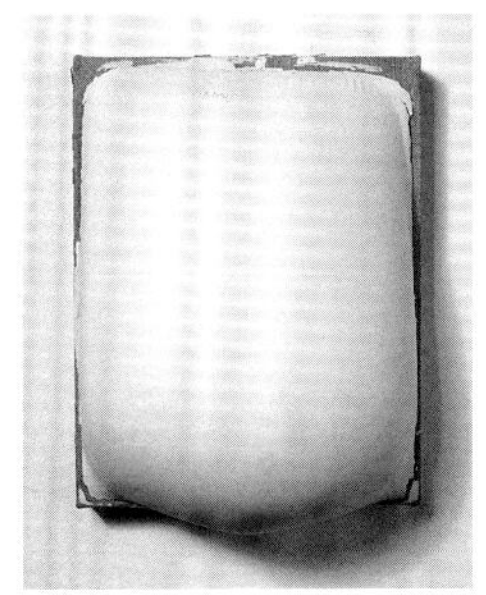
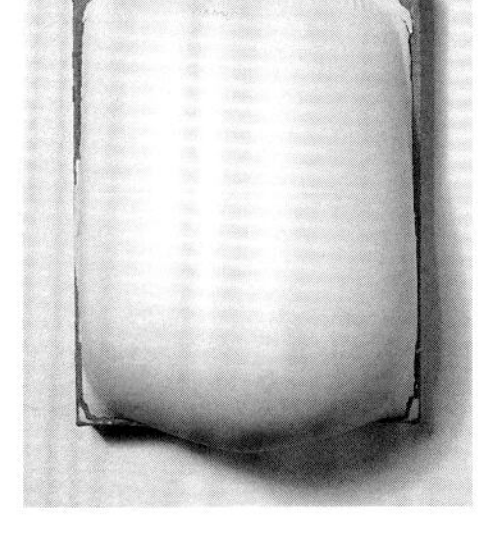

Byron Kim
(American, born 1961)
Belly Painting (White), 1998
Encaustic on linen
25.4 x 20.3 x 10.2 cm (10 x 8 x 4 in.)

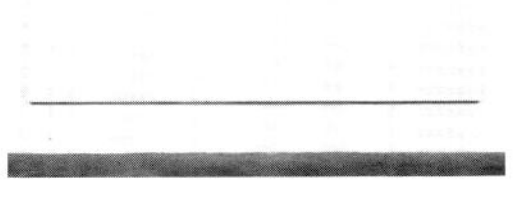

White Painting #3, 2001
Acrylic on canvas
228.6 x 228.6 cm (90 x 90 in.)

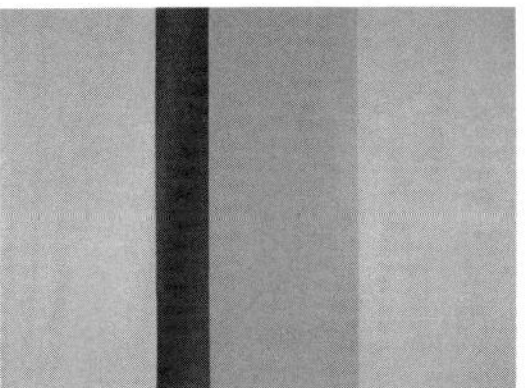

U.N. Building (Looking Downtown), 2008
Acrylic on canvas
121.9 x 172.7 cm (48 x 68 in.)
Promised gift, 2010
See pp. 80–81

Michael Krebber
(German, born 1954)
Beautiful Woman Beautifully Painted, 2002
Lacquer on canvas
120 x 100.3 cm (47 ¼ x 39 ½ in.)
Promised gift, 2010
See pp. 82–83

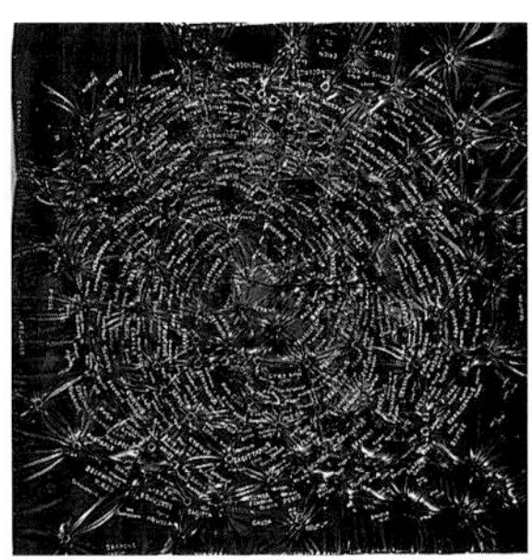

Guillermo Kuitca
(Argentine, born 1961)
Heaven, 1992
Mixed media on mattress
188 x 190.5 x 11.4 cm (74 x 75 x 4 ½ in.)

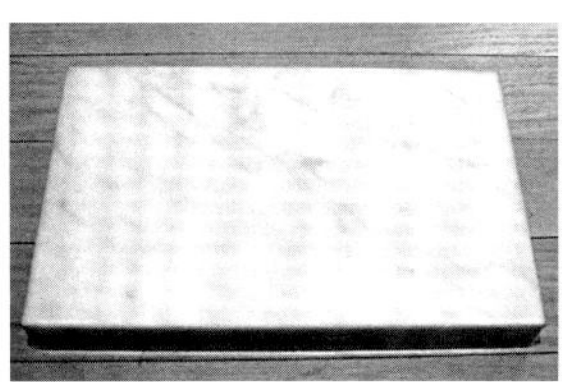

Wolfgang Laib
(German, born 1950)
Milkstone, 1976/77
Marble and milk
24.8 x 29.2 x 6.4 cm (9 ¾ x 11 ½ x 2 ½ in.)

Judy Ledgerwood
(American, born 1959)
Red Pine, 1990
Oil and encaustic on canvas
228.6 x 365.8 cm (90 x 144 in.)
Promised gift, 2010
See pp. 84–85

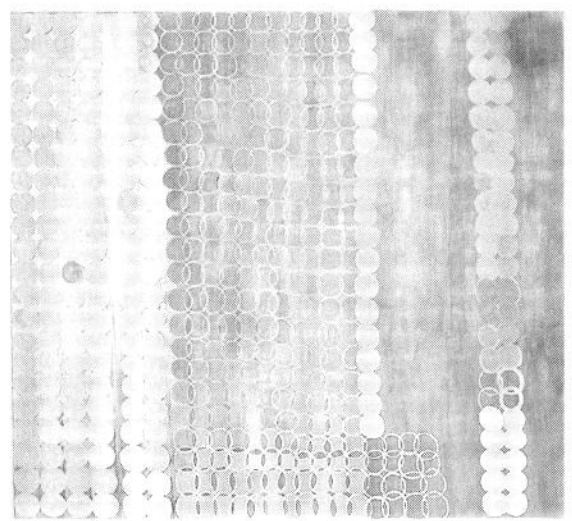

Flamenco Sketches, 1998
Oil on canvas
243.8 x 274.3 cm (96 x 108 in.)

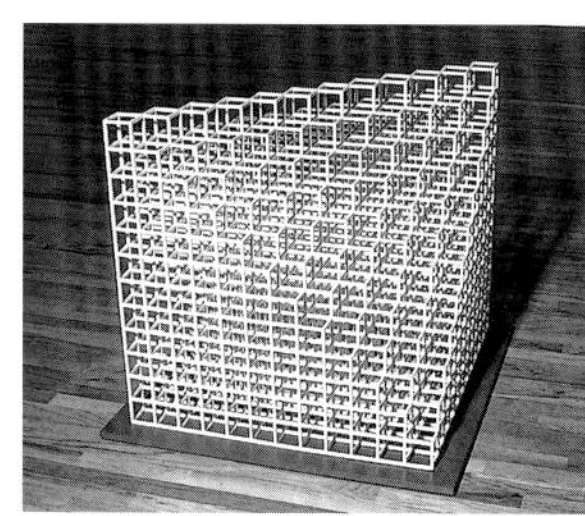

Sol LeWitt
(American, 1928–2007)
Progressive Pyramid, 1997
Painted wood
Structure: 72.4 x 72.4 x 72.4 cm
(28 ½ x 28 ½ x 28 ½ in.)
Base: 2.5 x 84.5 x 84.5 cm
(1 x 33 ¼ x 33 ¼ in.)

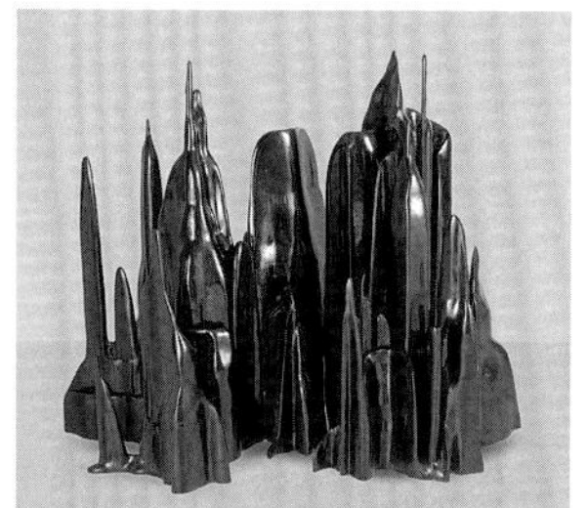

Splotch #1, 1999
Painted fiberglass
121.9 x 152.4 x 99.1 cm (48 x 60 x 39 in.)
Promised gift, 2010
See pp. 86–87

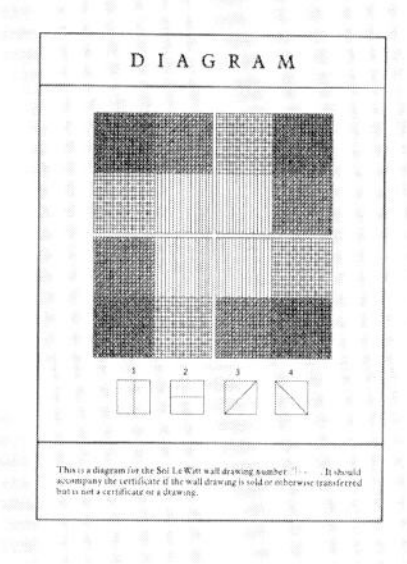

Wall Drawings #966–67: Drawing Series I 24 (B), 2001
Black pencil (#966) and colored pencil (#967)
Dimensions variable
Shown: Diagram for #966

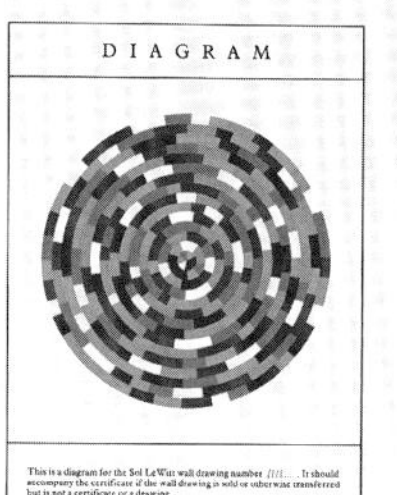

Wall Drawing #1111: Circle with broken bands of color, 2003
Acrylic
Dimensions variable
pp. 88–89
Shown: Diagram

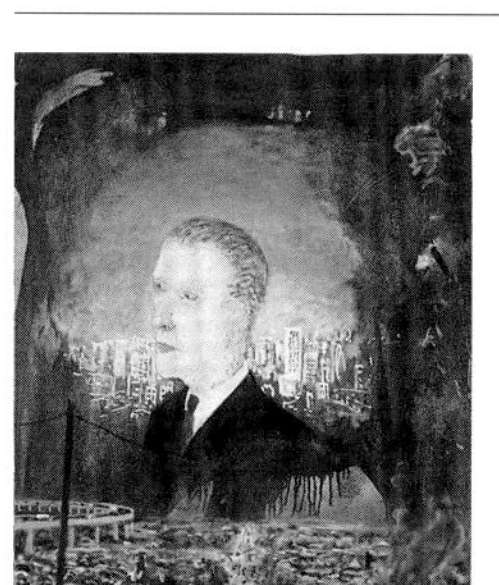

Jim Lutes
(American, born 1955)
The Recipients, 1986
Oil on canvas
68.6 x 55.9 cm (27 x 22 in.)

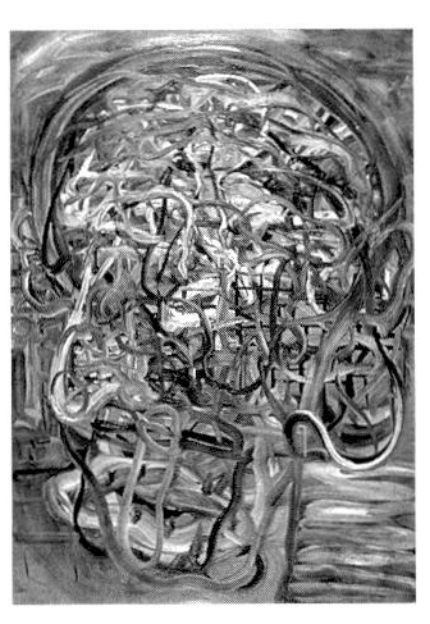

Organization Man, 1990
Oil on linen
124.5 x 94 cm (49 x 37 in.)

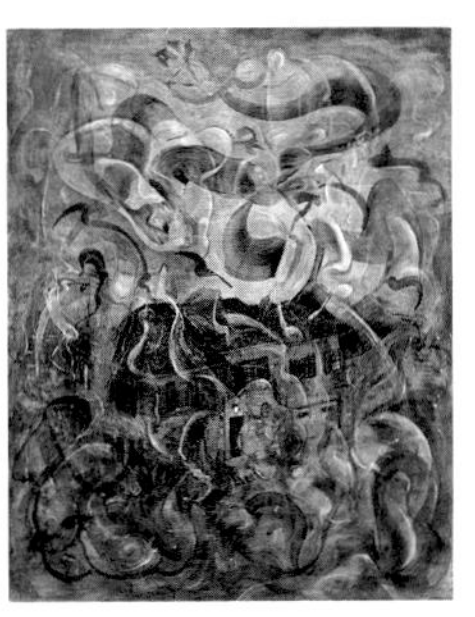

Bubble, 2009
Tempera and oil on panel
151.8 x 121.3 cm (59 ¾ x 47 ¾ in.)

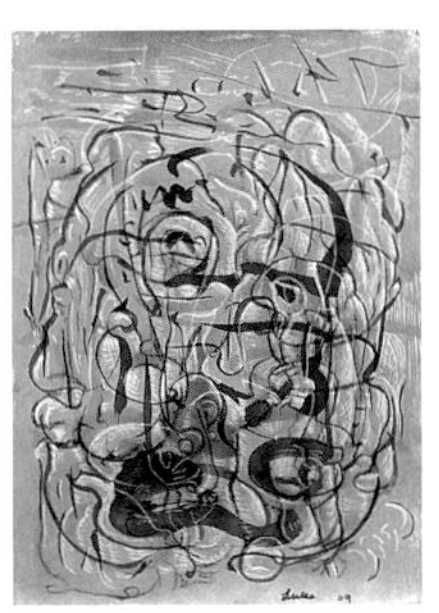

Untitled, 2009
Gelatin, pigment, ink, and tempera on paper
31.8 x 23.5 cm (12 ½ x 9 ¼ in.)

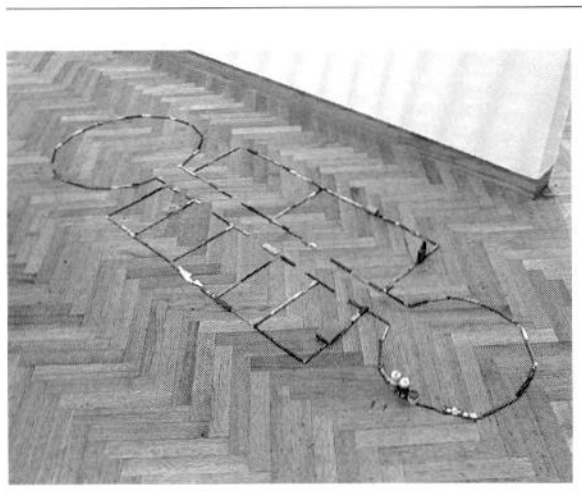

Mark Manders
(Dutch, born 1968)
Inhabited for a Survey (first floor plan from "Self-Portrait as a Building"), 1986
Writing materials, erasers, painting tools, and scissors
8 x 267 x 90 cm (3 ⅛ x 105 ⅛ x 35 ⅜ in.)
Promised gift, 2004

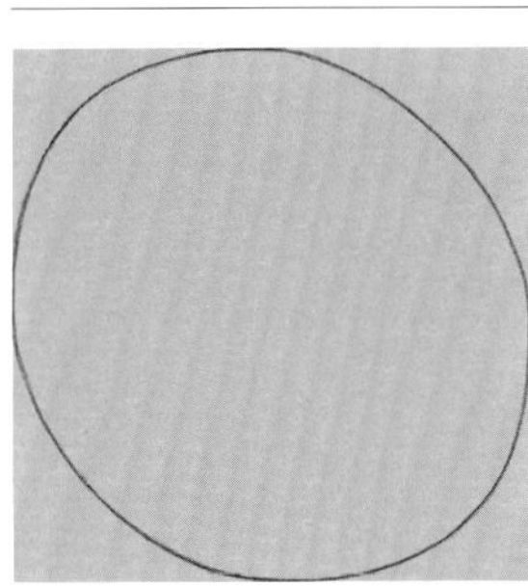

Robert Mangold
(American, born 1937)
Distorted Circle within a Square (Grey), 1972
Acrylic and black pencil on canvas
50.8 x 50.8 cm (20 x 20 in.)
See pp. 90–91

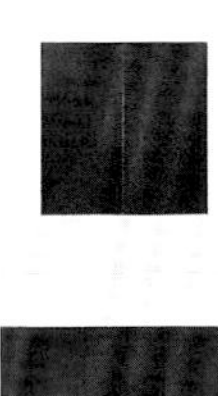

Brice Marden
(American, born 1938)
Untitled (Two Drawings), 1971
Graphite on paper
28.9 x 38.7 cm (11 ⅜ x 15 ¼ in.)
29.2 x 39.4 cm (11 ½ x 15 ½ in.)

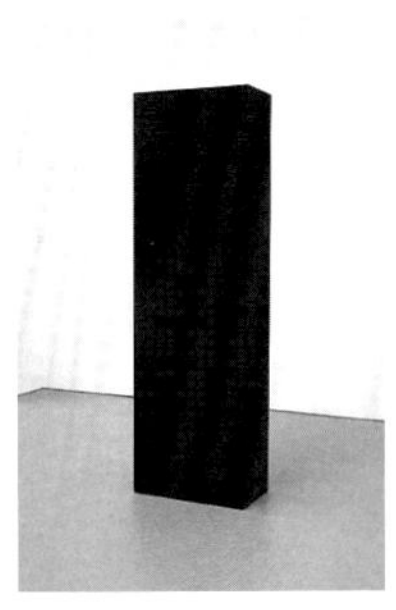

John McCracken
(American, born 1934)
Wave, 2004
Polyester resin, fiberglass, and plywood
243.8 x 76.2 x 40.6 cm (96 x 30 x 16 in.)

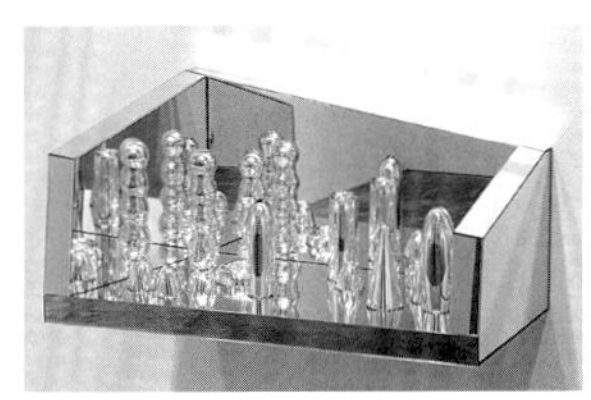

Josiah McElheny
(American, born 1966)
Scale Model for a Totally Reflective Landscape (Towers), 2007
Hand-blown mirrored glass, low-iron mirror, and wood
48.3 x 99.1 x 61 cm (19 x 39 x 24 in.)

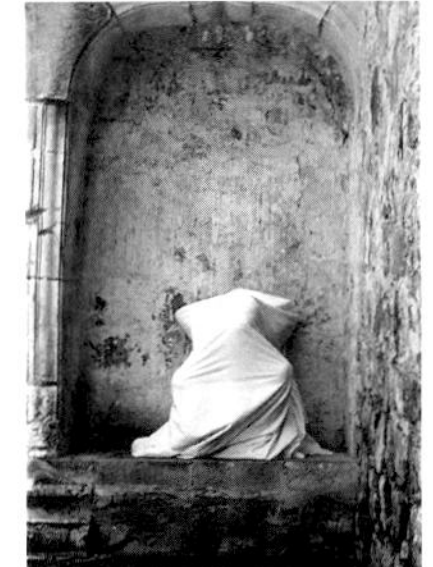

Ana Mendieta
(Cuban, 1948–1985)
Untitled, 1973
Black-and-white photograph
25.4 x 20.3 cm (10 x 8 in.)

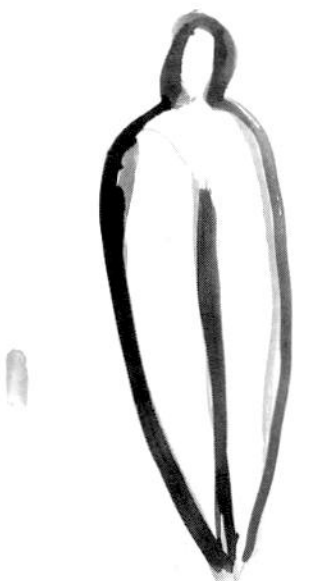

Untitled, 1983/85
Wash on paper
33 x 21.3 cm (13 x 8 ⅜ in.)

Donald Moffett
(American, born 1955)
#6 (Lot 060900), 2000
Oil on linen
50.8 x 63.5 cm (20 x 25 in.)

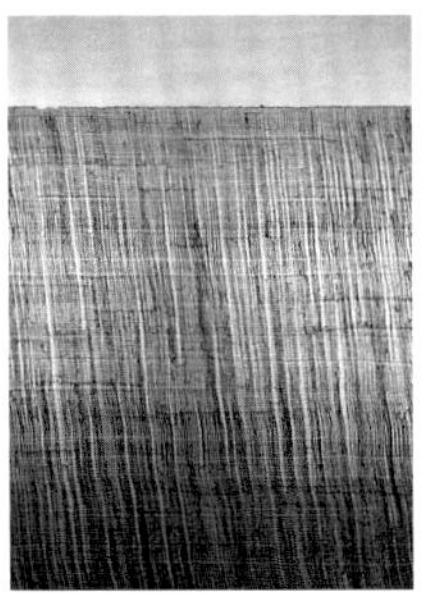

Untitled (We the People #3), 2001
Oil on linen
188 x 137.2 cm (74 x 54 in.)

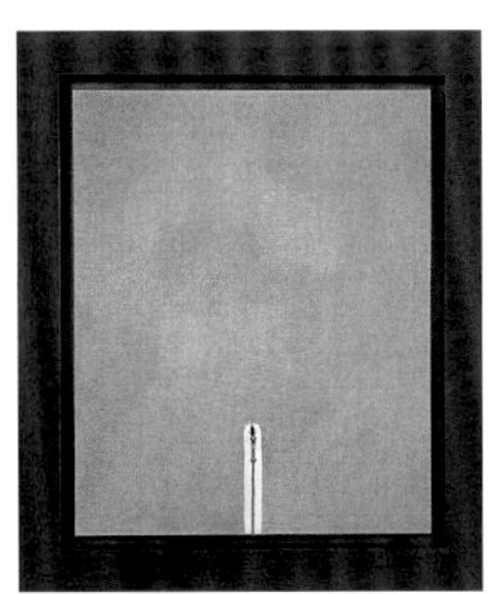

Lot 1011006, 2006
Rabbit skin glue and metal on linen and rayon with wood panel support; artist's frame
80 x 69.9 cm (31 ½ x 27 ½ in.)

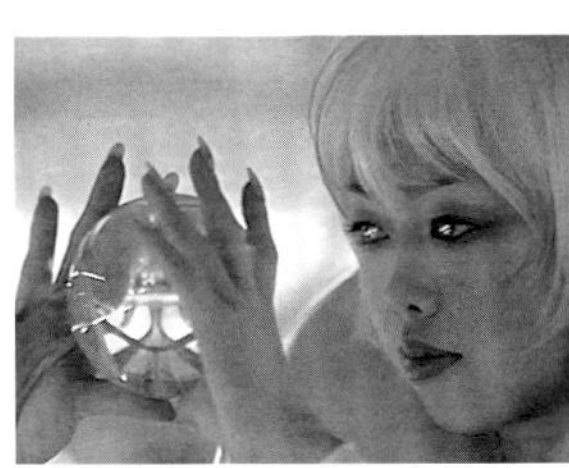

Mariko Mori
(Japanese, born 1967)
Miko No Inori, 1996
Color video with capsule and crystal (edition of 100); 29:23 min.
Gift, 2007

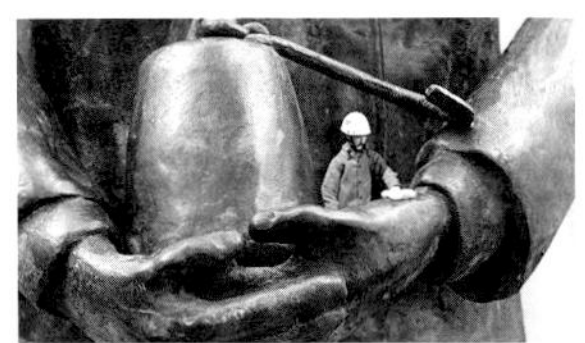

Joshua Mosley
(American, born 1974)
A Vue, 2004
High-definition digital color video, sound (projection) (edition of 5); 7:30 min. loop
Gift, 2007

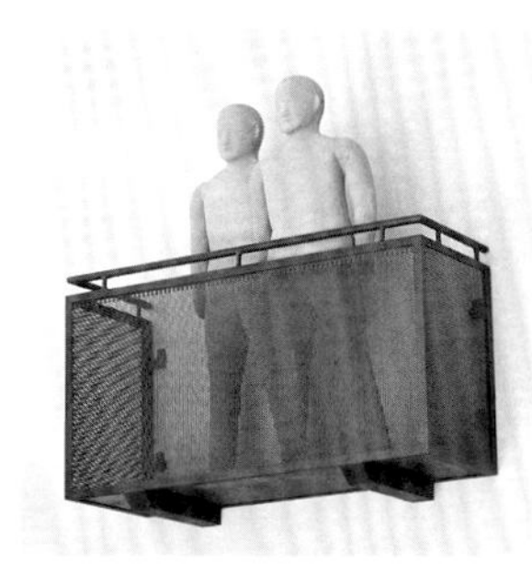

Juan Muñoz
(Spanish, 1953–2001)
Balcony, 1991
Iron and baked clay
100 x 100 x 34.3 cm
(39 ⅜ x 39 ⅜ x 13 ½ in.)

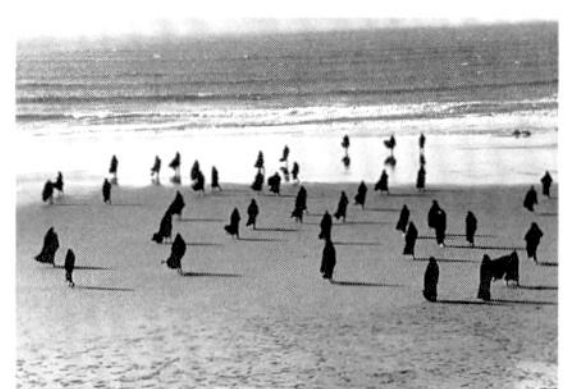

Shirin Neshat
(Iranian, born 1957)
Rapture, 1999
Two-channel black-and-white video, sound (projection) (edition of 5); 13 min. loop
Gift, 2007

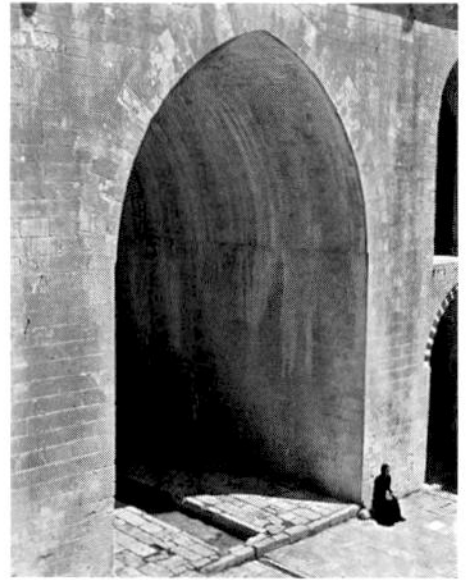

Untitled (Soliloquy Series), 2000
Chromogenic print (edition of 5)
153 x 111.8 cm (60 ¼ x 44 in.)

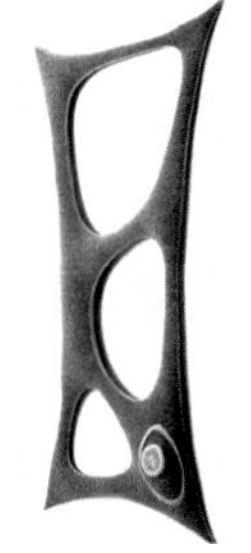

Ernesto Neto
(Brazilian, born 1964)
Small Skin with Lavender, 2001
Lycra tulle and lavender
93 x 42.1 x 4.9 cm
(36 ⅝ x 16 9/16 x 1 15/16 in.)

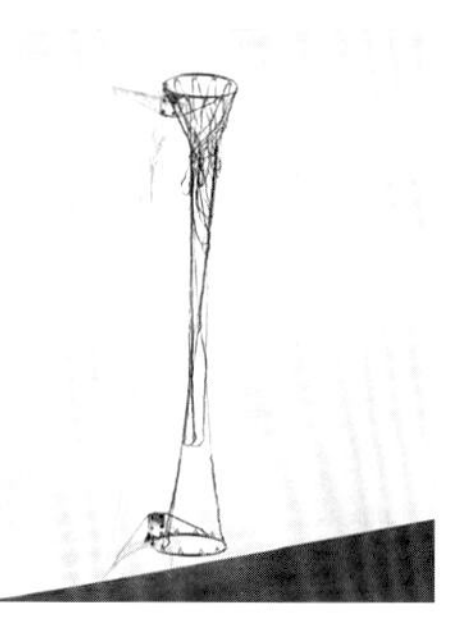

Kori Newkirk
(American, born 1970)
Suggett, 2000
Nickel-plated basketball hoops, pony beads, and synthetic hair
274.3 x 45.7 x 58.4 cm (108 x 18 x 23 in.)

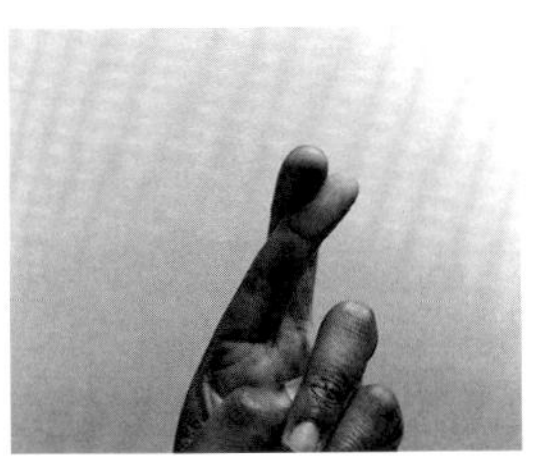

Void of Silence, 2001
Chromogenic print (edition of 5)
101.6 x 127 cm (40 x 50 in.)
Promised gift, 2009

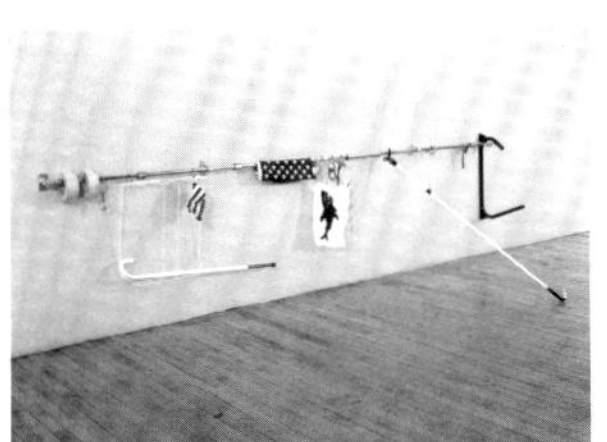

Cady Noland
(American, born 1956)
The Big Slide, 1989
Mixed media
86.4 x 375.9 x 165.1 cm (34 x 148 x 65 in.)
Promised gift, 2010
See pp. 92–93

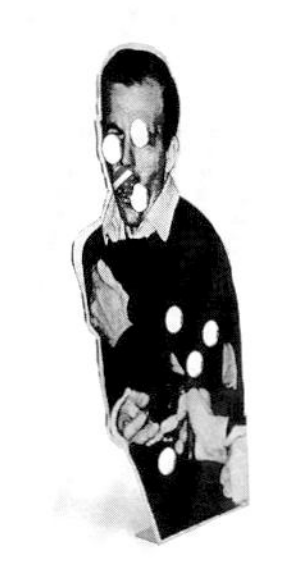

OOZEWALD, 1989
Ink and cloth on aluminum plate
(edition of 4)
182.9 x 91.4 x 17.8 cm (72 x 36 x 7 in.)
See pp. 94–95

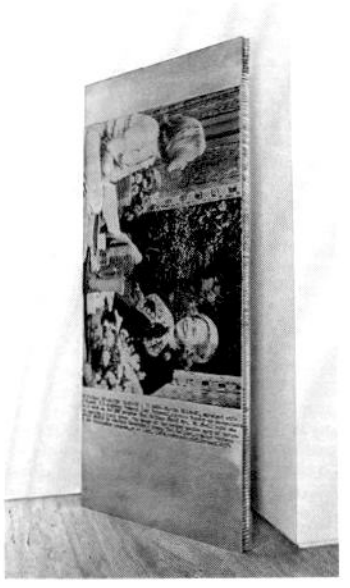

Managing Rubble, 1994
Silkscreen on aluminum
141 x 66 x 3.2 cm (55 ½ x 26 x 1 ¼ in.)

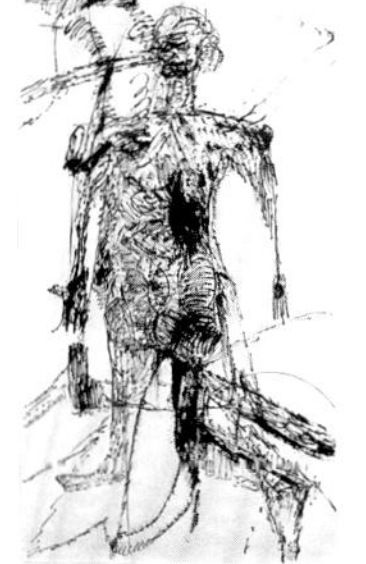

William J. O'Brien
(American, born 1975)
Temptation, 2007
Ink on paper
203.2 x 121.9 cm (80 x 48 in.)

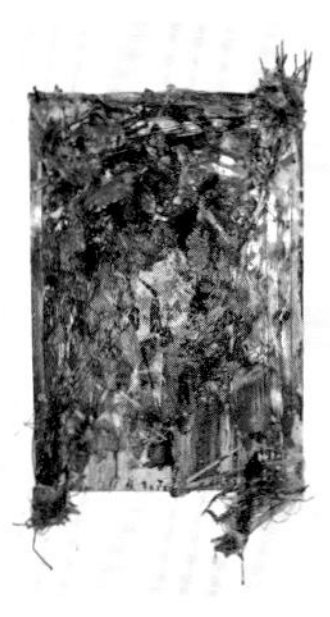

Touchdown, 2007
Mixed media on wood panel
205.7 x 109.2 x 25.4 cm (81 x 43 x 10 in.)

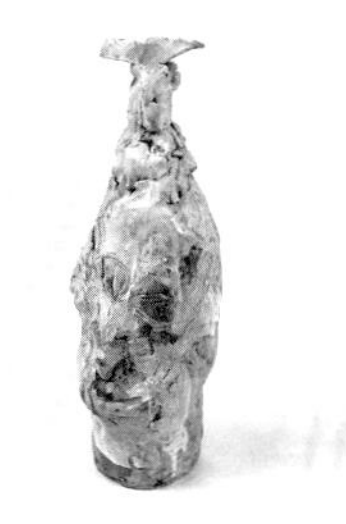

Untitled, 2008
Ceramic
15.2 x 12.7 x 38.1 cm (6 x 5 x 15 in.)

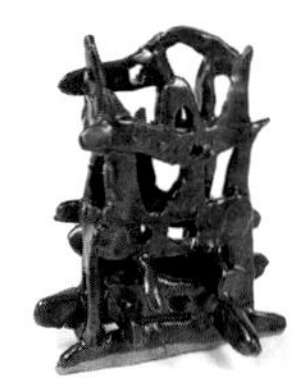

Untitled, 2008
Ceramic
22.9 x 16.5 x 30.5 cm (9 x 6 ½ x 12 in.)

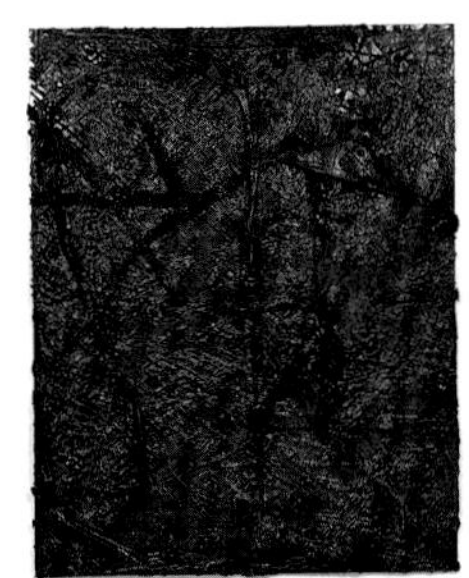

Untitled, 2008
Enamel and fabric on board and
wood support
213.4 x 165.1 cm (84 x 65 in.)

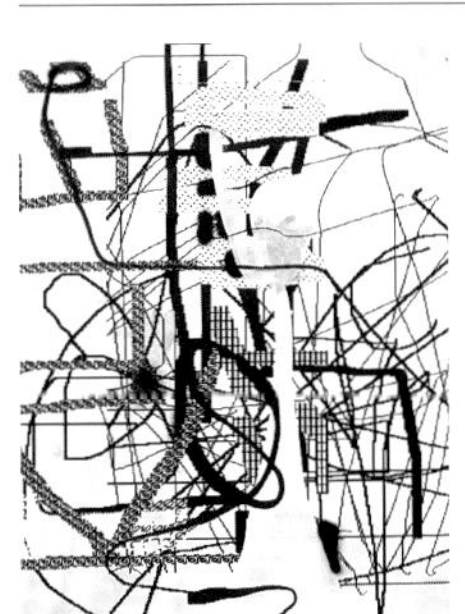

Albert Oehlen
(German, born 1954)
Untitled, 1997
Computer screen print, acrylic, and oil
on canvas
245 x 190.5 cm (96 7/16 x 75 in.)
Promised gift, 2009

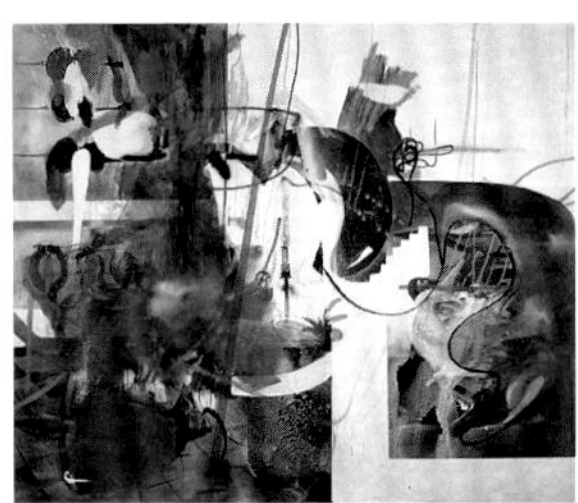

Treppe, 2006
Acrylic and oil on canvas
280 x 340 cm (110 1/4 x 133 7/8 in.)

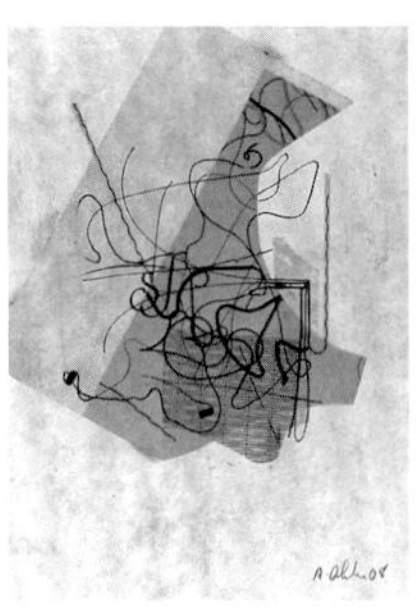

Untitled, 2008
Mixed media on paper
29.9 x 21.6 cm (11 3/4 x 8 1/2 in.)

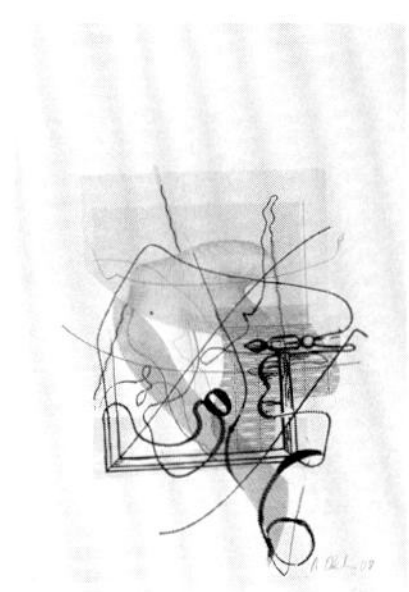

Untitled, 2008
Mixed media on paper
29.9 x 21 cm (11 3/4 x 8 1/4 in.)

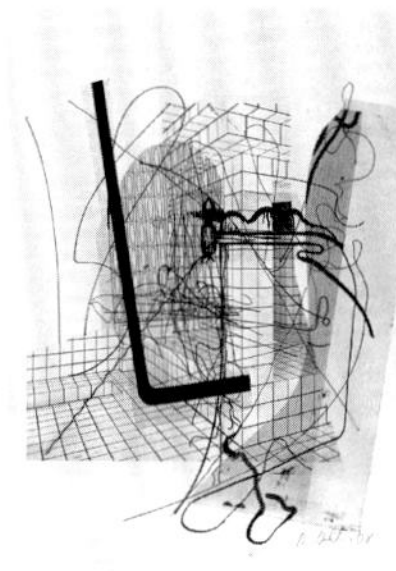

Untitled, 2008
Mixed media on paper
27.3 x 21 cm (10 3/4 x 8 1/4 in.)

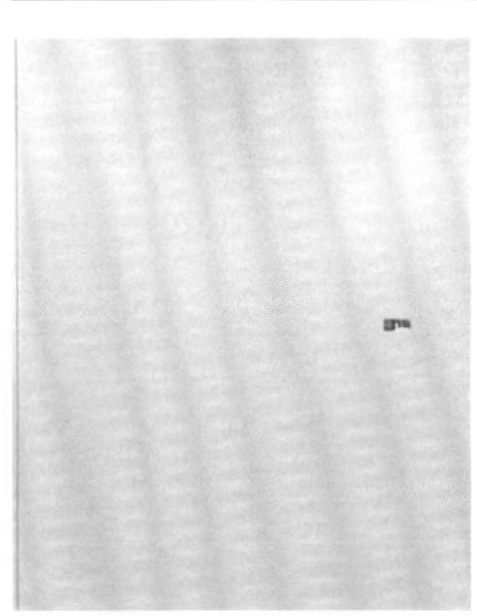

Catherine Opie
(American, born 1961)
Untitled #9 (Icehouses), 2001
Chromogenic print (edition of 5)
127 x 101.6 cm (50 x 40 in.)

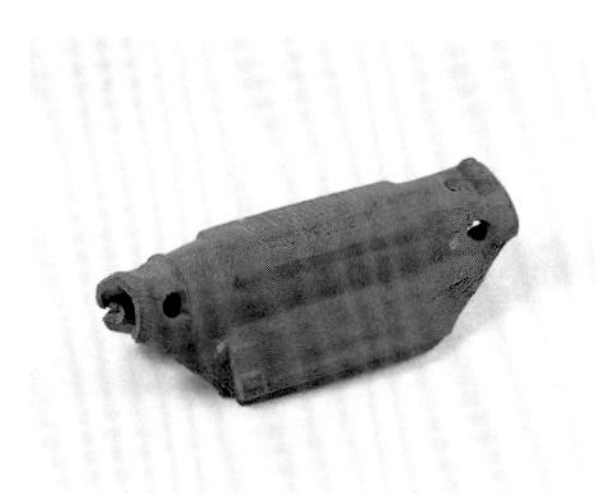

Gabriel Orozco
(Mexican, born 1962)
Made in Belgium, 1993
Terracotta (edition of 14)
12.1 x 20 x 32.1 cm (4 3/4 x 7 7/8 x 12 5/8 in.)
Promised gift, 2010
See p. 104

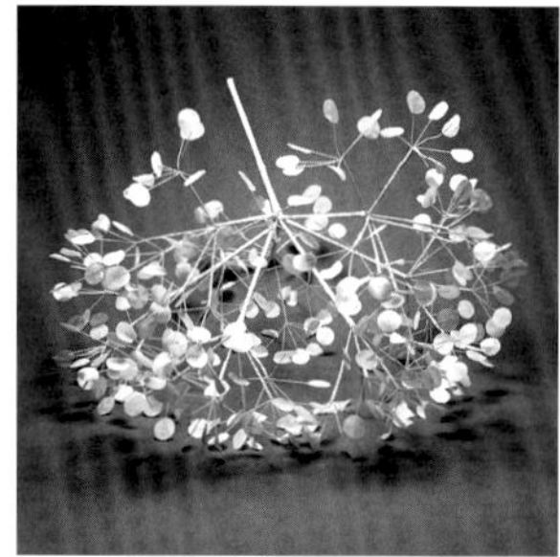

Dent de Lion, 1998
Fabric discs and metal stalks (edition of 10)
74.9 x 100 cm (29 1/2 x 39 3/8 in.)
Gift, 2010
See pp. 98–99

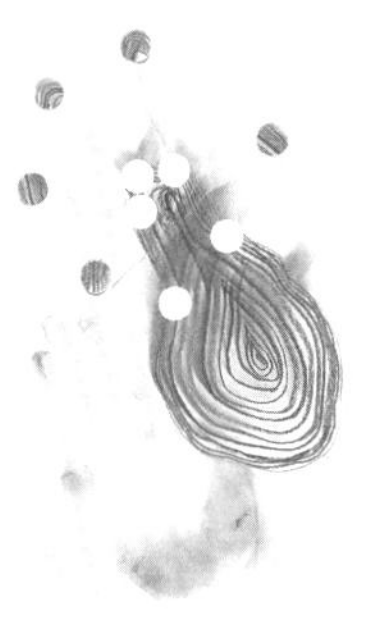

Untitled, 1998
Collage and colored pencil on paper
29.8 x 21.3 cm (11 3/4 x 8 3/8 in.)
Promised gift, 2010
See p. 96

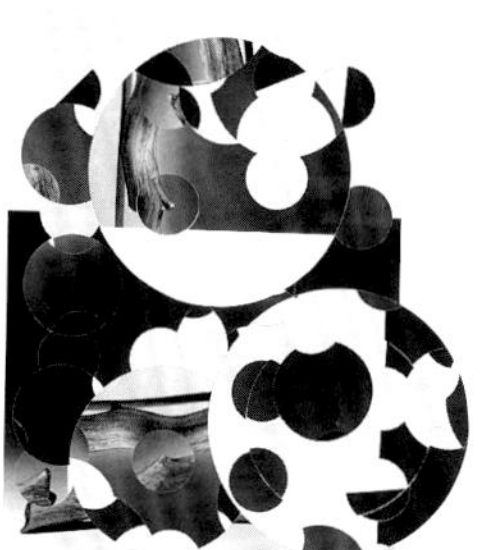

Eroded Suizekis 9, 1999
Collage
28.9 x 24.8 cm (11 3/8 x 9 3/4 in.)
Promised gift, 2010
See p. 96

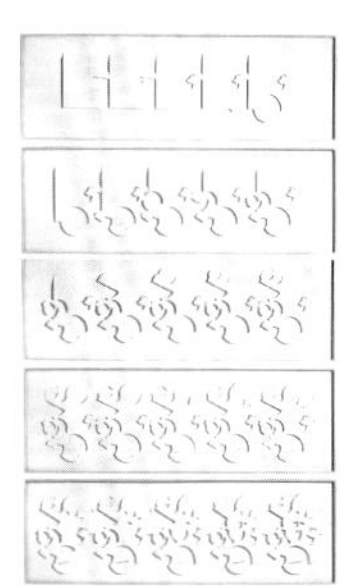

Paper Foam Waves, 1999
Paper collage (suite of five, individually framed)
56.8 x 171.1 cm (22 3/8 x 67 3/8 in.)
Promised gift, 2010
See pp. 100–01

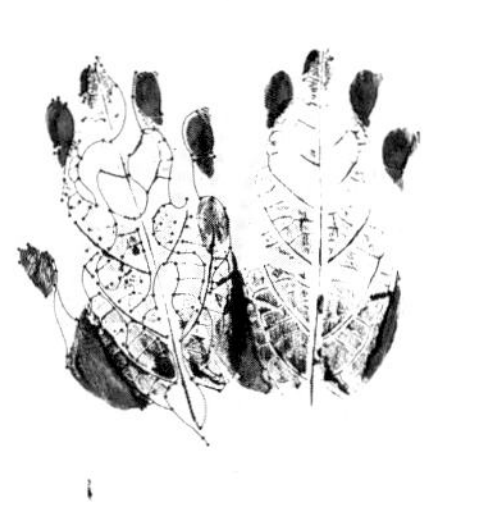

Palm, 2001
Ink on paper
27.9 x 21.6 cm (11 x 8 ½ in.)
Promised gift, 2010
See p. 97

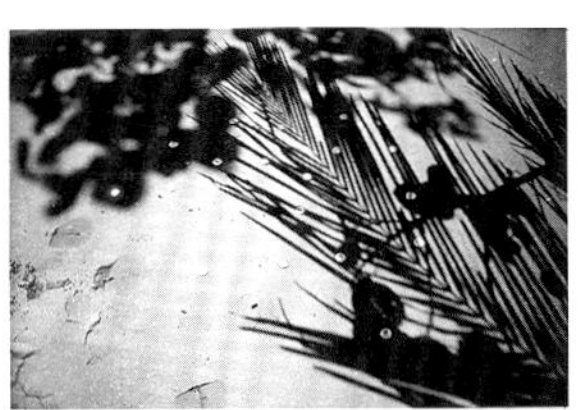

Star Caps, 2001
Cibachrome print (edition of 5)
40.6 x 50.8 cm (16 x 20 in.)
Promised gift, 2010
See p. 102

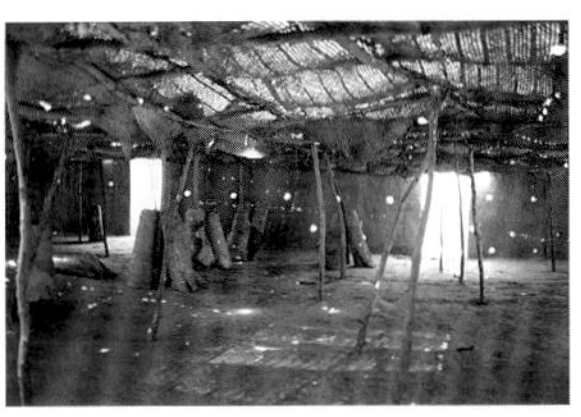

Total Perception, 2002
Chromogenic print (edition of 3)
85.7 x 118.8 cm (33 ¾ x 46 ¾ in.)
Gift, 2010
See p. 103

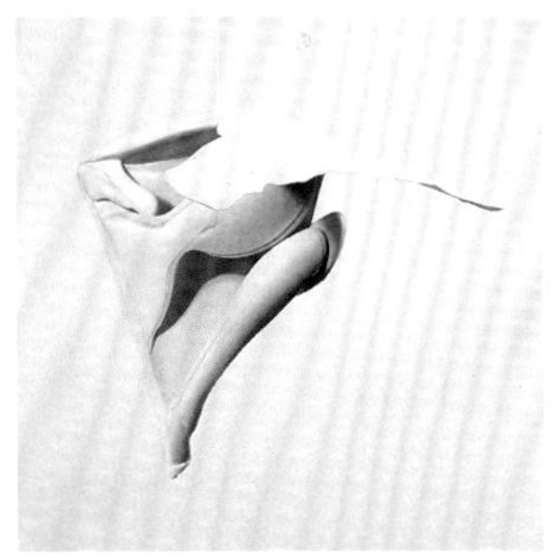

Under Tow, 2003
Polyurethane foam
94 x 132.1 x 83.8 cm (37 x 52 x 33 in.)
Gift, 2010
See p. 105

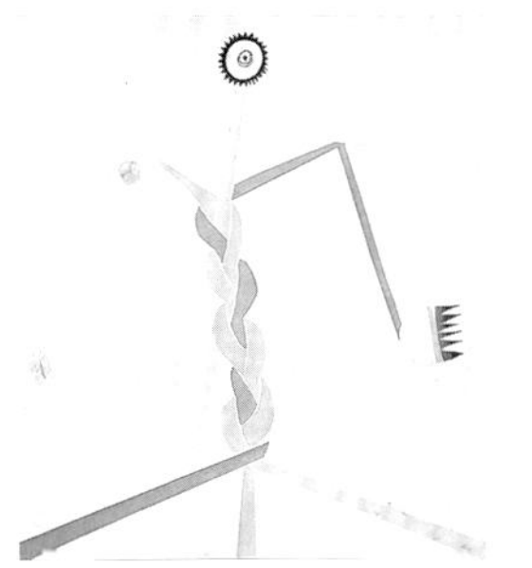

Laura Owens
(American, born 1970)
Untitled, 1998
Oil, acrylic, and pencil on canvas
213.4 x 193 cm (84 x 76 in.)

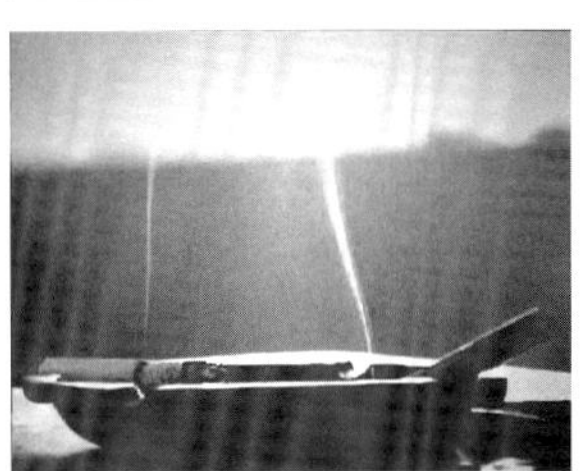

Hirsch Perlman
(American, born 1960)
Two Affect Studies, 2000–01
Two color videos, sound (projection)
(edition of 3); 15 min. loop
Gift, 2007

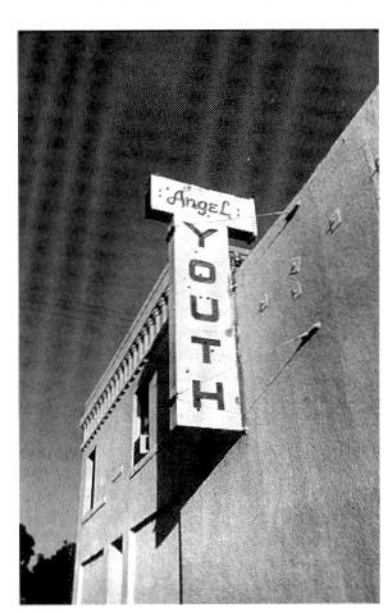

Jack Pierson
(American, born 1960)
Angel Youth, 1995
Portfolio of thirteen chromogenic
prints (edition of 25)
Each: 50.8 x 76.2 cm (20 x 30 in.)
Gift, 2002
Shown: Detail

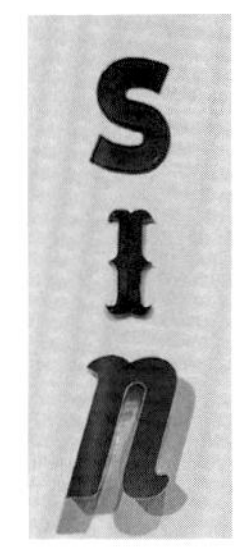

Sin, 1995
Metal and plastic
48.3 x 96.5 x 13.3 cm (19 x 38 x 5 ¼ in.)
Promised gift, 2010

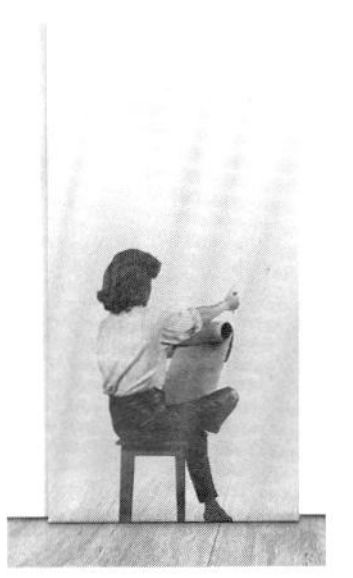

Michelangelo Pistoletto
(Italian, born 1933)
Girl Drawing, 1979
Silkscreen on stainless steel
229.9 x 124.9 cm (90 ½ x 49 3/16 in.)
Promised gift, 2010
See pp. 106–07

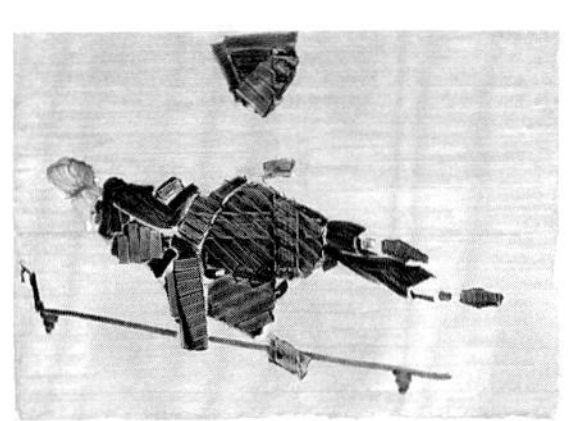

Magnus Plessen
(German, born 1967)
Lying Figure, 2003
Oil on canvas
64.8 x 94.8 cm (25 ½ x 37 ⅓ in.)
Promised gift, 2005

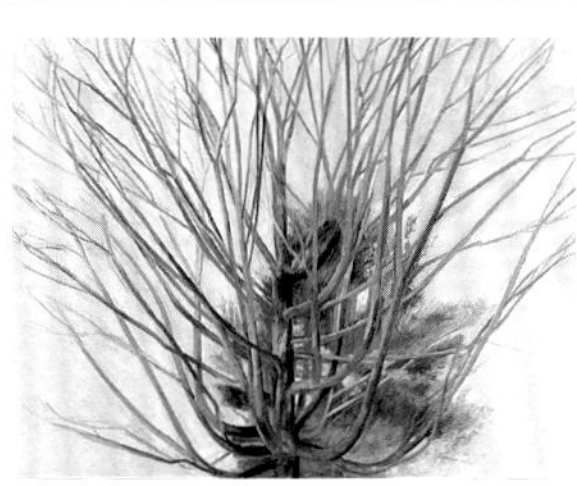

Sylvia Plimack Mangold
(American, born 1938)
The Maple Tree with Pine, 2005
Oil on linen
76.2 x 101.6 cm (30 x 40 in.)
Promised gift, 2010
See pp. 108–09

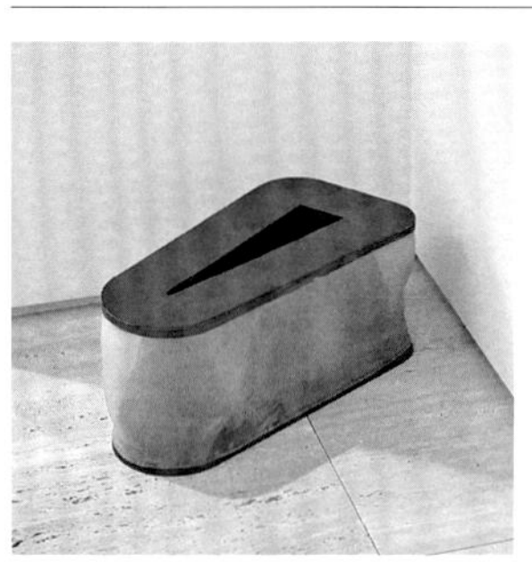

Richard Rezac
(American, born 1952)
Elevation (after Ninsei), 1989
Cast bronze and dyed silk
18.4 x 40.6 x 20.3 cm (7 1/4 x 16 x 8 in.)

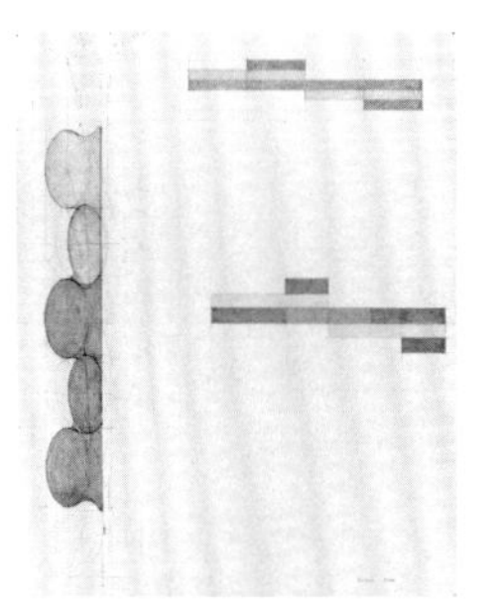

Study for "Untitled (08-04)," 2008
Colored pencil and pencil on paper
55.9 x 43.2 cm (22 x 17 in.)

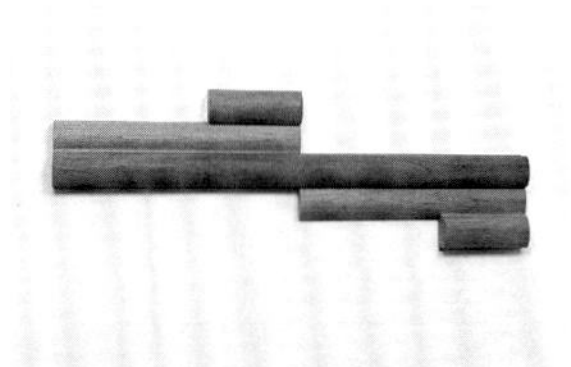

Untitled (08-04), 2008
Cherry
52.1 x 152.4 x 7.6 cm (20 1/2 x 60 x 3 in.)

Gerhard Richter
(German, born 1932)
Gray, 1973
Oil on canvas
250.2 x 200 cm (98 1/2 x 78 3/4 in.)
Promised gift, 2010
See pp. 110–11

Abstract Picture, 2000
Oil on canvas
175 x 250 cm (68 7/8 x 98 7/16 in.)
See pp. 112–13

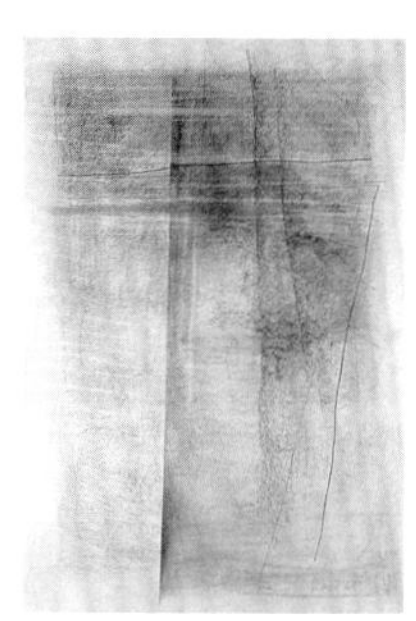

Drawing 1, from *Set of Four Drawings*, 2005
Graphite and charcoal on paper
151.1 x 102.6 cm (59 1/2 x 40 3/8 in.)
Promised gift, 2009

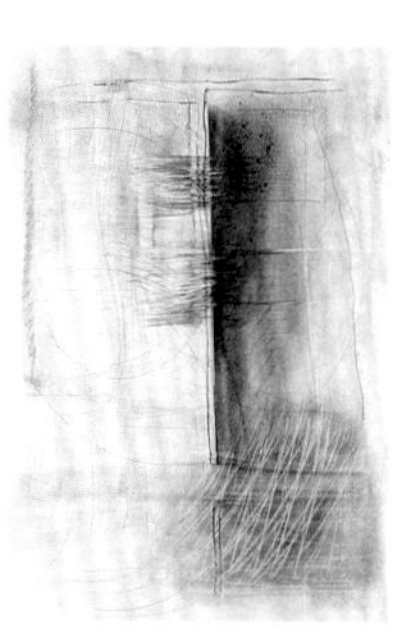

Drawing 2, from *Set of Four Drawings*, 2005
Graphite and charcoal on paper
151.1 x 102.6 cm (59 1/2 x 40 3/8 in.)
Promised gift, 2009

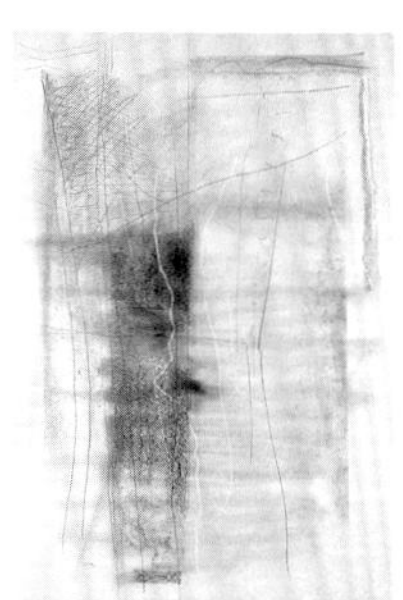

Drawing 3, from *Set of Four Drawings*, 2005
Graphite and charcoal on paper
151.1 x 102.6 cm (59 1/2 x 40 3/8 in.)
Promised gift, 2009

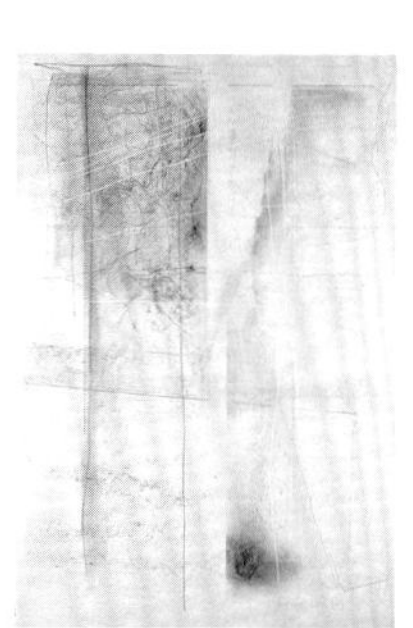

Drawing 4, from *Set of Four Drawings*, 2005
Graphite and charcoal on paper
151.1 x 102.6 cm (59 1/2 x 40 3/8 in.)
Promised gift, 2009

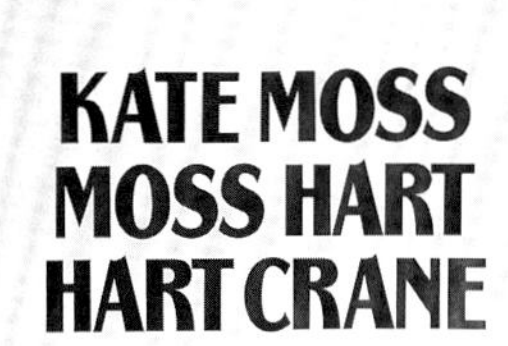

Kay Rosen
(American, born 1949)
A Rolling Stone, 1999
Graphite on paper
41.3 x 58.4 cm (16 ¼ x 23 in.)

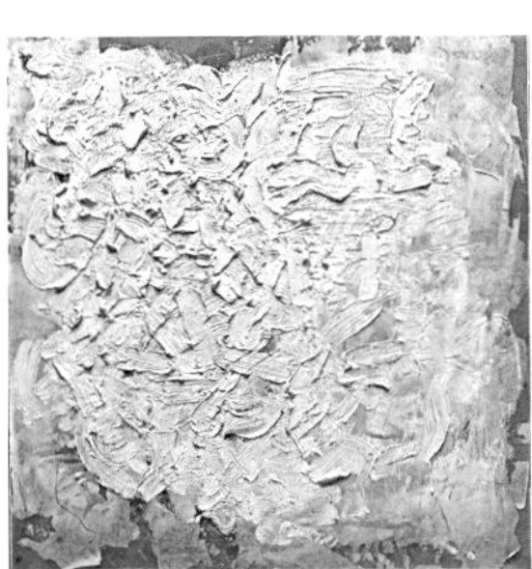

Robert Ryman
(American, born 1930)
Untitled, 1961
Oil on paper mounted on Masonite
30.8 x 30.8 cm (12 ⅛ x 12 ⅛ in.)
See pp. 114–15

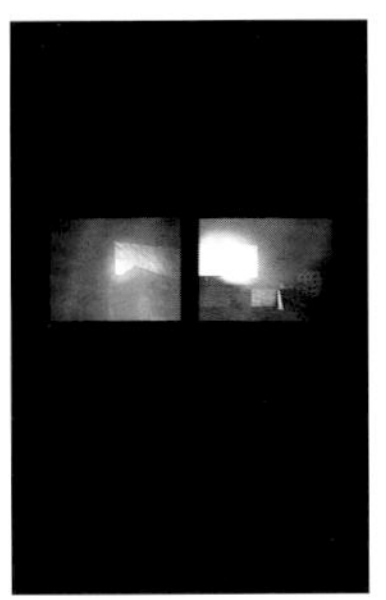

Anri Sala
(Albanian, born 1974)
Blindfold, 2002
Two-channel digital color video, six-channel digital sound (rear projection on two Plexiglas screens); 15 min. loop
Gift, 2007

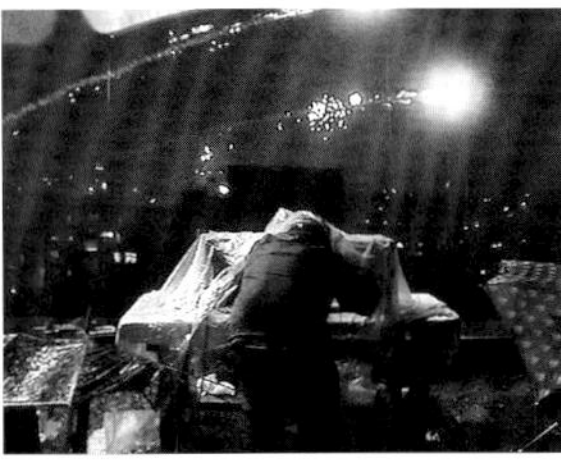

Mixed Behavior, 2003
Digital color, sound (projection); 8:17 min. loop
Purchased with the Donna and Howard Stone New Media Fund, 2005

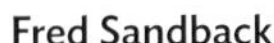

Fred Sandback
(American, 1943–2003)
Untitled, 1967, 1967
Gray-painted elastic cord
Dimensions variable
Promised gift, 2010
See pp. 116–17

Helium, from *Eight-Part Sculpture for the Dwan Gallery (Conceptual Construction)*, 1969
Typed text on paper
27.9 x 21.6 cm (11 x 8 ½ in.)

Xenon, from *Eight-Part Sculpture for the Dwan Gallery (Conceptual Construction)*, 1969
Typed text on paper
27.9 x 21.6 cm (11 x 8 ½ in.)

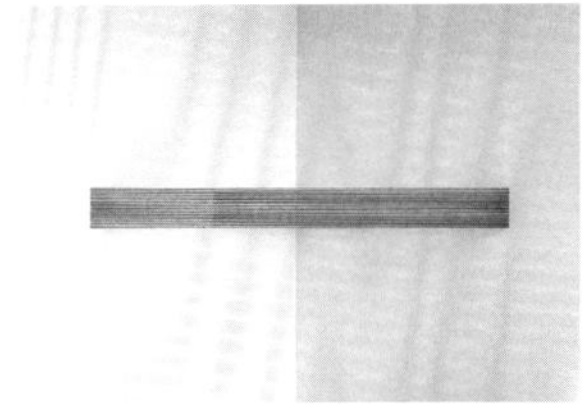

Untitled (Sculptural Study, Corner Construction), 1972/2008
Yellow and green acrylic yarn
Dimensions variable

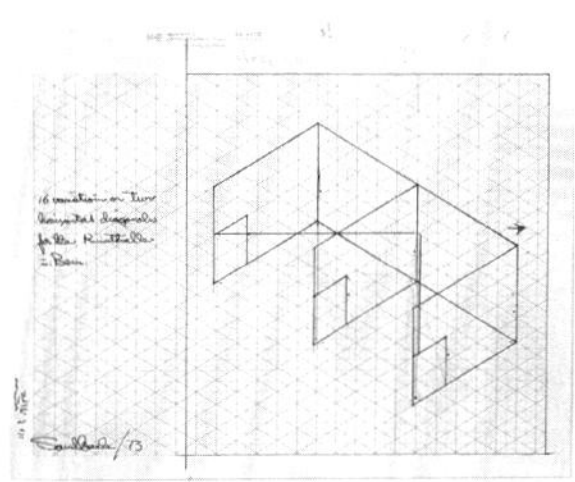

Untitled, 1973
Felt pen and pencil on graph paper
21.6 x 27.9 cm (8 ½ x 11 in.)

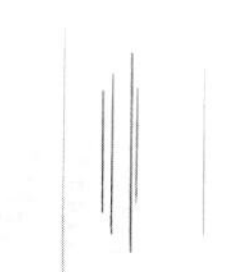

Untitled, 1987
Colored pencil on paper
43.2 x 55.9 cm (17 x 22 in.)

Untitled, Cut Drawing, 1994
Scored illustration board
40.6 x 50.8 cm (16 x 20 in.)

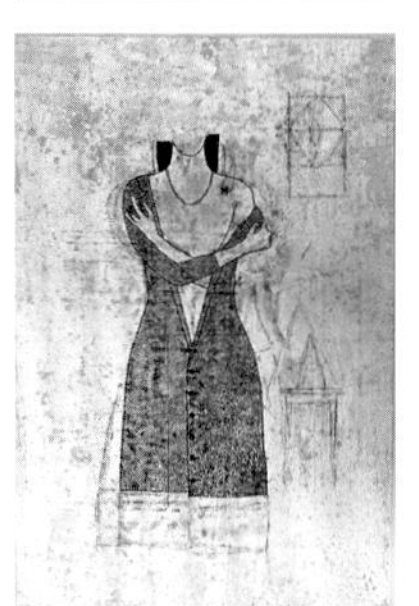

Julião Sarmento
(Portuguese, born 1948)
The Cone Concealed a Blade, 1991
Mixed media on canvas
190.5 x 129.5 cm (75 x 51 in.)

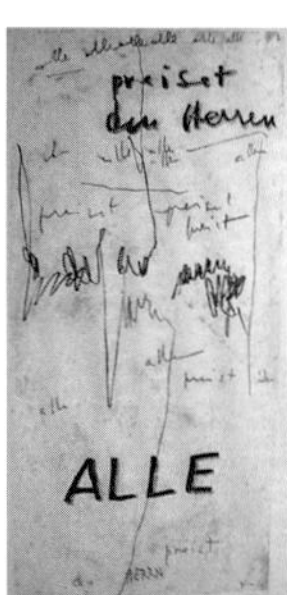

Mira Schendel
(Brazilian, born Switzerland, 1919–1988)
Untitled, 1964
Oil on rice paper
47 x 23 cm (18 ½ x 9 1/16 in.)

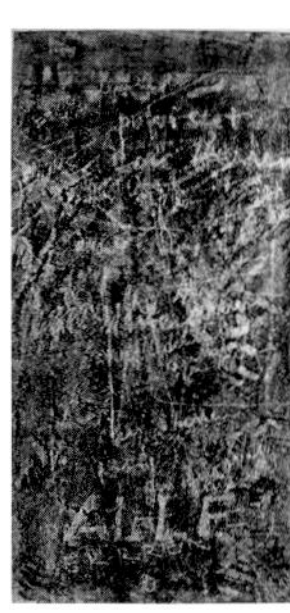

Untitled, 1965
Oil on rice paper
47 x 23 cm (18 ½ x 9 1/16 in.)

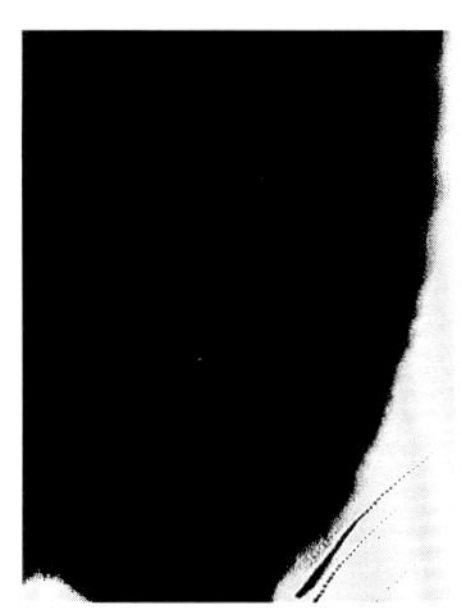

Scott Short
(American, born 1964)
Untitled (white), 2006
Oil on canvas
259.1 x 198.1 cm (102 x 78 in.)

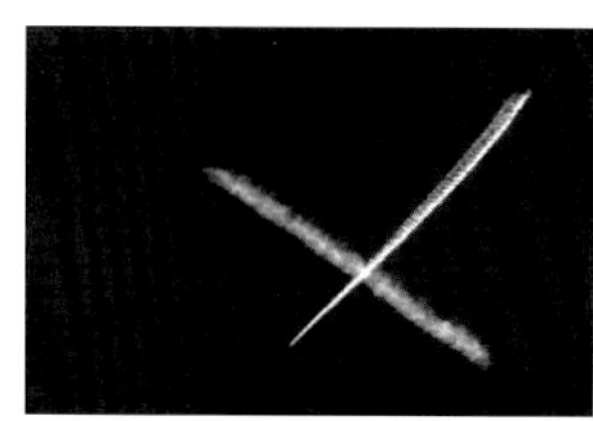

Gary Simmons
(American, born 1964)
Desert Blizzard, 1997
Digital color video (edition of 10); 8 min.

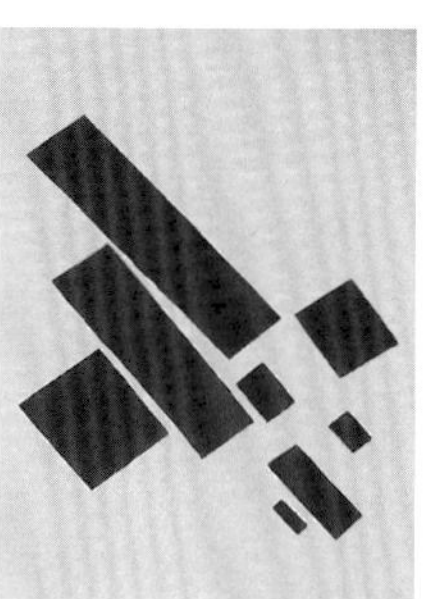

Buzz Spector
(American, born 1948)
Eight Red Rectangles, 1992
Enamel on aluminum inlay
33 x 35.6 cm (13 x 14 in.)

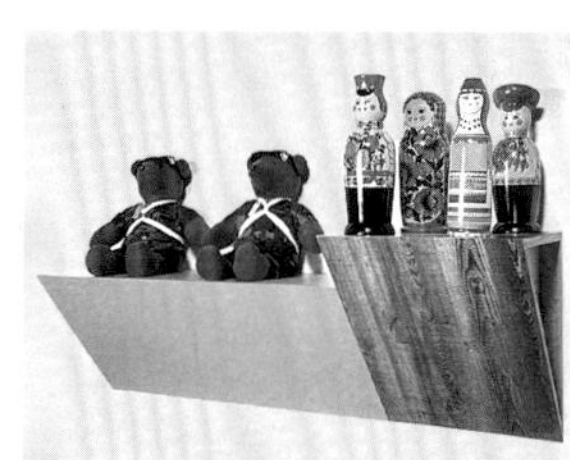

Haim Steinbach
(American, born Israel 1944)
say you, say me, 1986
Wood, formica, Parabears, Kuzbek liquor bottle dolls
86.4 x 139.7 x 41.9 cm (34 x 55 x 16 ½ in.)
Promised gift, 2010

Rudolf Stingel
(Italian, born 1956)
Untitled, 1996
Oil and enamel on canvas
106.7 x 96.5 cm (42 x 38 in.)

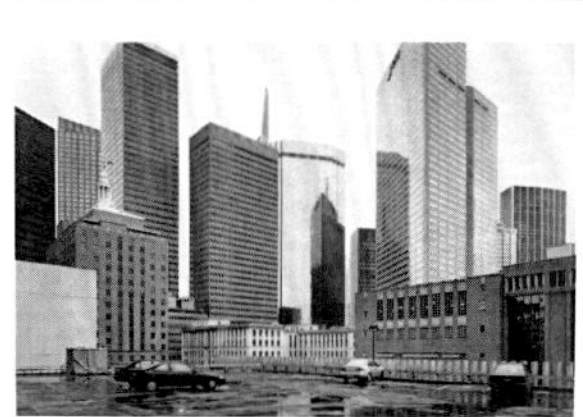

Thomas Struth
(German, born 1954)
Dallas Parking Lot, Dallas, 2001
Chromogenic print (edition of 10)
181.6 x 252.7 cm (71 ½ x 99 ½ in.)
Promised gift, 2010
See pp. 118–19

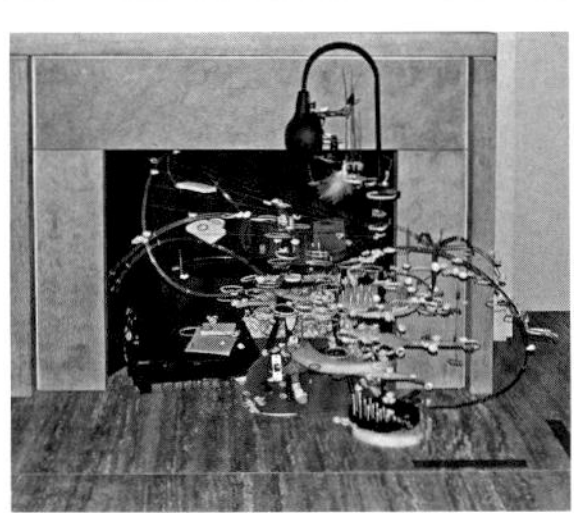

Sarah Sze
(American, born 1969)
Field and Frame, 2001
Mixed media
Dimensions variable

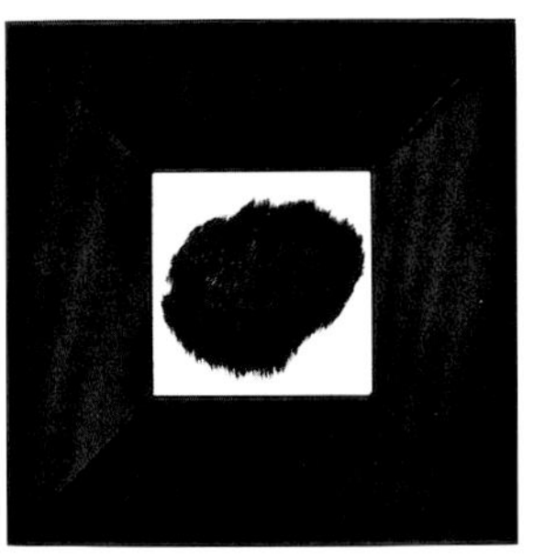

Tony Tasset
(American, born 1960)
Domestic Abstraction, 1986
Fur, framed
35.6 x 35.6 x 5.1 cm (14 x 14 x 2 in.)

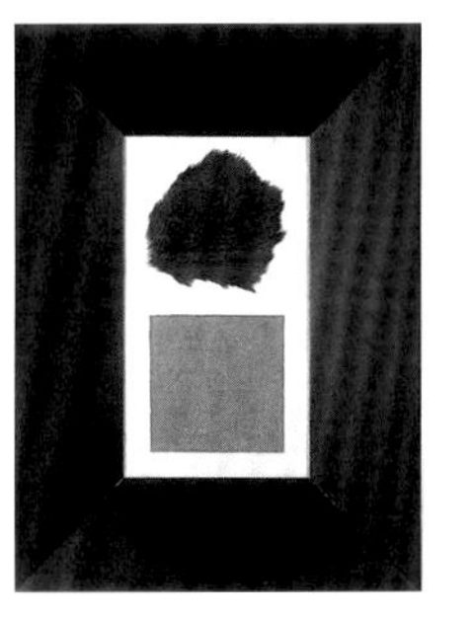

Domestic Abstraction, 1986
Fur, framed
35.6 x 53.3 x 5.1 cm (14 x 21 x 2 in.)

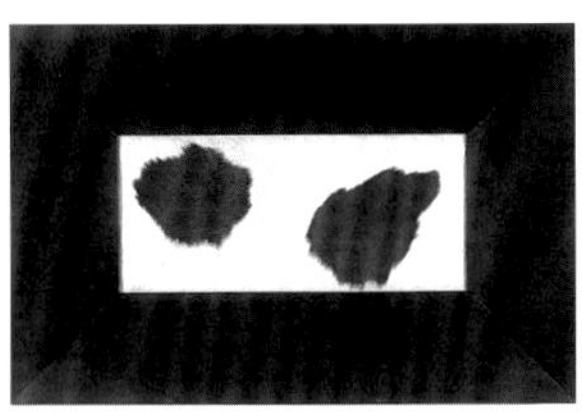

Domestic Abstraction, 1986
Fur, framed
50.8 x 83.8 x 5.1 cm (20 x 33 x 2 in.)

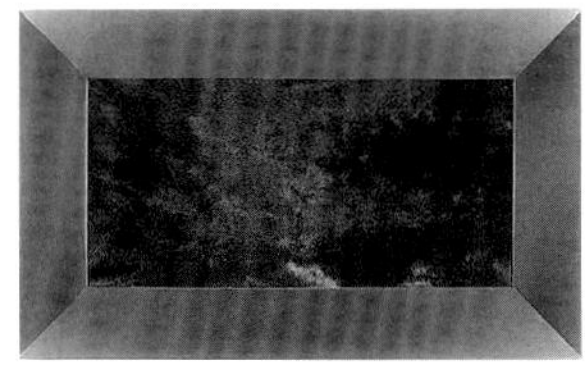

Domestic Abstraction, 1986
Fur and leather, framed
52.1 x 38.1 x 5.1 cm (20 ½ x 15 x 2 in.)

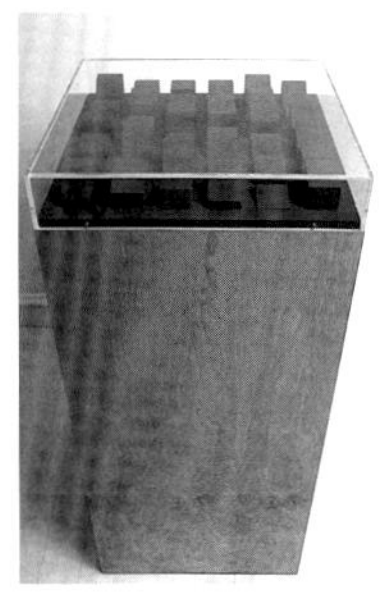

Display Sculpture with Thirty-Six Variations, 1991–93
Mixed media (green felt)
106.7 x 45.7 x 45.7 cm (42 x 18 x 18 in.)

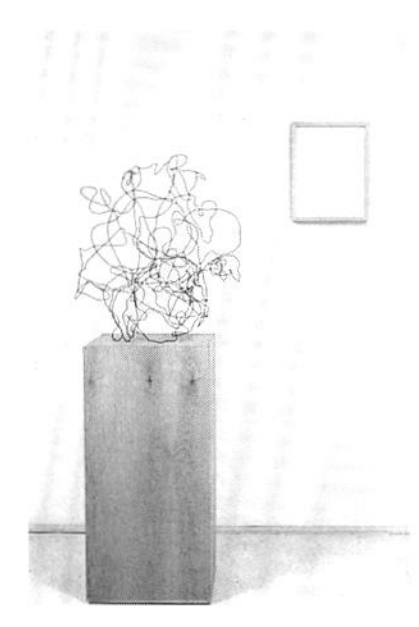

Wire Sculpture and *Untitled (Drawing for Wire Sculpture*, 1991–93
Steel, wood frame, and pencil on paper
Sculpture: 160 x 61 x 53.3 cm
(63 x 24 x 21 in.)
Drawing: 40 x 32.4 cm (15 ¾ x 12 ¾ in.)

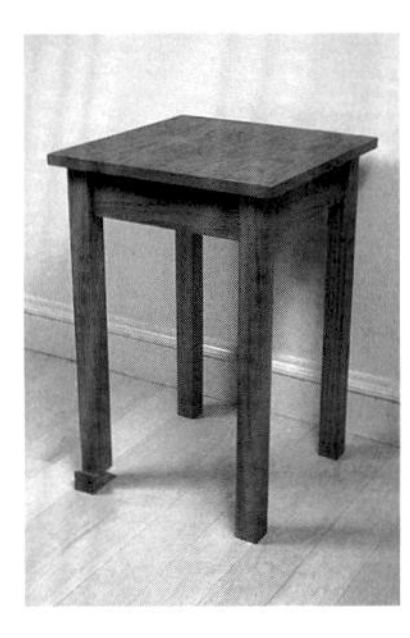

Table (Wedged), 1992
Oak (edition of 10)
66 x 45.7 x 45.7 cm (26 x 18 x 18 in.)

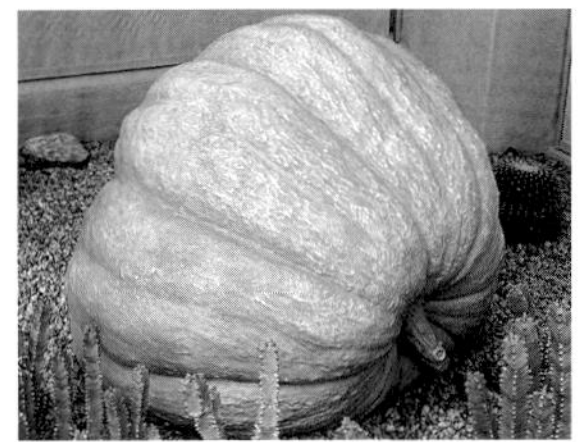

Pumpkin, 1998
Painted bronze (edition of 2)
88.9 x 99.1 x 99.1 cm (35 x 39 x 39 in.)
Promised gift, 2010
See pp. 120–21

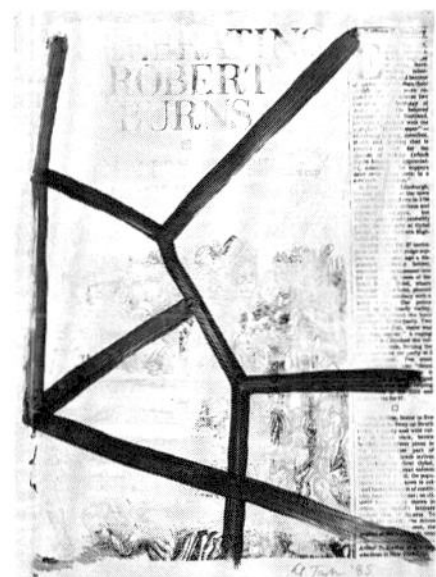

Al Taylor
(American, 1948–1999)
No Title, 1985
Acrylic paint on newsprint
31.8 x 24.6 cm (12 ½ x 9 ⅞ in.)

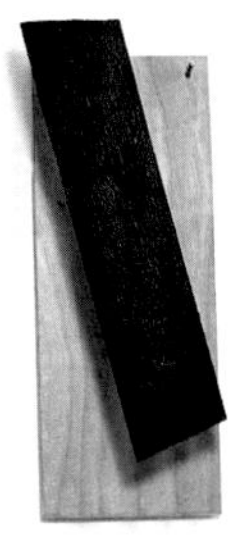

Untitled (Russian Tattoo), 1986
Wood, acrylic, and enamel paint, mounted on plywood
24.8 x 9.5 x 8.3 cm (9 ¾ x 3 ¾ x 3 ¼ in.)

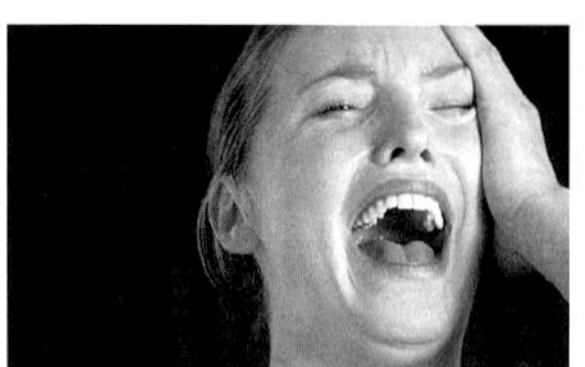

Sam Taylor-Wood
(English, born 1967)
Hysteria, 1997
16mm color film transferred to digital video (projection) (edition of 3); 8 min. loop
Gift, 2007

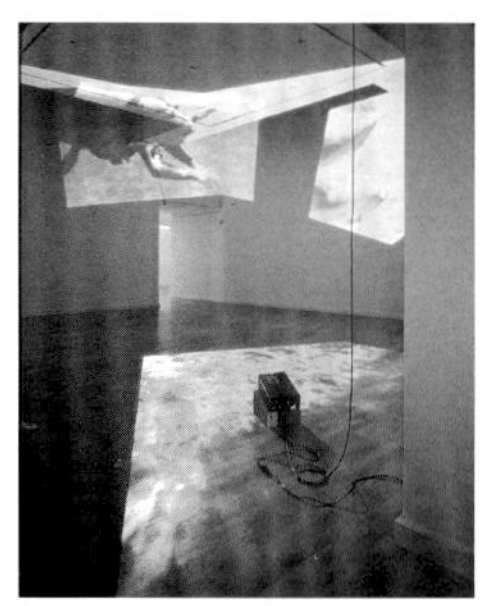

Diana Thater
(American, born 1962)
Delphine, 1999
Five-channel digital color video, sound (projection) with nine-monitor cube, light filters, and existing architecture (edition of 3); continuous loop
Purchased with the Donna and Howard Stone New Media Fund, 2005

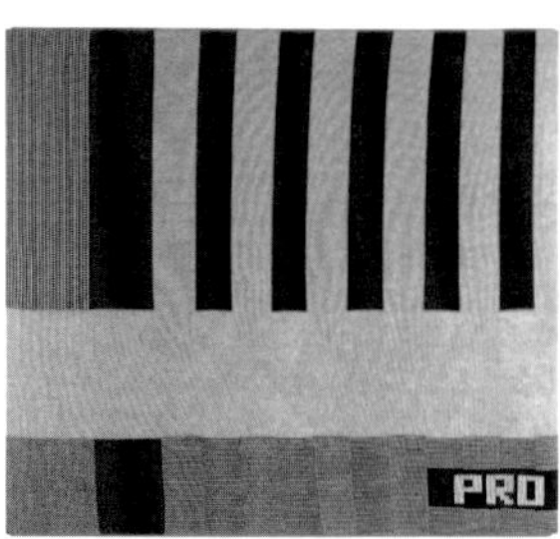

Rosemarie Trockel
(German, born 1952)
Untitled, 1986
Wool (edition of 3)
145 x 165 cm (57 ⅛ x 65 in.)
Promised gift, 2010
See pp. 122–23

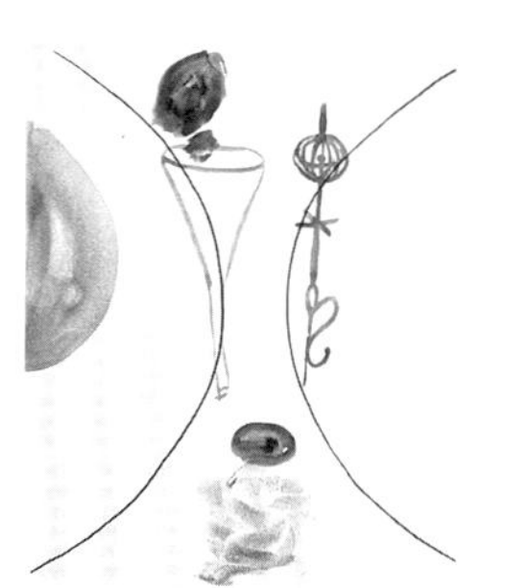

Untitled, 1987
Pencil on paper
25.4 x 20.3 cm (10 x 8 in.)

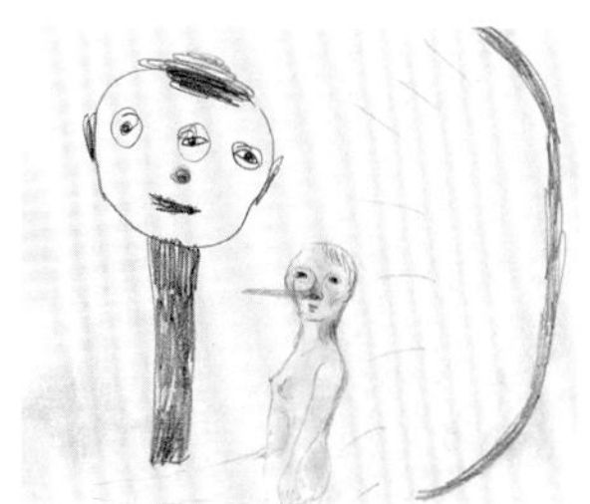

Untitled, 1987
Watercolor on paper
20.3 x 25.4 cm (8 x 10 in.)

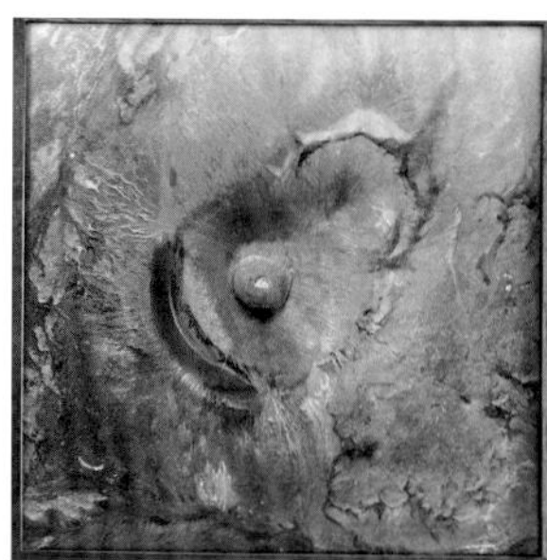

James Turrell
(American, born 1943)
1st Aerial Survey Photo with 10 Camera, 1983
Gelatin silver print in custom cherry frame
116.8 x 116.8 cm (46 x 46 in.)

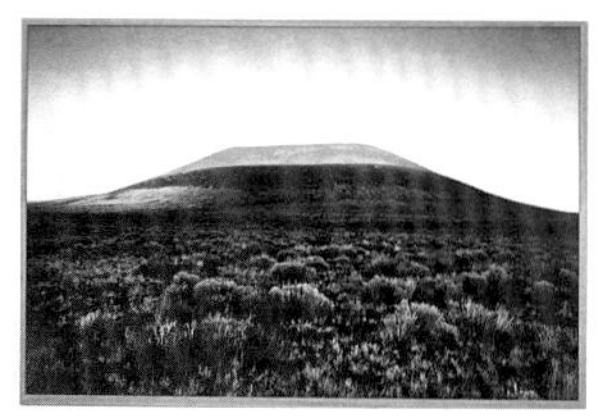

Roden Crater, 1986
Type-R photograph in cherry frame
124.5 x 186.7 cm (49 x 73 ½ in.)

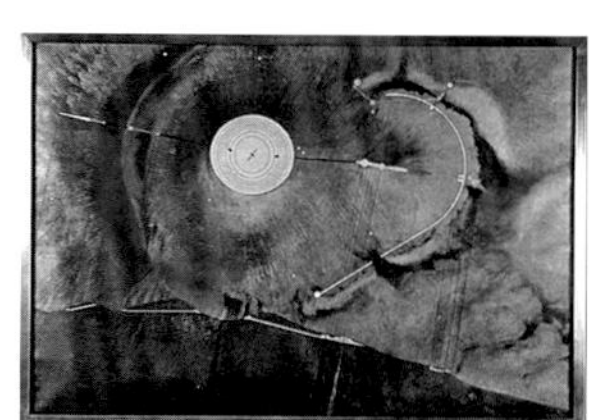

Site Plan with Projected Section and Survey Net, 1992
Beeswax, emulsion, ink, Liquitex, and wax pastel on Mylar in steel frame
101.6 x 152.4 cm (40 x 60 in.)

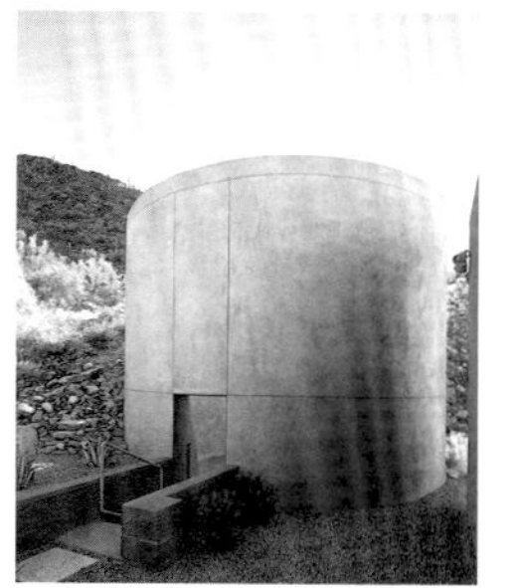

Stone Circle, 2001
Concrete and stone
487.7 x 670.6 cm (92 x 264 in.)

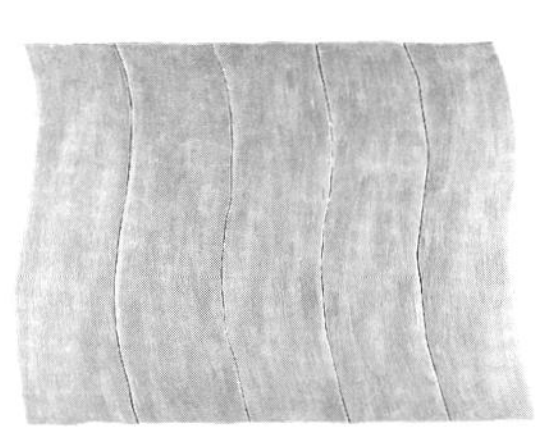

Richard Tuttle
(American, born 1941)
Twin River, 1965
Acrylic on wood
58.4 x 83.8 cm (23 x 33 in.)
Promised gift, 2010
See pp. 124–25

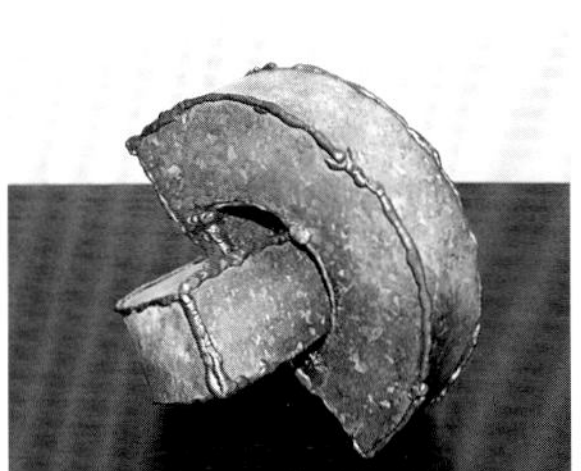

Untitled ("D"), 1966
Galvanized metal and solder
12.1 x 12.1 x 13.9 cm (4 3/4 x 4 3/4 x 5 1/2 in.)

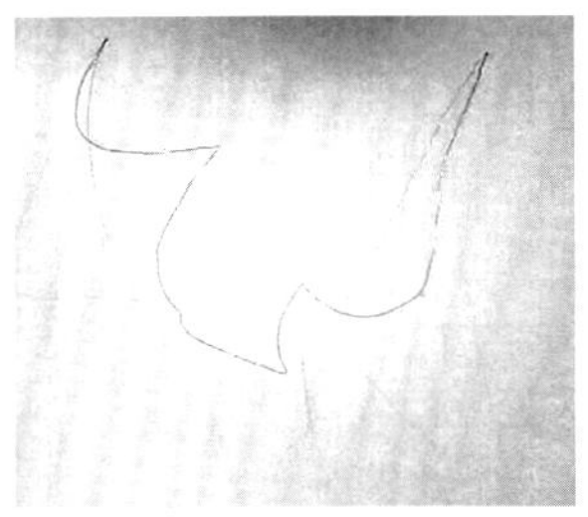

15th Wire Piece, 1972
Wire, nails, and graphite
Dimensions variable
Promised gift, 2010

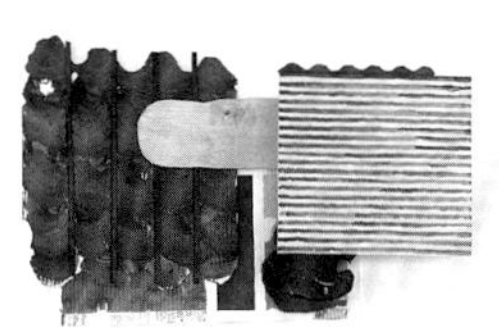

Yellow Backdrop, 1986
Plastic, paint, and foamcore
33.5 x 52 x 7.9 cm
(13 3/16 x 20 1/2 x 3 1/8 in.)
Promised gift, 2010

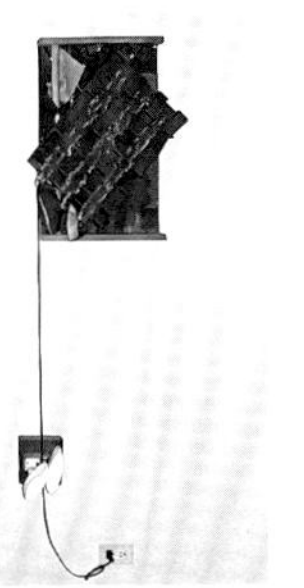

The Last Light Work, 1991
Wood, cardboard, lightbulbs, light fixtures, vinyl, and acrylic
139.7 x 50.8 x 17.8 cm (55 x 20 x 7 in.)
Promised gift, 2010

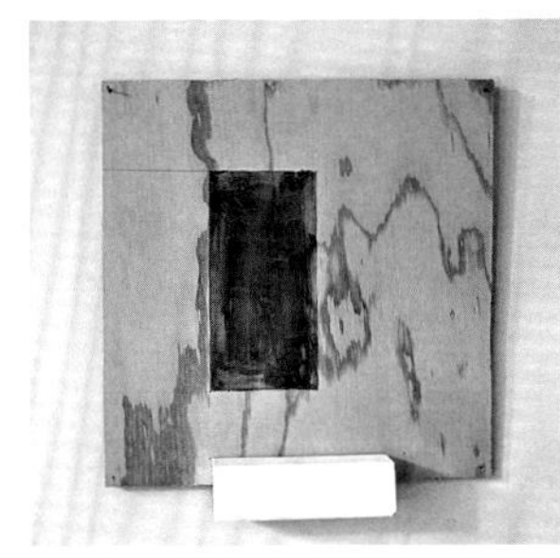

Two with Any Two, #14, 1999
Acrylic on fir plywood
29.5 x 27.9 x 4.4 cm (11 5/8 x 11 x 1 3/4 in.)
Promised gift, 2010

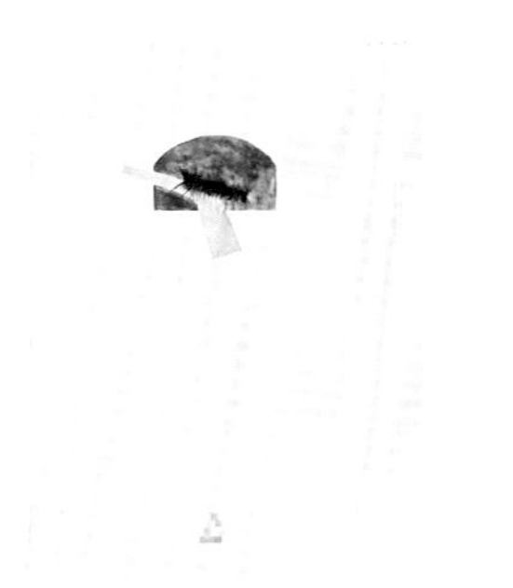

Up, to 7, 2000
Set of eight aquatint etchings
(edition of 20)
48.3 x 45.7 cm (19 x 18 in.)
Shown: (1)

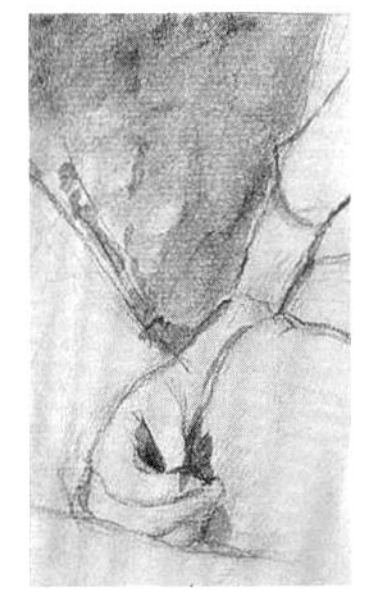

Luc Tuymans
(Belgian, born 1958)
Untitled, 1976
Watercolor on paper
14 x 8 cm (5 1/2 x 3 1/8 in.)

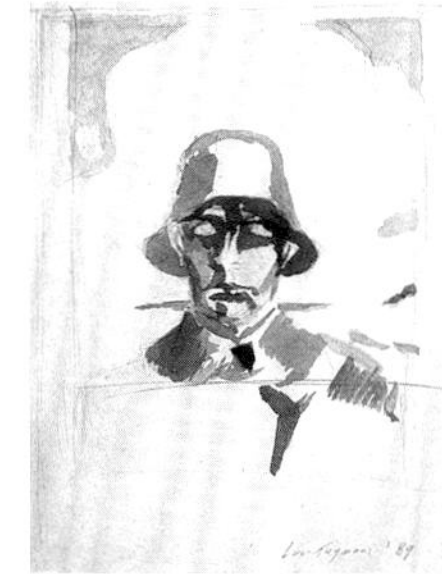

Untitled, 1989
Watercolor on paper
27.5 x 21 cm (10 13/16 x 8 1/4 in.)

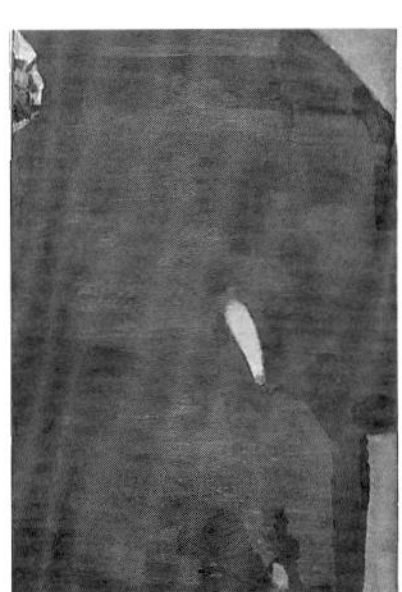

Shadow, 1994
Oil on canvas
57.8 x 39.5 cm (22 7/8 x 15 5/8 in.)
See pp. 126–27

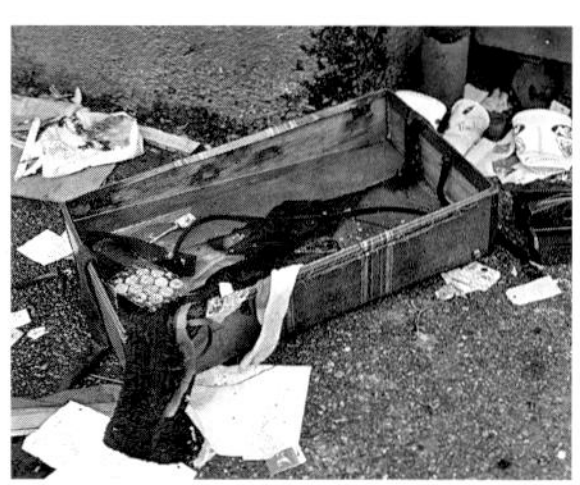

Jeff Wall
(Canadian, born 1946)
Rainfilled Suitcase, 2001
Silver dye-bleach transparency and aluminum light box
64.5 x 80 cm (25 3/8 x 31 1/2 in.)
Promised gift, 2010
See pp. 128–29

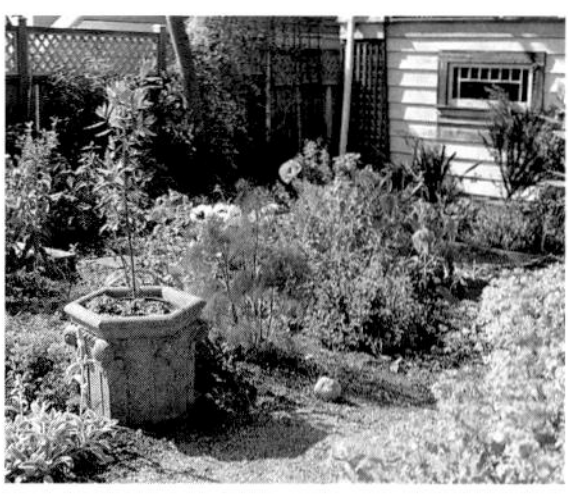

Poppies in a Garden, 2005
Silver dye-bleach transparency and aluminum light box
95 x 118 cm (37 3/8 x 46 1/2 in.)

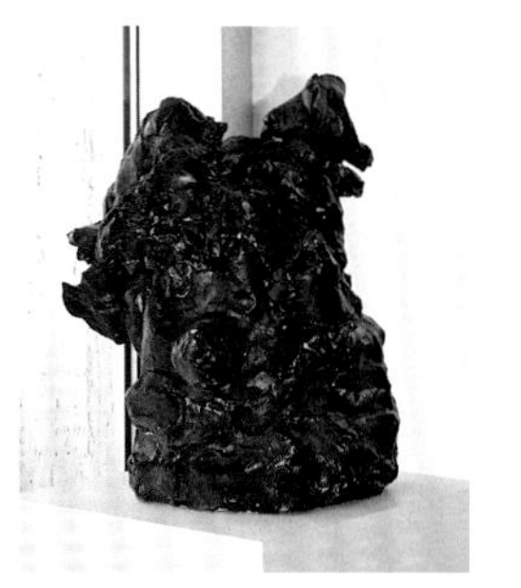

Rebecca Warren
(English, born 1965)
Invention of the Daguerreotype, 2005
Reinforced painted clay and plinth
43.2 x 33 x 43.2 cm (17 x 13 x 17 in.)

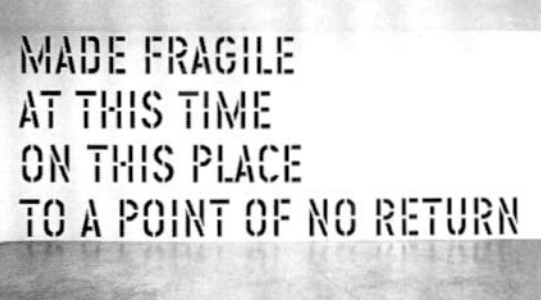

Lawrence Weiner
(American, born 1942)
MADE FRAGILE AT THIS TIME ON THIS PLACE TO A POINT OF NO RETURN, 2000
Installation at Regen Projects, 2002
Language and materials referred to
Dimensions variable
Promised gift, 2010
See pp. 130–31

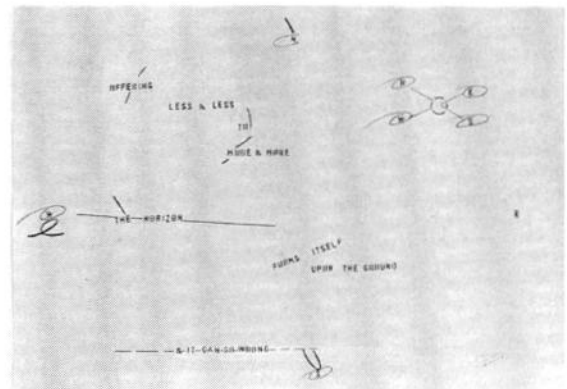

The horizon forms itself upon the ground, 2003
Pen, ink, and collage on paper
61 x 91.4 cm (24 x 36 in.)

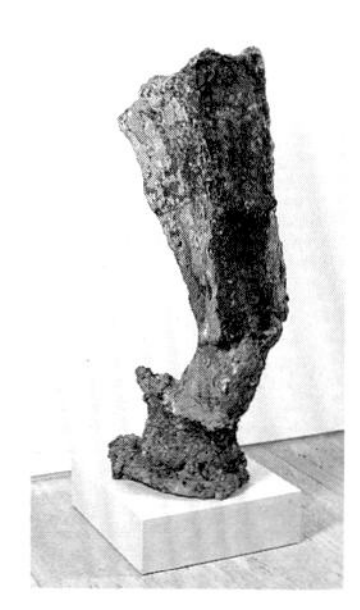

Franz West
(Austrian, born 1947)
Duktus, 1987
Papier-mâché and paint
100 x 33 x 45.6 cm (39 3/8 x 13 x 17 15/16 in.)
Promised gift, 2010
See pp. 132–33

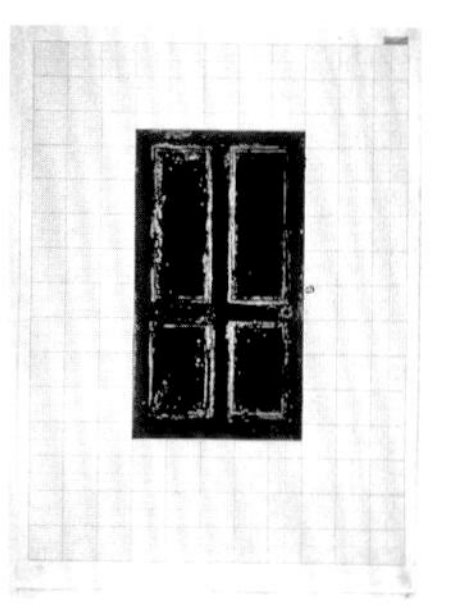

Rachel Whiteread
(English, born 1963)
Untitled (Black Door), 1991
Pencil and black ink on graph paper
45.7 x 30.5 cm (18 x 12 in.)

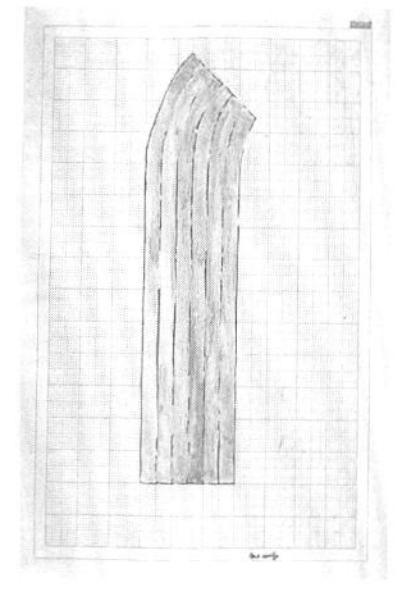

Untitled (Wax Corridor), 1992
Watercolor, ink, and correction fluid on graph paper
45.7 x 30.5 cm (18 x 12 in.)

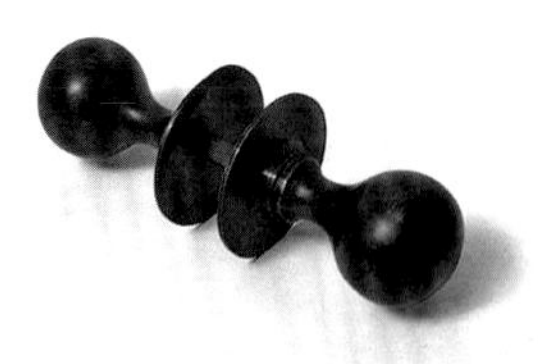

Untitled, 1993
Bronze (edition of 14)
6.4 x 6.4 x 17.8 cm (2 1/2 x 2 1/2 x 7 in.)

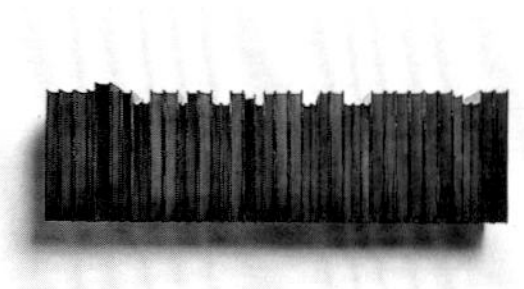

Untitled (Black Books), 1996–97
Black pigmented plastic and steel (edition of 10)
29.2 x 101 x 22.9 cm (11 7/8 x 40 x 9 1/8 in.)

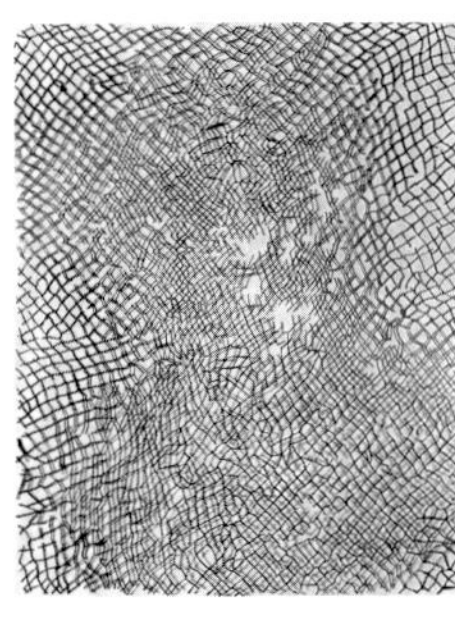

Untitled (Nets), 2002
Suite of five etched German silver (copper, nickel, zinc) sheet metal gratings (edition of 36)
Each: 65 x 52 cm (25 ½ x 20 ½ in.)
Shown: Detail

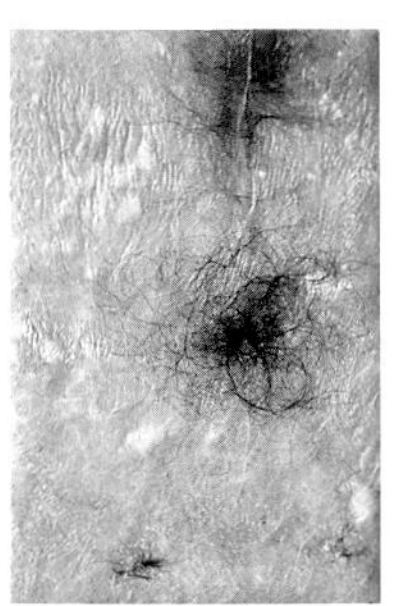

Anne Wilson
(American, born 1949)
Grafted and Dyed, 1991
Human hair, silk cocoon, and abaca (two components)
Each: 63.5 x 48.3 x 2.5 cm (25 x 19 x 1 in.)
Shown: Detail

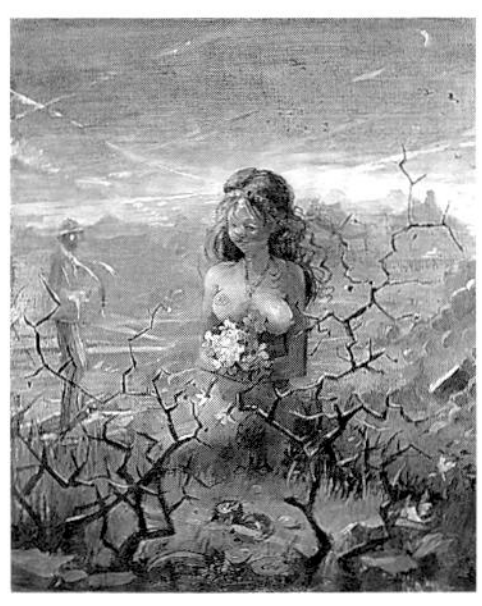

Lisa Yuskavage
(American, born 1962)
Tourist, 2008
Oil on linen
33 x 27.9 cm (13 x 11 in.)

Permissions to reproduce the artworks in this volume have been provided by the artists or their representatives. The following credits apply to all images for which separate acknowledgment is due. They are arranged alphabetically by artist. Unless otherwise noted, the credits for each artist apply to all works included in this catalogue. Every effort has been made to contact and acknowledge copyright holders for all reproductions; additional rights holders are encouraged to contact the Art Institute of Chicago.

Marina Abramović: © 2010 Marina Abramović, Courtesy of Sean Kelly Gallery / (ARS), New York. **Doug Aitken**: Courtesy 303 Gallery, New York. **Darren Almond**: © 1995 Darren Almond. **Carl Andre**: Art © Carl Andre/Licensed by VAGA, New York, NY. **Janine Antoni**: © Janine Antoni. Images courtesy of the artist and Luhring Augustine, New York. **Stephan Balkenhol**: Courtesy Regen Projects, Los Angeles © Stephan Balkenhol. © 2010 Artists Rights Society (ARS), New York / VG Bild-Kunst, Bonn. **Marie Krane Bergman**: © Marie Krane Bergman. **John Chamberlain**: © 2010 John Chamberlain / Artist Rights Society (ARS), New York. **Paul Chan**: Courtesy the artist and Greene Naftali Gallery. **Anne Chu**: Courtesy 303 Gallery, New York. **Gregory Crewdson**: Courtesy of the artist and Luhring Augustine, New York. **Rineke Dijkstra**: Courtesy of the artist and Marian Goodman Gallery, New York. **Jeanne Dunning**: © 1996 Jeanne Dunning. **Vincent Fecteau**: © Vincent Fecteau / Courtesy Matthew Marks Gallery, New York. **Tony Feher**: The Pace Gallery, New York, and D'Amelio Terras, NY. **Dan Flavin**: © 2010 Stephen Flavin / Artists Rights Society (ARS), New York. **Katharina Fritsch**: © 2010 Artists Rights Society (ARS), New York / VG Bild-Kunst, Bonn. **Maureen Gallace**: Courtesy 303 Gallery, New York. **Kendell Geers**: © The artist and courtesy the artist and Stephen Friedman Gallery, London. **Gaylen Gerber**: Three untitled works courtesy of the artist; *Support* courtesy of the artist and Rowley Kennerk Gallery. **Robert Gober**: © 2010 Robert Gober / Courtesy Matthew Marks Gallery, New York. **Daan van Golden**: Courtesy of Greene Naftali Gallery. **Nan Goldin**: © Nan Goldin / Courtesy Matthew Marks Gallery, New York. **Felix Gonzalez-Torres**: *"Untitled" (Portrait of Ross in L.A.)* © Felix Gonzalez-Torres Foundation. Courtesy of Andrea Rosen Gallery, New York; *"Untitled" (Paris)* © Felix Gonzalez-Torres Foundation. **Dan Graham**: Courtesy of the artist and Marian Goodman Gallery, New York. **Mary Heilmann**: Courtesy 303 Gallery, New York. **Arturo Herrera**: © Arturo Herrera. **Roger Hiorns**: Courtesy: Corvi-Mora, London. **Thomas Hirschhorn**: © 2010 Artists Rights Society (ARS), New York / ADAGP, Paris. **Jim Hodges**: *Untitled (Study for Gray)* © Jim Hodges. Photo courtesy of Gladstone Gallery, New York. **Jenny Holzer**: © 2010 Jenny Holzer, member Artists Rights Society (ARS), New York. **Pierre Huyghe**: Courtesy of the artist and Marian Goodman Gallery, New York. © 2010 Artists Rights Society (ARS), New York / ADAGP, Paris. **Isaac Julien**: Courtesy of the artist and Metro Pictures. **Ellsworth Kelly**: © Ellsworth Kelly / Courtesy Matthew Marks Gallery, New York. **William Kentridge**: Courtesy of the artist and Marian Goodman Gallery, New York. **Raoul De Keyser**: Courtesy David Zwirner, New York and Zeno X Gallery, Antwerp. **Michael Krebber**: Courtesy of Greene Naftali Gallery. **Wolfgang Laib**: Courtesy of the artist and Sean Kelly Gallery, New York. **Sol LeWitt**: © 2010 The LeWitt Estate / Artists Rights Society (ARS), New York. *Progressive Pyramid* image courtesy of Rhona Hoffman Gallery. **Jim Lutes**: *Organization Man* and *The Recipients* © Jim Lutes; *Bubble* © Jim Lutes / courtesy of the artist and Valerie Carberry Gallery. Photo by Tom Van Eynde. *Untitled* © Jim Lutes / courtesy of the artist and Valerie Carberry Gallery. Photo by Vanesa Zendejas. **Robert Mangold**: © 2010 Robert Mangold / Artists Rights Society (ARS), New York. **Brice Marden**: © 2010 Brice Marden / Artists Rights Society (ARS), New York / Courtesy Matthew Marks Gallery, New York. **John McCracken**: Courtesy the artist and David Zwirner, New York. **Josiah McElheny**: Courtesy Donald Young Gallery, Chicago. **Ana Mendieta**: © The Estate of Ana Mendieta Collection. Courtesy Galerie Lelong, New York. **Donald Moffett**: © Donald Moffett. **Mariko Mori**: Courtesy of Deitch Projects, NY, Galerie Emmanuel Perrotin, Paris. **Joshua Mosley**: Courtesy Donald Young Gallery, Chicago. **Juan Muñoz**: Courtesy: Estate of Juan Muñoz, Madrid, and Marian Goodman Gallery, New York. **Shirin Neshat**: Courtesy Gladstone Gallery, New York. **William J. O'Brien**: Courtesy of the artist, Marianne Boesky Gallery, New York, and Shane Campbell Gallery, Chicago. **Albert Oehlen**: Four untitled works courtesy Galerie Max Hetzler, Berlin. *Treppe* (original in color) courtesy of the artist and Luhring Augustine, New York. **Gabriel Orozco**: Courtesy of the artist and Marian Goodman Gallery, New York. **Hirsch Perlman**: Courtesy of the artist and Blum & Poe, Los Angeles. **Magnus Plessen**: Courtesy Gladstone Gallery, New York. **Sylvia Plimack Mangold**: Courtesy of Alexander and Bonin, New York. **Gerhard Richter**: Courtesy of the artist and Marian Goodman Gallery, New York. **Kay Rosen**: © 1998 Kay Rosen. **Robert Ryman**: © Robert Ryman, courtesy The Pace Gallery, New York. **Anri Sala**: Courtesy of the artist and Marian Goodman Gallery, New York. **Julião Sarmento**: © Julião Sarmento. Courtesy the artist and Sean Kelly Gallery, New York. **Rudolf Stingel**: © Rudolf Stingel. Courtesy Paula Cooper Gallery, New York. **Thomas Struth**: Courtesy of the artist and Marian Goodman Gallery, New York. **Al Taylor**: © 2010 The Estate of Al Taylor; courtesy David Zwirner, New York. **Diana Thater**: Courtesy David Zwirner, New York. **Rosemarie Trockel**: © 2010 Artists Rights Society (ARS), New York / VG Bild-Kunst, Bonn. **Richard Tuttle**: © Richard Tuttle, courtesy The Pace Gallery, New York. **Luc Tuymans**: Two untitled works courtesy Zeno X Gallery, Antwerp. *Shadow* courtesy David Zwirner, New York, and Zeno X Gallery, Antwerp. **Jeff Wall**: Courtesy of the artist and Marian Goodman Gallery, New York. **Rebecca Warren**: © Rebecca Warren / Courtesy Matthew Marks Gallery, New York. **Lawrence Weiner**: © 2010 Lawrence Weiner / Artists Rights Society (ARS), New York. *MADE FRAGILE AT THIS TIME ON THIS PLACE TO A POINT OF NO RETURN* courtesy Regen Projects, Los Angeles. **Rachel Whiteread**: Courtesy of the artist and Luhring Augustine, New York. **Lisa Yuskavage**: Courtesy David Zwirner, New York.